# Santería

# Santería

Correcting the Myths and Uncovering the
Realities of a Growing Religion

Mary Ann Clark

Westport, Connecticut
London

**Library of Congress Cataloging-in-Publication Data**

Clark, Mary Ann.
  Santería : correcting the myths and uncovering the realities of a growing religion /
  Mary Ann Clark.
    p. cm.
  Includes bibliographical references and index.
ISBN 978–0–275–99079–4 (alk. paper)
1. Santeria. I. Title.
BL2532.S3C52  2007
299.6'74—dc22          2007000059

British Library Cataloguing in Publication Data is available.

Library of Congress Catalog Card Number: 2007000059
ISBN–10: 0–275–99079–6
ISBN–13: 978–0–275–99079–4

First published in 2007

Praeger Publishers, 88 Post Road West, Westport, CT 06881
An imprint of Greenwood Publishing Group, Inc.
www.praeger.com

Printed in the United States of America

The paper used in this book complies with the
Permanent Paper Standard issued by the National
Information Standards Organization (Z39.48-1984).

10 9 8 7 6 5 4 3 2 1

**Copyright Acknowledgments**

Portions of the glossary in this volume were adapted from: Mary Ann Clark, *Where Men Are
Wives and Mothers Rule: Santería Ritual Practices and Their Gender Implications* (Gainesville:
University Press of Florida, 2005), pp. 163–68. Reprinted with permission of the University
Press of Florida.

# Contents

# Introduction

Many years ago my godfather called me. He had just done a reading for an African American woman who knew practically nothing about the religious tradition commonly known as Santería. Although he was very well read himself, he wanted to know if I could recommend any books about the religion suitable for her to read. We both knew that although the tradition was an oral one in which newcomers were expected to listen and learn, Americans generally wanted to read about subjects they had developed an interest in. As we discussed the possibilities, we decided that there were not very many good options. Many fell into the "easy read" category and contained much misinformation and focused too much on the most exotic elements of the tradition. Other scholarly works were well-researched but would put off some readers. And there were some materials for Spanish-speakers, but often there were no English versions or the translations were poorly done.

Since that time there has been an explosion of works about Santería and related traditions, most of it done by scholars who are also participants at some level in the traditions they are describing. Although these generally are quite well done, written to meet the rigorous demands of scholarly inquiry, they tend to focus on some important aspect of the tradition and often do not provide the introductory material newcomers are looking for. Were my godfather to call me today we'd still have a hard time finding something that presents an accurate and sympathetic introduction to this religious tradition while drawing on the current scholarly research but isn't filled with the jargon we scholars are so fond of using.

Santería is one of the religions developed by Africans and brought to the Americas. It is part of a religious system generically called "Orisha worship" that has spread from Africa to the Americas and around the world. There are variants of these traditions throughout the Americas, including on many islands of the Caribbean and Brazil. As they developed in Cuba, these traditions are commonly called Santería, but may also be known as *Lukumi* (or *Lucumí*), *Regla de Ocha*, Yoruba Traditional Religion, or Orisha. In the late 1980s Sandra Barnes estimated that more than 70 million African and American people participated in, or were familiar with, the various forms of Orisha worship, including traditional religions in West Africa, Vodun in Haiti, Candomblé in Brazil, Shango religion in Trinidad, Santería in Cuba, and of course variants of all of these in the United States.[1] Today there are practitioners of these traditions around the world including Europe and Asia. Mary Pat Fisher estimates that there are currently about 100 million practitioners in the U.S. and Latin America alone.[2]

Orisha worship is based on the indigenous religious traditions of the Yoruba-speaking people from what is now southwestern Nigeria and eastern Benin. It was brought to the Americas by enslaved peoples destined for the Caribbean and South America. Santería was developed in Cuba in the late eighteenth and early nineteenth centuries principally by the *gente de color*, that is the free people of color, living in Havana and the surrounding cities. Like many traditional religions Orisha worship is based on a cosmological system that recognizes a single great god, known as Olodumare, and many subsidiary deities. These secondary deities, known as the Orisha, are the focus of ritual attention, and every portion of the religion revolves around them. Although in their original African context most people were henotheistic, worshipping only a few of the innumerable Orisha, as the religion developed in Cuba the primary pantheon narrowed to encompass about 20 named deities who are known and worshipped by most practitioners, as well as many others that are rarer and less well-known.

The religion was brought to the United States in two principal waves. One was in the early 1960s after the Cuban Revolution, and a second with the *Marielitos* who escaped from the island in the 1980s during the so-called Mariel boatlift. Since then it has spread to the larger Hispanic community, to the African American community, and to America at large. Today practitioners can be found in every state in the union, and courses on Orisha and related traditions are taught in many colleges and universities. As the number of practitioners has grown, so has public awareness.

This book is intended to be a basic introduction to these traditions in the United States. It is designed to be appropriate for seekers like the young woman mentioned above since it assumes no prior familiarity with the religion or its traditions. Because of the secretive nature of the Orisha traditions (there are few public religious centers and most events are home-based and private), books such as this can provide an important service by answering basic questions about the tradition. It cannot, of course, take the place of interaction with knowledgeable members of these religious traditions. My hope is that this book will help seekers to learn more about basic elements of the religion including the Orisha, the place of divination and sacrifice, and the workings of religious congregations. However, those who want to participate in one of these traditions will need to seek out a religious community and ask for guidance from a properly initiated and trained priest.

Those who have been invited to a religious event and need a quick etiquette guide, what to wear, what to bring and what to expect, can turn to a list of do's and don'ts for participation at the event in the Basic Etiquette for Newcomers section at the end of Chapter 7, "Religious Rituals."

## WHAT'S IN A NAME?

Although Santería is the popular name for this religious tradition, many practitioners find that name offensive and prefer to use other terms, including Regla de Ocha (or simply Ocha), Lukumi (or Lucumi), Yoruba Traditional Religion, Ifa, or simply Orisha religion. Each of these terms represents a certain agenda and understanding of the tradition. The terminology used by Orisha practitioners is a mix of Yoruba (designated as Yr.), Spanish (Sp.), a creolized version of Yoruba known as Lukumi (Lk.), English, and some Kongolese (Kg.) words. Although calling the Orisha, the deities, *santos* or holy beings began quite early in Cuba, it appears that the terminology *Santería*, along with the corresponding identification of the priests as *santero* and *santera*, was developed in the mid 1930s by the Afro-Cuban scholar Rómula Lachatañeré to replace the earlier use of the terms *brujería* (witchcraft) and *brujo/a* (witch) in the popular press.[3] The terms *santero* and *santera* were existing Spanish words used to refer to people who dedicated their lives to the maintenance of certain shrines or to those who made their living creating the statues of the saints that were so popular at the time. The problem with attempting to replace a derogatory term with a more neutral one is that the neutral term often picks up the offensive nature of the original term. Thus it has been with *Santería*. For many practitioners, the new term is as insulting as the old term was.

For practitioners who are Spanish-speaking or who are associated with Spanish-speaking religious communities, the "official" name of the religion is *Regla de Ocha*. This is a mixed Yoruba-Spanish phrase. "Regla" or "rule" is used throughout Cuba to refer to different religious organizations, not only the Afro-Cuban groups but also the different Catholic religious orders. For example, the Central African traditions of Palo Monte and Palo Mayombe are known as Regla de Congo and the Franciscans as Regla de San Francisco (Rule of Saint Francis). "Ocha" is a contraction of the word "Orisha," so that Regla de Ocha means the rule or order of the Orisha. This is a more neutral term that is widely accepted both in its fullness and shortened to simply "Ocha."

Another long-standing designation is the term *Lukumi* (or its Spanish variant *Lucumi*), which was the name widely used to designate both the geographic area that was home to the Yoruba-speaking people and as the name of the people who lived there. Originally, the Lukumi were only the inhabitants of the ancient city of Oyo, but it soon was generalized to include all the Yoruba-speaking people from that area of West Africa. A long-standing term that shows up on some of the earliest maps of the area, *lukumi* also may have come from the Yoruba phrase *oluku mi*, "my friend." Practitioners who want to emphasize the African origins of the religion often prefer *Lukumi* to the Spanish-language designators.

Another way of calling attention to the religion's African roots is to refer to it as *Yoruba Traditional Religion*, although few in contemporary Nigeria would claim this as their own tradition, preferring other religious traditions. According to the CIA Fact Book's information on Nigeria, today only 10 percent of the people are adherents of what they call "indigenous beliefs." The remaining 90 percent are Muslim (50%) and Christian (40%).[4] This means that there are probably more followers of these traditions in the Americas than in the homeland of the Orisha. This terminology is misleading in that there was no single Yoruba traditional religion; rather, during precolonial times before Christian missionaries made the declaration of one's "faith" important, the Yoruba-speaking people worshiped in groups dedicated to one or more of the Orisha. There was no word for "religion," as these activities were tightly integrated into their day-to-day lives. As with many religious traditions around the world, the essential feature was not belief, but practice. One didn't believe in Shango or Oshun or Obatala, but rather served them.

The most general way of referring to this tradition and its sister traditions is *Orisha religion*. In addition to Santería and its many variants, Orisha religion includes the remnants of the traditions remaining in Nigeria as well as the traditions that developed in the Americas, including Candomblé in Brazil, portions of Vodou in Haiti, and Shango in Trinidad. While maintaining the African roots of the tradition, this term focuses on the deities rather than a geographic or ethnic designation. Although I will concentrate on the Orisha tradition as it has flourished in the United States, much of what I will be saying applies in whole or in part to the other Orisha traditions around the world. Although all of these names can be used, those who are involved with a local religious community should use the terminology that community prefers.

This religion is often described as having grown out of the Afro-Cuban experience of slavery, as an attempt by the Africans and their children to temporarily rise above their enslaved state by imagining themselves to be kings and queens, gods and goddesses. In spite of the fact that the religion as it exists today developed during the era of Cuban colonization and slavery, it is important to realize that it is closely aligned with the royal and popular practices of the precolonial Yoruba-speaking people, especially those from the capital city of Oyo. While it is true, as one of her informants told Lydia Cabrera, "to make Santo it is to make a king, and kariocha [initiation] is a ceremony of kings, like those of the palace of Lucumi kings,"[5] it is important to realize that this tradition was not developed in reaction to the servitude of the African peoples in Cuba. The traditions are much older and are based on a time when the Lukumi, the peoples of Oyo, were themselves the rulers of an extensive empire.

While many practitioners refer to themselves by the name of the tradition they follow ("I am Lukumi" or "I am Ifa") there are several additional terms that are used to identify practitioners of these traditions including santero/a, santerian, olorisha, babalosha, iyalosha, and babalawo. As with the different terms used to name the traditions, these terms reflect political and social agendas. For those who identify with Santería or Regla de Ocha, "santero" (male) or "santera" (female) can be used to identify practitioners. Even though these terms refer to initiate priests, they are often generalized to include anyone who participates in the tradition. Sometimes outsiders who are unfamiliar with the tradition will use the term "santerians" to refer to practitioners, but that is a neologism not used by practitioners themselves. For those who prefer African terminology, olorisha (one who owns an Orisha), babalosha (father of Orisha), and iyalosha (mother of Orisha) can be used to distinguish initiated priests, olorisha, from priests who have initiated others into the tradition, iyalosha and babalosha. Priests in the Ifa tradition are known as "babalawo" (father of mystery) or either iyanifa (mother of Ifa) or "iyalawo" (mother of mystery). There are also a group of Yoruba terms used in some communities to refer to those with different levels of involvement in the tradition, including "aleyo" (Yr. stranger) for someone with either no initiations or only the Necklaces ritual; "aborisha" (Yr. Orisha worshipper) for someone who has received an vivified Orisha icon, generally the Warriors, for worship in their own home; and "iyawo," which refers to a new priestly initiate during their one-year novitiate period. In this book I will generally use the term "devotee" to refer to anyone who is involved in one of the traditions, "practitioner" for someone who has received some rituals or initiations, and "priest" for an initiated priest.

## MAGIC, SUPERSTITION, AND RELIGION

It is common among both scholars and non-scholars to attempt to distinguish between the practices of religion and those of magic. Without a preexisting notion that a particular practice is religious or superstitious, observers are often at a loss to distinguish between the two. Familiar religious practices, then, become the model used to judge all religious practices.

Thus, for Americans familiar with Christian traditions, a group of people gathered in a church to pray for rain or for the health and well-being of a member of the congregation is perceived as a religious act, while a similar group of people gathered under the open sky to dance and chant for rain or making offering on the bank of a river is not. As a culture we tend to belittle unfamiliar traditions, calling them either evil, superstitious, and wrong, or silly, ridiculous, and foolish. Often the term "cult" is used to describe such traditions.

The word "cult" has legitimate scholarly uses in respect to religious traditions to describe groups of people who follow a single religious leader or whose worship centers on a single deity in a larger pantheon as in the "Jesus cult" or the "cult of Isis." The term is often used in older anthropological and sociological literature to describe the groups in strange and exotic areas. In popular culture, the word is most often used in a derogatory way to mean a group of people whose beliefs and practices are so far outside the mainstream that they are sinister, anti-social, and generally dangerous to either their members and the larger society or both. Many new religious movements and traditions, because they are have relatively few members, follow novel belief systems, and engage in idiosyncratic practices, are disparaged in the media as "dangerous cults."

The Orisha traditions are often lumped together with other African-based traditions and described as "Voodoo cults," which is doubly disparaging given the extremely negative connotations associated with the term "Voodoo." Vodun (also called Voudou, Vodou, Vudun, Vodoun and other phonetically equivalent terms) is an African-based tradition, similar in many ways to the Orisha traditions, which developed in Haiti by people taken from the West Africa, many from the kingdoms of Dahomey and Kongo. Although it is considered pejorative, some scholars use the term "voodoo" for a variant of the same tradition as it developed in New Orleans in the nineteenth century.[6] In the United States the term "voodoo" is widely associated with mysterious black magical practices including spells and potions, zombies, and the sticking of pins into dolls to punish errant lovers and spouses. "Voodoo" is so well understood in popular culture as a superstitious and misguided practice that certain non-religious practices can be disparaged simply by the addition of the modifier of "voodoo" as was done in the 1980s when certain economic theories were called "voodoo economics."

Accusations of "witchcraft" (Sp. *brujería*) are another way misunderstood and minority traditions are disparaged by the mainstream culture. Although the term has a variety of meanings, "witchcraft" generally has the connotation of the use of non-material powers for personal gain or to harm others. The first scholarly book written about the religious traditions of Afro-Cubans was called *Los negros brujos* (*The Black Witches*).[7] Writing at the beginning of the nineteenth century, the young lawyer Fernando Ortiz set out to prove that Cuba's black population was afflicted by immortality and witchcraft. Using the language of medicine, Ortiz condemned the whole of Afro-Cuban culture and practices as a social pathology that could be "cured" with the appropriate social hygiene. Even though Ortiz had little firsthand knowledge of the cultures he described in *Los negros brujos,* and in spite of the fact that he later became a sympathetic defender of Afro-Cuba traditions, the stigma of witchcraft continues to plague these traditions. At the time Ortiz was writing, Afro-Cuban sorcerers were believed to be killing young children and using their blood to create potions to extend their own lives and those of their clients. This hysteria was part of a larger panic in the period after the slaves had been emancipated and Cuba had won its freedom from Spanish colonial control when the relationship among the Cuban people of all racial backgrounds was being renegotiated. African and African-identified practices were suspect and subjected to wide-ranging and oppressive controls.

The connection between the practices of the Orisha religions and ideas about "black witchcraft" continues. "Black" in this instance refers both to the purported African underpinnings and to a way of distinguishing between this and so-called "white" or good witchcraft. In the common understanding, "black" magic is malevolent and self-concerned, caught up in wickedness and death. The generalized term for this doubly black magic is "voodoo," the form of sorcery brought from Africa and practiced by unsavory characters. This usage leads both the police and the media to describe any unusual or ritualistic crimes as involving "voodoo or Santería."[8]

These traditions are also often described as "syncretistic." Syncretism is formally defined as the attempt to combine two or more different systems of belief and practice together into a single system. Often the two belief systems are logically incompatible although individual devotees seldom question the internal inconsistencies. Sometimes such combinations are seen as transitions between the old and new ways of being religious, such as when missionaries allow converts to include elements of their old culture into their new religious practices. Examples include African drumming and dancing during services or the use of Native American smudging rituals. Sometimes syncretistic practices are considered a betrayal of the original purity of one or the other of the traditions, an example of ignorance, or of theological confusion. The Orisha traditions are often described as a syncretistic religion that combines elements of West African Orisha cults and Spanish colonial Catholic religious practice. Practitioners are commonly accused of either corrupting Catholicism with their own cosmology, practices, and language, or of inappropriately assimilating Catholicism into their practice of Orisha worship.

The Yoruba culture has been described as open, flexible, and incorporative rather than closed, rigid, and conservative.[9] This means that people from these cultures are generally ready to take on new ideas and practices and incorporate them into their lives and cultures. The people living in the

Yoruba-speaking area of West Africa often incorporated the ideas and practices from the surrounding cultures. When some of these people were brought to the Americas, they continued to incorporate elements of the cultures they found into their own lives. Thus we find elements not only of Catholic Christianity but also Bantu and native Caribbean cultures incorporated into the Orisha traditions. As I describe these traditions I will sometimes highlight syncretistic elements and sometimes discuss the efforts by some devotees to remove certain syncretistic elements from their practices. After describing these traditions, I will discuss the issues surrounding syncretism more fully in Chapter 10. As we explore the beliefs and practices of these traditions, we need to be careful about the ways we characterize them. In general, all religious traditions have beliefs and practices that an outside observer may find strange, even bizarre. In this book I will be approaching this tradition from its own point of view, not trying to judge it according to the standards of other traditions. I will explain practitioners' religious worldviews and why they find certain kinds of activities important to their religious practice. I ask that this material be approached with an open mind. As I tell my students, I'm not asking you to accept this worldview, but I am asking you to respect those who do.

## Advice for Seekers

Individuals come to the religions of the Orisha in many different ways and for many different reasons. Some people are born into families or communities of practitioners, so they learn about the traditions, beliefs, and practices as a natural part of their growing up. Others know someone who knows someone who is a devotee and seek their aid when their physical, mental, or emotional problems seem intractable. Still others learn about these traditions in classrooms and dance studios where dedicated teachers provide instruction into the cultures of Africa. For some people their first introduction to the world of the Orisha is scary, as everything seems alien and unsettling; for others there is a sense of coming home to the religious tradition of their forebears or of their own heart.

Many contemporary Americans have become disillusioned with the religious tradition of their childhood or, more generally, of the mainstream traditions they see around them. These seekers have a vast assortment of traditions to explore, from alternative forms of Christianity and Judaism, to Islam or Baha'i, to Asian traditions such as Hinduism or Buddhism, to modern versions of the ancient Pagan traditions of Europe, Greece, Rome, and Egypt, to new traditions developed in the United States or elsewhere. For some people, their practice of these traditions takes on a smorgasbord appearance: a little from this one and a little from that. Others spend long years in one tradition acquiring knowledge and gaining the titles bestowed on the leaders of that tradition. Some of these traditions are very structured and rigid in their organization and practice. Other traditions are more free-form, allowing flexibility and spontaneity in beliefs and practices.

Many of these people, after having had experience in one or more of these different types of traditions, discover the Orisha and want to participate in their worship. However, the Orisha traditions are different both from mainstream traditions and from the many alternative traditions seekers may be familiar with. These are hierarchical and secretive traditions. Regardless of their previous training or background in another tradition, everyone enters these traditions at the lowest level and is expected to defer to those with higher levels of initiations, regardless of their chronological age, spiritual experience, educational level, gender, race, or other personal characteristics. Having gained a high-ranking position in another tradition doesn't give anyone an advantage in these traditions. Through participation and initiation one can move through the ranks of the tradition, but there will always be those who are your senior, to whom you must defer.

Many priests of the Orisha are natural teachers and enjoy sharing their knowledge about the Orisha and their worship with others. However, some of the best and most knowledgeable are not. There is no obligation for anyone to teach newcomers anything, and even the most willing of teachers is constrained by a culture of sacred secrecy that limits what one can know and do according to one's initiatory level. These traditions are based on oral culture where the student is expected to watch and listen to learn indirectly while doing the work of religion. Demanding information is not only rude but also counterproductive toward the development of the kind of respectful relationship where teaching and learning happen naturally.

Many priests are also distrustful of seekers who come to them armed by knowledge gained from books like this one and others. Although there are many books written by sincere and knowledgeable people, there is also a vast library of inaccurate and misleading information easily acquired from the local library or online bookseller. These are oral traditions where real learning happens person-to-person in the course of doing all the work required to perform the many rituals of an active religious household. While books can give a basic introduction to the Orisha and their worship, real learning can only happen through the sharing of a knowledgeable priest who has agreed to teach and train the seeker. In this book I have tried to give a good grounding in these traditions; however, every priest and every religious household will have practices and customs that deviate from what is described here. Seekers should not try to tell priests the "right way" to do something or question their expertise based on something they read in a book. Reading can give one a basic understanding of these traditions but can never take the place of a knowledgeable godparent.

These are not traditions of belief but ones of practice. When devotees speak of *serving* the Orisha, they are expressing the reality of Orisha worship. Although prayer and meditation are important parts of many devotees' practice, it is the physical work of preparing for, performing, and cleaning up after rituals and events that forms the major portion of one's practice in these traditions. Much of this work requires advanced levels of initiation; however, there is much that those with entry-level initiations and even the uninitiated can do. A great deal of this work is hard, grimy, physical labor: helping in the kitchen by plucking chickens or making refreshments for the other workers, cleaning, or running errands. Not what many of us might think of as "spiritual" work. Every Orisha community depends on the work of its members to provide the rituals and events required by the deities. It is in conjunction with this work that most of a newcomer's training takes place, as they learn how and often why certain things are done. Seekers must be willing to work with the members of the community, fetching and carrying with their eyes and ears open, listening and learning by watching and doing.

As in all hierarchal communities where some members have real or imagined power over others, abuses can occur. Although there are relatively few reports of sexual abuses with Orisha communities, there are exceptions. In general, the members of these communities are fairly conservative in their approaches to sexuality. Strong marriages and families are encouraged even in areas where single parent families are more common. Gay, lesbian, bisexual, and transsexual members are welcomed in many communities, and some of the most well-known and highly respected priests, past and present, are gay men and lesbians. Sexual activity between godparents and their godchildren and other types of sexual impropriety is improper and scandalous. Thus most communities forbid priests initiating anyone with whom they have had a sexual or familial relationship, including former and current spouses, children, parents, siblings, current or potential lovers, or sexual partners. Diviners are also discouraged from divining for individuals with whom they have a sexual or familial relationship, and diviners or other priests who demand sexual favors are strongly censured.

If a person decides that she wants to become involved in an Orisha community, she must put herself under the authority and protection of a priest or priestess who will become her spiritual guardian, her godparent teaching her in the ways of the Orisha and giving her the initiations she needs to fulfill her life's destiny. The relationship between godchild and godparent is extremely important and not to be entered into lightly. As in all religious traditions there are some well-respected leaders and some people who put themselves forward as leaders who are unsavory or unscrupulous. In many other traditions the organizational hierarchy certifies its priests, ministers, imams, or rabbis. Although there are groups who have begun to certify Orisha priests, there is no centralized authority that can tell a seeker whether someone is a legitimate priest or whether they are the right person to manage *his* spiritual development.[10] Before a seeker places himself under the guidance of someone he must make sure that they are who they say they are, that they are active in and acknowledged by the larger community, and that they will provide *him* with the spiritual guidance he needs. A seeker should remember that someone might be an excellent and well-respected priest but not be able to provide the kind of thoughtful, caring spiritual guidance *he* needs. Someone wanting to learn more should go to events, especially drummings and birthday celebrations, talk to the people there, watch, and listen. He should observe both the priest's interaction with his or her equals and with his or her godchildren.

Seekers should take things slow, remembering that the relationships formed through initiations are life-long and absolute. Santeros and other Orisha priests are not saints. Neither are they substitutes for medical doctors, therapists, or marriage counselors. They are common people who have dedicated themselves to the worship of the Orisha. When choosing a godparent, the priest who will guide a newcomer's work with the Orisha, a person should choose someone who seems to be a generally good person, someone who commands respect. If you make a mistake and marry the wrong person you can get a divorce; once you commit to a godparent and become fully initiated that relationship is forever. Just as you cannot change the person who gives you birth, you cannot change the person who brings you to spiritual birth through the Orisha.

## Money Concerns

Everything in these traditions costs money. Divination costs money, initiations cost money, participation in many ritual events costs money. In spite of the fact that all religious traditions must somehow pay for the goods and services they use in conjunction with their religious mission, many people come to Orisha communities expecting that they should receive love, support, and spiritual guidance for free. While it is true that one can attend many mainstream churches without contributing to their ongoing maintenance, every religious institution must have a way of funding its activities, paying rent and utilities on its building, paying for the supplies it buys, and paying its religious specialists. Many churches depend on tithing by their members and donations from those who have more wealth to subsidize the needs of those who have less.

In general (there are exceptions), the Orisha traditions are pay-as-you-go societies. Every person must pay for the goods and services they need as they need them. Costs of divination pay for the time and skill of the diviner. Costs of rituals include the price of all of the goods needed to complete the ritual, including religious icons and other items, animals to be sacrificed, refreshments for the participants, and some small payment for the time and skill of the priests involved. Prices vary across country and from community to community, but simple divination sessions should generally be in the two-figure range (less than $100). Major or complex divinations will cost more. Getting one's head marked by babalawo (which requires at least three diviners) will cost more than getting one's head marked by an itelero. Although simple baths and cleansing rituals may cost in the two-figure range, Warrior, Neckla- ces, Hand of Ifa, and other more complex rituals will be in the hundreds of dollars. Major initiations can be very expensive. The so-called "crowning" ceremony that makes one a priest lasts for a week, and requires between 10 and 20 priests and thousands of dollars.

All rituals and divination sessions should be done face-to-face. Seekers should be suspicious of priests who offer to do ceremonies of any kind over the phone, Internet, or email. They should also be suspicious of priests who insist that they must travel to Cuba, Haiti, Brazil, or Nigeria in order to receive the initiations and other religious ceremonies that they need. Because these are community-based traditions, if one receives her initiations thou- sands of miles from her hometown, she will have a difficult time finding a community that will help her learn what she should know to worship the Ori- sha. This is a problem for devotees living in American towns and cities who may once have been members of communities but now live far from the cen- ters of Orisha practice. It makes religious life almost impossible for those whose religious community is on another continent.

Similarly, seekers shouldn't go to Cuba, Haiti, Brazil, or Nigeria with the plan of being initiated by "somebody there." The potential for long-term problems is enormous. Unless he is familiar with the communities in his tar- get country and knows the language well, such a religious tourist will have no assurance that he is working with legitimate priests and getting the initiations he is paying for. In all of these traditions, the actual initiation event is only the beginning of a series of rituals that make one a full-fledged priest. Unless he plans on relocating to his target country the tourist will have a hard time completing both his initiation and the training he needs. I can't say it too often that these are community-based traditions. If someone is initiated by one community, members of other communities have no responsibility to work with her or train her in the practices of the tradition. Many people have gone off to another country either because they thought the rituals would be less expensive or more powerful, only to return to find that the local commu- nity they bypassed would have nothing to do with them and would not rec- ognize their foreign initiations.

Seekers should also be wary of priests who work alone and have no god- children, elders, or religious siblings to help with their ceremonies. One can- not self-initiate or practice solo in these traditions. Although one might find someone living far from her Orisha community who maintains her obliga- tions in the absence of a supporting community, she should look to a reli- gious community somewhere and travel to that community on a regular basis. This is particularly true of someone who is working with clients and other seekers.

## COMING UP

In the remainder of this book I will explore the Orisha traditions as they are found in the United States. Of necessity this book will generalize and simplify these very complex traditions in an effort to provide a readable introduction. Throughout, I will suggest additional sources for those who want to dig deeper into this or that portion of the material. I will begin by looking at the history of these traditions in an effort to see where they came from and how they found their way to the contemporary United States. Then I will explore the underlying cosmology, followed by a more detailed introduction to the Orisha, the focal point of all religious practice. With that introduction, I will then explore how these traditions are actually practiced. I will begin by discussing the relations between the Yoruba concept of destiny, the ways that one can discover and moderate their destiny through divination, and the part that sacrifice plays in the working out of one's destiny. Ancestors and other invisible beings continue to play an important part in the practice of Orisha religion. In Chapter 6, "Life, Death, and the Afterlife," I discuss more fully the way that Yoruba, European, and Asian ideas about what happens when one dies have all influenced contemporary views of the ancestors and the reverence due to them. Then I will look at the more common religious rituals, including initiation rituals and the organization of religious communities into families of practice. Finally, in the last chapter I will look at some of the controversial issues surrounding these traditions and suggest the ways these traditions will develop in the twenty-first century.

## ACKNOWLEDGMENTS

This book would never have been possible without the ongoing cooperation of the Orisha and their priests and devotees Mafererfun Yemaya, maferefun Eleggua, mafererfun Oshun, mafererfun Ogun, mafererfun gbogbo Orisha, mafererfun all those olorisha and their godchildren who have allowed me into their lives. Special thanks to my parents, Daniel and Marilyn Clark, who gave me life and taught me how to live, and my godparents, Ode Kan (Sandra Cersonsky) and Chango Ladé (Anthony DeQuinzio), who gave me the Orisha and sustained me along this great journey.

This project would never have gotten off the ground (or been completed) without the kindness and patience of my editor, Suzanne Staszak-Silva, and her associates at Greenwood Press. This project would never have been possible without all of those who supported my work over the years, including Dr. Edith Wyschogrod, who believed in me and mentored my career from the beginning, Dr. Elias Bongmba, who has become a great friend and colleague, Dr. Mary Curry, whose calm and steady presence continue to support me even though I am no longer graced by her physical presence. Dr. Alice Wood deserves special recognition. You have been a role model, sounding board, and best friend since my first days in graduate school. Sweet Alice, I could never have done this project without your loving presence and incisive questions.

Finally, my husband deserves the highest recognition for his constant loving support in this and all my endeavors. You are the wind beneath my wings, the rock that holds me firm.

# History of the Tradition

The religion that is known as Santería was brought to the Americas by enslaved West Africans who lived in the Yoruba-speaking regions of the southwestern area of the contemporary nation of Nigeria. Although Africans were brought to the Americas with the earliest voyages of Columbus, the majority of the Yoruba-speaking people brought to the Caribbean arrived in the mid 1800s.

It is important to remember that our view of Yoruba culture comes from two sources: anthropology and colonial history-making. The principal sources for our understanding of Yoruba culture at the time of the slave trade are the works of William Bascom, including *The Yoruba of Southwest Nigeria* along with many articles and monographs, and the Reverend Samuel Johnson, whose *History of the Yoruba* is still one of the most important publications about the Yoruba-speaking peoples.[1] Like all anthropologists of his time, Bascom wrote in a form known as the "ethnographic present." When one reads these materials (and materials like those below, based on that work), it appears as though the people and culture described have always and everywhere been the way they are when described. Simple common sense tells us that this is not true. All people have a history both before and after their encounter with anthropologists. Every culture changes, grows, and declines based on changes in its circumstances and the people who create and maintain it. The Yoruba people today are one of the many ethnic groups that form the country of Nigeria. Their contemporary lives and cultures have been greatly influenced by their encounters with the British who colonized their area. Only about 10 percent of the population of contemporary Nigeria claims traditional religions, while 40 percent claim Christianity and the remaining 50 percent claim Islam. Similarly, few live the way their ancestors did in the sixteenth, seventeenth, eighteenth, and nineteenth centuries during the times of the slave trade and the subsequent research into their cultures by anthropologists and other scholars.

The Reverend Johnson was a native of the city of Oyo and former captive freed in Sierra Leone who was educated in CMS (Church Missionary Society) schools. He wrote his *History* at the turn of the century in order to highlight the role of Christianity in promoting cultural change among his people. His attitude toward traditional religious and cultural practices is always influenced by his European, Protestant, colonial education. Like many modern educated Nigerians, Johnson saw the work of missionaries and other Europeans as a civilizing force that brought his people from barbarism to modernity.

In the pre-colonial period the Yoruba-speaking people were a culturally diverse group who identified themselves as citizens of particular city-states. Although they did not think of themselves as a single people until the British colonized them in the nineteenth century, they shared certain fundamental social, political, religious, philosophical, and artistic concepts. They also claimed a common origin from the city of Ile-Ife.

Our knowledge of this area is sketchy until the 1600s, which saw the rise of the Oyo Empire. By the eighteenth century these people were among the most urbane of all of the peoples of West Africa. Anthropologists know that as early as 500 BCE people living in this area of Africa had the technology to produce sophisticated stone carvings and that by 800-1000 CE there were complex city-states, including the two important city-states of Ile-Ife and Oyo, headed by sacred rulers, councils of elders, and chiefs. Both men and women were included among these rulers and their council of elders.

Although Ile-Ife is generally accepted to be the birthplace of Yoruba culture, it was the city of Oyo that became the political leader. Lead by empire-building kings, wars between Oyo and the surrounding towns it was attempting to subordinate grew in intensity between the 1600s and the 1800s. Rather than killing their enemies or locking them up in camps, both sides in these conflicts sent their prisoners of war to the coastal cities where they were sold to the Europeans who were plying the waters off what was aptly called the Slave Coast. Most of these captives were taken to northern Brazil and the islands of the Caribbean. During the latter part of this period, as the demand for slaves to work the cotton and sugar fields of the America grew, wars were waged not only in the service of empire-building but also in order to participate in the lucrative slave trade. It is important to understand that the Yoruba people were masters of empire building whose internal wars were responsible for so many of them coming to the Americas.

During the early years of this period the island of Cuba was a relative backwater, used mainly to re-provision ships arriving from Europe and Africa and as the last port for provisioning ships heading back to Europe or Africa. However, after the Haitian Revolution in 1794, the center of the Caribbean sugar industry moved from Haiti to Cuba. At the same time, sugar, which had entered Europe as a luxury available only to the most well-to-do, was also developing as an international commodity in demand throughout the world. Increased demand required increased production. Increased production called for an increase in the number of laborers to meet that demand. The combination of more Yoruba-speaking captives available in the African slave markets and greater demand for laborers in Cuba brought the greatest influx of Yoruba peoples to Cuba in its history. By 1886 (when slavery was finally abolished in Cuba), between 500,000 and 700,000 Africans had been transported to Cuba. During the final years of the slave trade in Cuba, between 1850 and 1870, over a third of these were designated as Lukumi, that is, Yoruba-speakers.[2]

## RELIGIOUS ORGANIZATION IN YORUBALAND

Many people have the mistaken notion that in pre-colonial Africa initiates worshipped only one or two Orisha, while in the New World each individual worships multiple Orisha. Sometimes this understanding is extended to suggest that devotees in each African city-state focused ritual attention on a single Orisha: Shango in Oyo, Oshun in Osogbo, etc., and that in pre-colonial times each village in Yorubaland had its own deity that was worshipped exclusively. It has been suggested that if one wanted or needed to worship a different deity, one would have been required to travel to a neighboring village. This view lead to the assertion that one of the major innovations undertaken by those who reconstructed Orisha religions in the Americas was the uniting of the devotees of all the Orisha into a single organization.[3]

Although it is true that every Yoruba city and town was under the patronage of either a single Orisha or a small group of related Orisha, that did not prevent devotees of other Orisha from developing in the community. In his book *The Sociological Role of the Yoruba Cult Group*, William Bascom describes the organization of Orisha worship in Yorubaland.[4] The Yoruba lived in family compounds that included a man, his wives and under-aged children, the wives and children of his sons, his unmarried daughters, and often, unrelated visitors. According to Bascom's research, at the household level, different members of a compound may worship a variety of gods. Each household had one or more lineage deities accepted as "belonging" to that compound. Although a woman marrying into the household may adopt the Orisha of her husband, she may also continue the worship of her own deities—or both. Since the Yoruba are exogenous—that is, one marries outside the family or clan—the woman would have come from another lineage, perhaps another village. Although a woman may choose to abandon the Orisha of her birth family upon marriage it is not necessary that she do so. Strangers, that is people living in a compound who are not a part of the lineage, may also introduce new Orisha into the worship pattern of the compound. A child may inherit the worship of an Orisha from one or both of his parents after their deaths, he may be "called" to the worship of an ancestral Orisha, or he may be initiated into the worship of the deities of other members of the compound. Parents (who may themselves worship different Orisha) may select one or more of their children to continue the worship of their personal deities, training that child in the worship procedures, taking him to festivals, making sacrifices for him, and the like. When old enough the child would worship the Orisha independently. (It should also be understood in this description that not all children were trained in such a way, nor was every child trained in the worship even of the lineage deity.) If a woman made a sacrifice to an Orisha in an attempt to bear a child that child was considered to have been given to her by the Orisha, and was said to have come from heaven worshipping that Orisha. This Orisha may or may not be in the mother's personal pantheon. A desperate woman may sacrifice to several Orisha before becoming pregnant. Also, children were said to belong to an Orisha because of unusual circumstances surrounding their birth. Certain abnormalities were associated with an Orisha; albinos, for example, were associated with Obatala, while a certain pattern of hair growth indicated an association with Dada. Again the mother would aid such children in their worship until they were old enough to worship on their own. Finally, Bascom tells us a person may discover that he or she "belongs" to an Orisha later in life when illness, economic loss, or a series of deaths in the family prompt him (or her) to consult a diviner who might suggest the worship of a hitherto neglected Orisha. At the same time, groups and individuals may abandon the worship of one or more Orisha for any number of reasons. Thus, over time, worship patterns evolved. An individual may, over the course of her life, worship several Orisha. In fact, according to Bascom, most Yoruba worshipped a group of five or six deities acquired under different circumstances. And regardless of how one came to the worship of an Orisha, he or she was often eligible to become a priest of that Orisha. This suggests that the worship of several Orisha either simultaneously or serially was common in the African environment.[5]

One might be the only devotee of an Orisha in a neighborhood or city, worshipping it within one's own household. Lineage deities were given shrine areas in the family compound. The family head or his designated representative generally led their worship. If there was a small group of worshippers in an area, they would gather together for worship at shrines in the compounds of their members. A larger group might petition for shrine space within the town, while the town patrons, the Orisha worshipped by the king, and other major Orisha, would have their own temples and shrines. Sometimes political changes brought new Orisha to the city as new rulers or refugees from wars and natural disasters brought their own Orisha. A foreign deity might gain adherents for a variety of social, political, or economic reasons. It was also common to find antagonistic relationships among the many different worship communities, particularly when some were associated with new political leaders or other changes in the social structure.

It is important to keep in mind that during this time there was no single, unified Yoruba religion. Each region, each city, and each town quarter may have held one or more related, and sometimes antagonistic, religious groups. There was no Orisha that was universally worshipped, and any individual might worship a single Orisha, several Orisha, or even none at all. Major groups had temples and a related priesthood organized in a hierarchy modeled on the local political organization led by one or more high priests. In some cases, this hierarchy extended beyond the town to include priests, shrines, and devotees from neighboring towns. It was common for the king's Orisha to have shrines in all of his vassal cities. In these cases, the priests at the shrine in the capital city would have authority over those in the subordinate towns.

In pre-colonial Yorubaland, each Orisha was worshipped by a more or less independent and self-sufficient community. Although any individual might be a member of multiple such groups, the groups themselves were generally autonomous. Although each group of devotees tended to establish their own shrines and priestly orders, in some towns the worshippers of a related group of Orisha joined together into a single larger group. The number and prestige of a group's members determined the prestige and power of a group. Orisha that were worshiped by many powerful people who could hold large, extravagant festivals were more prestigious than those with just a few more humble worshippers. Most of these groups had both male and female members, and both men and women rose to positions of leadership within them. Women were the majority in many of these groups, and often the most powerful person in such a group, the "high priest," was a woman or a male and female pair.

Although there were thousands of Orisha worshipped in Yorubaland, there are far fewer worshipped in the Americas because in many cases there were not enough devotees to reestablish the requisite communities. Cities and towns that were at the center of the wars for empire that raged through Yorubaland during the nineteenth century contributed the majority of devotees to the reconstruction of Yoruba religious traditions in the Americas. Those cities and towns that were less involved in these wars contributed fewer devotees. Consequently, a majority of the Orisha worshippers in the Americas come from the city of Oyo and its subordinated towns, while there were far fewer citizens of Ife and its environs since they generally did not participate in these wars.

## CUBAN CABILDOS

Slavery and the slavery codes in the Caribbean were different from those of British-controlled North America. The people of the Spanish peninsula had a history of slavery even before Columbus's voyage, and these codes were instituted in the American colonies as slavery was established there. Between the years 1263 and 1265 (centuries before Columbus's fateful voyage), the comprehensive *Las Siente Partidas del Rey Don Alfonso el Sabio* were compiled under royal direction. Under these codes, slaves were given certain rights, including the right to marriage and the right to manumission. Manumission is the process by which a person can buy his own or another's freedom from slavery. According to *Las Siente Partidas*, a person could request that the court establish the price of his or her freedom. When someone came forward with the required amount, the person would be manumitted or freed.

*Las Siente Partidas* controlled the institution of slavery as it developed in the Spanish colony that became Cuba. The rights given to slaves, particularly the right of manumission, had an important effect on the development of Cuban culture. This provision was of little use to those working on the sugar plantation where individuals had little opportunity to earn their own money. However, for those living in the cities (principally Havana and Santiago de Cuba), their working conditions enabled them to work independently and earn the money necessary to manumit themselves or their friends and relatives. In addition, it was common for Spanish slave owners to free especially favored slaves either during their lifetimes or as part of their wills. On the plantation, old or injured slaves might be manumitted to relieve their owners of "unprofitable" property. As a consequence of all these practices, by the middle of the nineteenth century when there were few free blacks in the United States, over a third of the black population of Cuba was *gente de color* ([free] people of color). These were the people who developed the religion of Santería based on the beliefs and practices they, their parents, and their grandparents brought from their African homeland.

From as early as 1573, free and enslaved Africans in Cuba had organized themselves, with the blessings of both the colonial and church authorities, into clubs called *cabildos*.[6] These cabildos were social clubs where members of the same African ethnic group, called *nación*, could meet and socialize together. They were also quasi-political governmental bodies whose leadership was responsible to the Spanish city council for the behavior of their members. Cabildos provided a variety of services to their members, including burial for those who died, help for widows and orphans, funds to manumit members or their families, and social and spiritual guidance.

By law and custom, the members of each cabildo were members of the same African "nation" whose dances, drum types, and songs were considered ethnically significant symbols. The Cuban authorities hoped to provide a safety valve against discontent based on the members' social conditions while inserting a wedge between groups based on their different customs. The reconstruction of their religious traditions was an unintended consequence of the development of the Cuban cabildos. West African religions are danced religions. Rather than praying either silently or in unison, practitioners of these religious use drumming, song, dance, and possession trance to summon and worship their deities. To the Spanish authorities that were more familiar with Catholic church-based religious services, these rituals probably appeared more social than religious, but to the practitioners of these traditions these dances were potentially intense religious events. By encouraging the members of the different cabildos to maintain their drumming and dancing traditions, the colonial authorities were also encouraging them to reconstruct their religious traditions. Based on the importance of drumming and dancing to West African religious traditions, it is not surprising that by maintaining culturally homogeneous cabildos Afro-Cubans were able to provide a site for the development of new religious traditions based on the practices and traditions the members had known in their homeland. Since these activities were not recognized as "religious" by Europeans, the different African groups were able to reestablish their spiritual traditions in a relatively benign cultural context.

## PERSECUTION

There is little evidence of religious persecution of the Afro-Cuban cabildos or their members during the colonial period. However, in the nineteenth century as the colony was moving toward independence, the authorities began (rightly) to perceive the cabildos as the breeding grounds for anti-colonial and abolitionist activity. After slavery was abolished in 1886 and Cuba gained its independence from Spain in 1898, the new governmental authorities became increasingly concerned about the population of black and mulatto (mixed-race) Cubans who had expected full equality in the new administration.[7]

In November 1906, the disappearance of a toddler named Zoila Días was blamed on three members of the *Cabildo Congos Reales*, who, it was said, wanted to use the child's blood and body parts for sacrificial or curative purposes. The tumult around this and similar cases was the beginning of a twenty-year period of repression and persecution of all of the African-based religious groups in Cuba. During this period, Cubans became obsessed with the idea that the white civilized population must defend itself against the barbarianism and savagery of its black and mixed-race lower classes. The young lawyer Fernando Ortiz's *Los negros brujos*, published in 1906, outlined the rise and continuation of African-based "witchcraft" among Cuba's criminal element. It soon became the canonical text for recognizing such practices. (Surprisingly, in the 1920s, after learning more about the Lukumi societies in Havana, Oritz did a complete about face and become one of the leading figures in the new Afro-Cubanism movement that re-valorized Afro-Cuban culture.) Although religious secrecy was an element of Orisha religious practices in Yorubaland, it was during this period that heightened secrecy became an important element of these religions in Cuba.

Afro-Cuban religions, including Santería, Palo Monte, and Abakuá, experienced alternating periods of repression and tolerance throughout the twentieth century. In the 1960s and 1970s, the Castro government gave Afro-Cuban religions public recognition as "the people's folklore," and at the beginning of the twenty-first century they continue to regard these religions as an important part of their cultural heritage and as a source of tourist income.

## ORISHA RELIGION IN CUBA

Since there was no unified Yoruba culture in Africa, there was no single Yoruba Traditional Religion for Africans to reconstruct in the Americas. In fact, as citizens of warring towns, many of the Yoruba-speaking peoples arriving in Cuba could be expected to be antagonistic toward one another. However, the priests and devotees of the many deities whose stories were woven together in the Yoruba mythological tradition were able to work together to create a new religious system that integrated their numerous beliefs and practices.

Yoruba culture has always been incorporative, flexible, and eclectic. In addition to incorporating the religious practices of the different African worship communities, Yoruba peoples in Cuba also incorporated elements from the surrounding Spanish culture. Although this is generally presented as an attempt to deceive or mislead members of the dominant culture, the incorporation of alien religious powers into their religious pantheon had long been a practice among West African peoples. By incorporating Catholic saints, iconography, and sacramentals (that is, Catholic rituals of private devotion not associated with the sacraments of the Church) into their own practices, the Yoruba peoples in Cuba were able to domesticate these powerful spiritual forces for their own use. Although this mixing may have confused outsiders, Afro-Cubans and their contemporary descendents have never been confused by the presence of these appropriated images and objects.

It is not clear from the records that we have how Yoruba customs developed in the cabildos resulted in the religious forms we know today. We do know that all the elements necessary to develop a uniquely American version of Orisha worship was present in the cabildos, including a critical mass of individuals familiar with the worship styles associated with a key group of Orisha, the freedom to develop culturally satisfying social structures, and the encouragement to maintain certain significant activities, including drumming and dancing, which are central to Orisha worship. It appears that although the public face of the cabildos was male, internally they were governed by both men and women (often identified as kings and queens) with the women holding the superior position. That is, the "queens" had primary authority including the right to choose the "kings" who governed with them.[8] Women held important religious positions among the Yoruba-speaking peoples of Africa, so it should not be surprising to find that they were instrumental in the re-creation of their religious practices in Cuba. Contemporary santeros identify 11 African-born founders of Lukumi lineages: Efuche (Ña Rosalia, aka María Trujillo), Ainá (Ña Margarita Armenteros), Igoró (Ña Caridad Argudín), Apoto (Ña Belen González), Ma Monserrate (González), Francisca Entensa ("Palmira"), Obadimelli (Octavio Samar), José Pata de Palo (Urquiola), Los Ibeyi (the "Twins," Perfecto and Gumersindo), Monserrate Asiñabí, and Tía Julia Abonse.[9] Significantly, seven of these founders are women

There doesn't appear to be a direct connection between these lineages and the cabildos of the earlier period. During the early years of the repressive Republican period (1902-1958), many of the cabildos were disbanded or brought under more intense civic scrutiny. It appears that the practitioners of the African traditions, including the Yoruba-based traditions, moved their focus away from the cabildos and toward independent *casas de Ocha* (houses of the Orisha). Thus, in the early twentieth century, it appears that many of those who had been religious leaders in the cabildos gathered together the cabildos members they had initiated into new worship communities. Because of the initiatory nature of the religion, everyone looked to the person who performed their initiation as their religious leader and guide. The groups that formed under the guidance of these strong leaders evolved into the lineages and *casas de Ocha* of today. It appears that many of the founders of these lineages had worked together in the cabildos, and continued to work together in this later period.

It was during this time that worship of the Orisha in Cuba came together into a religious system that is the basis of the tradition we know today. Important to this reform movement were two women from Yorubaland who came to Cuba as free women in the late nineteenth century. They complained that the forms of worship they found in Cuba were not what they had known in their homeland, and worked to reorganize the community into a single religious system.[10] What had been independent communities focused on a single Orisha or a small group of Orisha in Africa were combined to form a unified worship system known as *Regla de Ocha* (Rule/Law of the Orisha) in Cuba. Under this system, rather than being initiated into as a priest of a single Orisha, each new priest was initiated into the worship of a standard set of between five to seven Orisha. Priests initiated under this system could not only initiate priests into the worship of their primary Orisha, but also into the worship of all the other Orisha.

Under the traditional system, the senior priests and priestesses were trained to perform the ceremonies and rituals associated with their individual Orisha. This new system of initiations required that ritual leaders be able to perform the ceremonies and rituals of all the Orisha. In time a group of highly trained ritual specialists developed to aid the priests in the performance of these ceremonies. They became known as *oba oriate*, or simply *oriate*. The oriate were trained to perform all ceremonies required for all of the different Orisha. Thus, they performed the role of the high priest (or priestess) for all of the individual worship groups, whether they themselves were members of the different groups or not. Because cowry shell divination was an integral part of many of these ceremonies, particularly the rituals of initiation, the oriate were also the highest trained practitioners of that divination system. Though several of the earliest oriate were women, it is the name Obadimelli (Octavio Samar Rodríguez) that is credited with the professionalization of this religious role. Obadimelli worked with the principal Ocha houses in Havana, and is considered to be the architect of the "modern" initiation system. Although the role of *oriate* originated earlier and Obadimelli was probably trained by the two women who were among Havana's great female oriates, he is recognized as the teacher of the most famous oriates of the twentieth century. Together with one of these women, Efuche, Obadimelli standardized initiation practices such that every priest was initiated to the worship of a set group of Orisha according to uniform ritual procedures. Because Obadimelli only trained other men as oriate, this important ritual role moved from the control of women to that of men.[11]

## BABALAWO

One group of priests was not completely incorporated into this unified system. Unlike the other priestly groups who welcomed both men and women, the priests of Orula (Orunmila in Africa) known as the *babalawo* (fathers of mystery) only allowed heterosexual men to be initiated into their priesthood. The babalawo were also exclusive in other regards. Although priests of the other Orisha could be initiated as babalawo, a babalawo could not receive any other Orisha initiations after his initiation in to the priesthood of Orula.

The babalawo are the owners of the divination system known as Ifa. In both Yorubaland and the Americas, they formed an all-male priesthood and ritual system that functions in parallel to the Orisha worship systems. Although much of the literature about the Orisha traditions suggests that the babalawo are the "high-priests" of Orisha worshippers, other priests say that the limitations imposed upon them reduce their influence. Babalawo who were initiated into the Orisha priesthood before their dedication to Orula can observe but not participate in the major portions of the *Asiento*, or priestly initiation ceremony, except for the *matanza* (sacrifice). Babalawo who were not initiated into the Orisha priesthood cannot even observe the central ceremonies. Although they are divination specialists, they are forbidden from performing diloggun divination (cowry shell divination), which is required as part of the initiation ceremonies. Babalawo may not participate in any other Orisha ritual, except as an observer. They may not divine with cowry shells or become possessed by an Orisha. Although they may construct icons for the warrior Orisha Eleggua, Ogun, and Osun, these icons cannot be used in the priestly initiations, and new icons must be created for the initiate.

While all of the babalawo are male, there are some female practitioners of the Ifa divination system in both Yorubaland and the Americas known as *iya-nifa* (Yr. mother of Ifa) or *iyalawo* (Yr. mother of secrets). These women are trained in the divination arts but are excluded from the highest ranks of the Ifa priesthood. The initiation of women into the ranks of the Ifa priesthood is controversial and not accepted by all devotees. Gay men are also ideally excluded from the ranks of the babalawo, although openly gay initiates into the priesthood of Ifa are not unknown.

Conflicts between the male-centric brotherhood of babalawo and the more female-centric Orisha worshippers are not unique to the Americas or the modern period. Some of the earliest records of the culture and religion of the Yoruba-speaking areas of West Africa noted the differences between the "Ifá priests" whom the missionaries seemed to respect and "fetish priests" upon whom they heaped their unalloyed contempt. In these early records, the babalawo were generally seen as religious professionals, sophisticated men with whom missionaries could engage in learned discussion, while the so-called fetish priests or *olorisha* (Yr. owners of Orisha) were presented as corrupt and ignorant, deceivers of the people who enriched themselves on the superstitions of others. That many of these fetish priests were women or cross-dressing men also lowered their standing in the eyes of the early Christian missionaries.[12]

In Cuba the earliest leaders of the religion were women (or like Obadi-melli, trained by women) who fit the description of African olorisha, that is, priests of the Orisha whose worship centered on rituals and possession trance. There were few active babalawo in Cuba until the twentieth century, and it was not until the 1930s that they did more than perform their trademark divination and the requisite ebos.[13] Only after they began marrying successful and renowned priestesses did they begin participating in initiation rituals.[14] Cuban-based babalawo look to back to five ancestors as the originators of their own lineages: Ño Carlos Adé (Ojuani Baká, "Crown gives Birth"), Ño Remigio Herrera Adechina (Obara Melli, "Crown Makes Fire"), Joaquin Cádiz Ifá-Omí (Ogundá Teturá, "Ifá of Water"), Olugueré Kó Kó (Oyekún Melli), and Francisco Villalonga Ifá Bí (Obe Ate, "Ifá Gives Birth").[15] Today, other babalawo lineages have developed as devotees have gone directly to Nigeria for initiation by African babalawo.

The principal function of the babalawo is to provide divination services. As the voice of Orula, who is called "the witness to creation," they can speak of the inquirer's destiny, his or her past, present, and future, unbiased by the needs or desires of any individual Orisha. While they can introduce one into the worship of Orula and a small number of other Orisha, they are precluded from direct participation in the rituals of the Orisha.

The incomplete assimilation of the priests of Orula into the larger Orisha community has lead to the development of two different organization styles that I call "oriaté-centered" houses and "babalawo-centered" houses. In an oriaté-centered house a babalawo is not used for any portion of the initiation process and is usually only consulted when his special type of divination is required. In these communities it is the oriaté who not only presides at the actual initiation, but also at all the preliminary rituals (determining the guardian Orisha and making the warriors, etc.) as well as at the required animal sacrifices afterward. Although only a babalawo can perform Ifá divination, such divination is not required for an Orisha initiation. Thus it is possible for an oriaté to conduct an entire initiation from start to finish without the assistance of a babalawo. Although the role of oriaté is a New World innovation, their exclusive use allows oriaté-centered houses to initiate new possession priests in the absence of any members of the divination priesthood.

In babalawo-centered houses, on the other hand, a babalawo does participate in these activities. He determines the guardian Orisha of the initiate, makes the initial set of warriors, performs other divination sessions before the initiation, and performs the sacrifice that feeds the new Orisha. He will generally also give members of the house the entry-level initiation into the cult of Ifá through a ceremony called "the hand of Orula." However, since babalawo cannot participate in some portions of the Orisha initiatory process, in babalawo-centered houses these initiation activities, including the *asiento* and the diloggun-based divination afterward, must also be presided over by an oriaté. In addition to these pure forms, there are other ways to distribute the responsibility for the different activities between the babalawo and the oriaté. And, in spite of the fact that it is considered extremely unorthodox by the most traditional and conservative practitioners, there are babalawo in the United States who directly participate in all aspects of Orisha initiation.

## SANTERÍA IN THE UNITED STATES

There were some santeros in the United States before the Cuban revolution. The earliest was the babalawo Francisco (Pancho) Mora, who came to the U.S. in 1946. The first American woman initiate to the religion was the Cuban-born Mercedes Noble, who was initiated in 1958. The first African American from the United States initiated was Walter King, who later took the name Osejiman Adefunmi. He was initiated along with Christopher Oliana in Matanzas Province, Cuba in 1959. Leonore Dolme, another Cuban santera, initiated Margie Baynes Quiniones, the first African American woman, in Queens in 1969. Assunta Seranno, a Puerto Rican priestess who was initiating priests in Adefunmi's temple, initiated the author Judith Gleason, the first Anglo-American priestess initiated in the United States.[16]

Two major emigration movements from Cuba, the first in the early 1960s after the Cuban Revolution and later in the 1980s during the so-call Mariel boatlift, were instrumental in bringing Cuban refugees and the Orisha to the United States. In Cuba the religion of the Orisha was generally considered to be a lower class phenomenon, even though it attracted devotees from all segments of society. The majority of Cubans fleeing the country after the Revolution were from the upper classes of Cuba who had were not involved in the tradition. However, many became devotees to the Orisha in the U.S. as they saw it as a part of the cultural heritage that could help them adjust to life in a strange new country.

In 1980, Fidel Castro declared the port of Mariel "open" and permitted any person who wanted to leave Cuba free access to depart from there. Approximately 124,000 undocumented Cuban migrants entered the United States between April and October of that year. Many of these were poorer and darker than those who arrived earlier. And many had been practitioners of Orisha religion before their departure. In spite of conflicts between the first and second wave of immigrants, these new arrivals reenergized the practices of Orisha traditional religion in the United States. Many look to these "Marielitos" as the founders of their community, and in many communities the religion has become more visible because of their activities. Since the 1980s, Orisha worship has spread throughout the country. Although the highest concentrations of devotees are still in the Miami area, along the eastern seaboard particularly in the New York City and New Jersey areas, Chicago, Los Angeles, Oakland, and Seattle, there are smaller communities in all of the major and many of the secondary American cities. Additionally, small pockets of devotees can be found throughout the country even in the smaller cities and towns of the heartland.

## PUBLIC FACES OF THE RELIGION

Although the Orisha communities in Cuba and the United States tend to be private and anonymous, two communities have played an important part in the public history of the religion: Oyotunji Village in South Carolina and the Church of the Lukumi Babalu Aye in Florida.

### OYOTUNJI VILLAGE

Walter Serge King was already immersed in African culture when he traveled with his friend Christopher Oliana to Matanzas Cuba, and in August of 1959 became the first African American from the United States to be initiated as a priest of the Orisha.[17] As part of his initiation, he was given the name Efuntola Oseijeman Adefunmi. He had been dancer with the Katherine Dunham Dance Company, and had studied the Afro-Haitian religion of Vodou as well as ancient Egyptian religion. He was learning Swahili, the trade language of Eastern Africa. As part of his exploration of his African heritage, he had established the Order of the Damballah Hwedo, and had begun to wear and sell dashikis on the streets of Harlem. However, when he discovered the Orisha he discovered his most important connection to the African homeland, and eventually his life's work. After his return from Cuba in 1959, Osejiman Adefumni founded a series of Orisha-centric organizations in New York City, including the Shango Temple and African Theological Archmininstry, which came to be called the Yoruba Temple.

In the 1960s, his practice of Santería became more and more entwined with the Black Nationalist movement of the time. Black Nationalists maintained and promoted their identity as African people and attempted to repudiate the influences of non-African (White/European) culture in their lives. Adefunmi begin wearing Yoruba clothing and using more Yoruba (rather than Spanish) in his practice of the religion. He also rejected Catholic saints and statues that he saw as Cuban rather than African icons, replacing them more Afrocentric images. All of this soon brought him in conflict with his Santería elders, some of whom viewed Cuba (rather than Africa) as the primary home of the Orisha, and Spanish as its sacred language. Eventually, he broke with the Santería community, founding his own Orisha lineage.

As a Black Nationalist, Adefunmi felt that African Americans needed to separate themselves from mainstream American culture, so in 1970 he established Oyotunji Village in Beaufort County, South Carolina. Oyotunji Village (the name means "Oyo returns") was designed to be the reincarnation of the great city of Oyo on American soil. In 1972, Adefunmi was initiated into the Ifa priesthood in Nigeria, and later that year was proclaimed the Oba (king) of the Village. Until his death in 2005, Adefumni led the Village in its effort to create an authentically African "kingdom" within the confines of the United States. Although the actual population of the Village has been small (no more than five to nine families during the last 10 years of Adfumni's life), it has had a lasting effect on the face of Orisha worship due to the large number of priests and priestesses who were initiated in the system he established. The religious practice that developed at the Village, although based on Santería precedents, was tailored to meet the needs of African American devotees. This lineage is often known as Orisha Voodoo since it incorporates not only the beliefs and practices of the Yoruba people as they were preserved in Cuba, but also practices based on contemporary Yoruba culture and the beliefs and practices from other West African peoples. Under the leadership of Adefunmi, the Village reinstituted several Yoruba cultural institutions that had been lost in Cuba, including the Egungun Masquerade honoring the ancestors, male and female secret societies, and worship groups for individual Orisha.

In July 2005, the second Oba (king) of Olotunji, Adelabu Adefunmi II, Adefumni's 28-year-old son, was crowned. He inherited a village that is much smaller than the 200 people who lived there in the 1970s and 80s, but whose reach extends throughout the country as many of those who no longer live in the village maintain close ties and loyalties to the village and its leaders.

## CHURCH OF THE LUKUMI BABALU AYE

The Church of the Lukumi Babalu Aye (CLBA) was founded in 1974 in a suburb of Miami by a small group of Spanish-speaking devotees, including Iyalosha Carmen Pla, Babalosha Raul Rodriguez, Oba Ernesto Pichardo, Babalosha Fernando Pichardo, and Attorney Gino Negretti.[18] In 1987, the Church celebrated the pre-opening of its first public location. This was a radical change from the predominate form of Orisha communities, which is home-based and very private. The Church immediately became the center of a political uproar. The city of Hialeah eventually enacted a series of ordinances that banned ritual animal sacrifice. These ordinances made it illegal "to unnecessarily kill, torment, torture, or mutilate an animal in a public or private ritual or ceremony not for the primary purpose of food consumption." Since the city allowed the killing of animals for a host of other reasons "'even if you're tired of taking care of them,' as long as the purpose was not sacrifice," these ordinances appeared to be an effort to suppress CLBA. The Church sued the city, and in 1993, the United States Supreme Court, in a landmark ruling, overturned the lower courts in favor of CLBA, declaring Hialeah's city ordinances were a denial of the Church members' constitutional rights.[19]

CLBA has attempted to create an organizational structure that could be sustained over time and better fit within what they call "the eurocentric secular framework" of the American religious landscape. By separating the corporate administrative functions from the religious functions, they hope to create a series of check and balances that will sustain the community beyond the lifetimes of the founders. Like Oyotunji Village, CLBA is attempting to create an organization style that works for Americans, one that is free from colonial Catholic fusion. Whereas Oyotunji Village looks to its understanding of traditional Yoruba culture for models, CLBA looks to the Cuban cabildo period for a model structure while drawing on some American business practices to sustain the business side of the organization. In addition to providing an actual "home church" for those in the Miami area, they also support what they call traditional "home worship groups". Toward that effort, CLBA provides membership status to devotees across the nation and provides a certification service for priests and priestesses. Certified priests can obtain a clergy identification card and inclusion in CLBA's list of certified priests available to those exploring the religion. In addition, members can register their ceremonies (baptisms, marriages, and Orisha ceremonies) and receive a certificate from CLBA.

Although the CLBA is committed to the abandonment of syncretistic retentions and the reestablishment of traditional rites and values, it has incorporated many of the outward forms of the American religious scene, including identifying the Necklaces ritual as a "baptism," Ifa or dilogun divination as "confession," and developing and performing several types of rituals not known among practitioners in Cuba, such as marriages and baby-naming ceremonies. By establishing a storefront "church" and developing many familiar religious forms, CLBA is on the forefront of the movement toward the "protestantization" of the tradition.

## WEB PRESENCE

In addition to establishing themselves in the United States, the Orisha have communities of devotees around the world including Europe, Asia, and Latin America. They have also found a home on the Internet. A quick search for "Orisha" on google.com yields in excess of 300,000 entries, including personal webpages, information from museum exhibits, and online *botanicas* (stores catering to devotees). There are also innumerable message boards and discussion groups for devotees, and even private areas for members of certain Orisha communities. As with all internet sources, the quality of these sites is mixed both in terms of the web layout and design and in terms of the information provided. Many sites offer a marketplace of goods and services. Although many are legitimate sources, one must always be careful when purchasing both goods and services from an unknown source. One should be especially wary of sites offering online or distance readings. For more information about online sources, refer to the Online Resources section in the Bibliography.

# Cosmology

The worldview of santeros and other Orisha devotees is based on the cosmology of the ancient Yoruba people. According to this view, the cosmos is singular. There is no this world and another world, but a single world with visible and invisible elements. Visible elements include living people, plants, animals, rocks, stars, rain, the ocean, everything that can be perceived with the basic senses. The invisible elements include those who have died and those waiting to be born, the Orisha and Olodumare. Sometimes the visible world is called *Aiye* (Yr. earth) and the invisible world *Orun* (Yr. sky or heaven), but with the understanding that earth and sky are of a single piece, not two separate worlds as is commonly believed in Western cultures.

The Yoruba imaged the visible and invisible worlds as a giant calabash. A calabash is a type of gourd that is often grown for use as a container. The calabash of the cosmos is imaged to be a spherical calabash cut along its equator to form two halves containing the visible and invisible portions of the world. There are two ways of understanding the calabash of existence. One is using the concept of *ashé*, the energy of the universe. The other is by looking at the different types of beings that inhabit the visible and invisible portions of the calabash and describing the interactions between them. These two understandings are mutually exclusive, so that it seems as though if one is correct the other can't be. However, both explanations can be found within the mythology of the Yoruba and neither explanation is complete in itself. This is similar to the strategy modern physicists use to explain the actions of atoms which sometimes exhibit the characteristics of waves and sometimes those of particles.

Yoruba religions can sometimes be described as a type of monism focusing on the energy of ashé and sometimes as a polytheism focusing on the Orisha, without being limited it to either of those positions. Each has a partial truth but neither holds the whole truth. Consequently, I will describe the calabash of existence first in terms of *ashé* and then in terms of the beings inhabiting it in order to come to the fullest understanding of these ideas.

## Ashé as the Focus of the Religion

Monistic religious traditions conceive of reality as a single unified whole that is grounded in a single basic substance or principle. If there are deities in these traditions, they merely represent portions of that whole. Although this is a difficult concept for those of us who grew up within a theistic tradition in which ultimate reality is seen as one or more personal beings or gods, it is not entirely alien. The worldview of the Star Wars films presents a popular form of monism.[1] For Luke Skywalker and his companions, the Force is a type of universal energy that stands behind and encompasses the cosmos. As the focus of the quasi-religious brotherhood of the Jedi Knights, the Force can be manipulated for good or evil, while "may the Force be with you" serves as a type of blessing among the people.

Among the Yoruba the Force is called *ashé*. Ashé can be understood as the energy of the universe. Modern physics teaches us that everything is merely energy moving at different rates of speed. Although the total energy in the universe cannot be changed, one can change portions of the universe by adding and removing energy from that portion, for example, by adding or removing energy from the air used to heat and cool our homes and offices. By understanding these principles of energy we have the power to control our environment.

Within the Orisha, one can learn to control the movement of this sacred energy. Just as the Jedi knights can access and control the Force, Orisha priests can learn to understand and control the movement of ashé within the whole calabash of existence. Ashé itself is neither good nor evil, rather it is the force of the universe that maintains balance and order. This balance is not static, but is a dynamic force that is constantly changing. It is not the balance of a rock firmly embedded in the earth, but of a tightrope walker whose continuous subtle movements allow him to maintain equilibrium. If the tightrope walker should quit moving he would lose his balance and fall. When a portion of the calabash is out of balance, people experience emotional, physical, or economic disorder. They may vacillate wildly or fall off the path of their destiny. By manipulating ashé, Orisha priests can bring such people back into to the balance that expresses ashé in their lives. Much of the work of the religion is restoring and maintaining balance and order in the lives of devotees.

Joseph Murphy describes ashé as the movement of the cosmos toward completeness and divinity. Quoting the words of the anthropologist Pierre Verger, he says that it is "all mystery, all secret power, all divinity." It is without beginning and end, cannot be enumerated or exhausted. It is not a particular power but Power itself. While ashé is the absolute ground of reality it is also absolute movement and thus no ground at all.[2]

Santería worship considers drumming and dancing as essential to religious ritual. Santería is a danced religion because dancing expresses the fundamental dynamism of ashé. By dancing, the practitioner expresses the ashé of the universe, calls into presence the ashé of the Orisha, and moves more surely into his or her personal destiny, his or her personal ashé. In the same way that one can change the world by an understanding and manipulation of physics, by understanding the principles of ashé one can dance one's true destiny. Through prayers, rhythms, offerings, and the observation of his or her taboos, Murphy says that an initiate of Santería is "lifted out of the self-absorption and frustration of ordinary life into the world of power where everything is easy because all is ashé, all is destiny."[3]

## ORISHA AS THE FOCUS OF THE RELIGION

The worldview of the Yoruba is not only expressed in abstract notion of ashé, but also in beings that embody this energy. When the universe came into existence, ashé was expressed in a wide variety of beings that have responsibilities toward one another. It is the interaction between these beings that maintains the balance of the world, which keeps the ashé in motion. In this view, the calabash of the cosmos is divided into two spheres: *Orun*, the invisible world sometimes called heaven, and *Aiye*, the visible world sometimes called earth. Even though the translation of these words uses the common worlds "heaven" and "earth," it is important to understand that Orun and Aiye are two parts of the unified cosmos. "Heaven" and "earth" are not two separate places, but part of a single cosmos that contains within itself all that is. Within this world there are beings located at five different levels of power: Olodumare, the Orisha, the ancestors, human beings, and the lowest group that includes plants and animals as well as natural and manufactured items.

## OLODUMARE

At the highest, most powerful level, practitioners understand that ashé, the ground of being, is something rather than nothing. They call this something Olodumare, the Supreme Being, the owner of Heaven, the Owner of all Destinies. Olodumare can be seen as the chief source of power and is often referred to as a great god, a deistic being beyond human comprehension, the God behind all the lesser gods. Although many scholars and practitioners refer to Olodumare as "father" and use male pronouns in their discussions,

Olodumare is beyond all categories including that of gender. It is only the limitation of our language that encourages this usage. The Yoruba language has no gendered pronouns, making it easier to speak without assigning gender to a genderless being.

As the most remote of beings, Olodumare is never approached directly, no shrines are erected in the name of Olodumare, no rituals are directed toward Olodumare, and no sacrifices are made to Olodumare. However, Olodumare is not otherworldly, rather it is Olodumare as the personification of ashé who sustains all the rest of the universe. The name of Olodumare is invoked within every ritual, and Olodumare is present in all shrines and partakes of all sacrifices. Olodumare is the owner of heaven in the metaphysical sense of possessing a sacred power or being the source of a mystery. It is the power of Olodumare that guides the evolution of the cosmos and thus is present everywhere. Because Olodumare includes all that is and all that is not, Olodumare is beyond human comprehension. In this way, Olodumare fulfills the description of a transcendent or "high" god. It is the breath of Olodumare that maintains life in all living things, and the energy of Olodumare that sustains the whole of the universe. Thus, although transcendent, Olodumare is, at the same time, ultimately immanent, present in the butterfly, the earthworm, the newborn child.[4]

## ORISHA

The ashé of the universe, however, is not all the same; it collects and forms into nodes of power we recognize as forces of nature (wind, ocean, and thunder), power sites (rivers and mountains), and aspects of human life (our roles as mothers, kings, and warriors). In the Yoruba traditions these forces have been given human form as a group of beings or demigods called the *Orisha*. The Orisha are multi-dimensional beings that represent the forces of nature, act as archetypes, and function as sacred patrons or "guardian angels." As knowable aspects of Olodumare, they represent a level of power that is approachable though ritual action and so provide one very important focus for Yoruba religion.[5] The Orisha have attributes and stories similar to the stories and attributes used to describe the ancient Greek and Roman deities. Their stories tell us how the world came to be the way it is (why thunder and wind are often found together) and how to live a good life (sometimes you can persuade better with honey than with a sword). However, unlike the Greek gods, the Orisha are not remote deities living high on a mountain peak, rather they are living beings present in the everyday life of their followers. It is around the Orisha that most Yoruba and Santería religious activity focuses. Most of the Yoruba mythology tells of the time when the Orisha lived upon the earth.

Although it is common to describe the Orisha in terms of a hierarchy that places Olodumare at the top and some Orisha superior to others, that is an incomplete description of both the Yoruba case and the ways Orisha religions have developed in the Americas. There are three organizational schemes that anthropologists developed to describe these traditions in Yorubaland.[6] The Triangular model conforms most closely with the hierarchical model presented in much of the literature. In this model Olodumare sits at the top of a pyramid while the Orisha occupying the space below are graded according to their importance and power. Orunmila, who is also known as Ifa or Orula, is the Orisha of divination who is often placed toward the top of the pyramid along with Eshu, the spirit of divine unpredictability. This model focuses on the unity and continuity of divine power embedded in the Orisha. It tends to support a rationalized univeralist monotheism that undercuts the place of the individual Orisha and their groups of worshippers.

The Circular model seems to better reflect the cosmology found in the sacred praise songs of the Orisha. It has an upper hemisphere that is similar in organization to that found in the Triangular model. Olodumare sits above the Orisha while Eshu and Ifa have a special position side by side between Olodumare and the other "sky" Orisha. In the lower portion are the earthly spirits and Onile, the Earth goddess who is often absent from description of the Triangular model. This model restores Onile and recognizes the special positions of Eshu and Ifa in the mythology, but it ignores the links between the so-called "sky gods" and the earth and leads to a form of dualism that associates the upper hemisphere with "light" and lower hemisphere with "darkness."

Pierre Verger, who collected the single largest number of *oriki* (sacred praise songs) and chants suggested that neither of these models accurately reflected the Yoruba worldview.[7] Rather, he suggested what can be called the Ashé model. In this conception, ashé is the all-encompassing force that envelops all of the Orisha and their worship groups. There is no hierarchical relationship between Orisha; rather, each is a separate and complete deity in the fullest sense. Verger suggests that rather than a pantheon, the Orisha form individual juxtaposed theisms, or even monotheisms. While this model undervalues the interrelatedness between different worship groups and the specialization of the priests of Ifa and Esu, it gives the same valuation to all of the Orisha and perhaps overvalues the place of ashé.[8]

Again, each of these models provides a partial view of the way the Yoruba people understand the relationship between and among the Orisha. Some of the same ambiguity continues to exist in the Americas. Americans seem to have developed a fourth model that combines features of the three Yoruba models. From the Triangular model they take the idea that Olodumare is the high god who sits above the other Orisha who are arrayed below. However, there is no consensus as to the relationship among the Orisha below. Many, but not all, would accord Orula a special high position, and most would say that Obatala stands as a father to the rest of the Orisha. However, there is no distinction made between sky-god and earth-gods, and few Orisha devotees in the American would be able to place the Orisha into those categories. In addition, the Earth Goddess, Onile, is not worshipped in the Americas.

When the religion of the Orisha was standardized in Cuba in the early twentieth century, the major Orisha were arranged into a list for the purposes of ritual invocation. However, that arrangement doesn't imply any hierarchical relationships between them; that is, Orisha invoked first are not considered superior to those invoked later. In many ways, contemporary Orisha devotees think of the Orisha in terms of a modified Ashé model in which Olodumare and perhaps Ifa are considered superior, but all of the other Orisha are each considered to be separate and complete deities in the fullest sense. For many priests, the Orisha of their head is the head of a personal pantheon that includes all of the Orisha they have received.

## HUMAN BEINGS

As part of the creation cycle, the story is told of the coming of human beings. It is said that Olodumare commissioned Oshanla, whose name means the great or principal Orisha, to make the bodies of human beings in order that Olodumare might breathe the breath of life into them. In this way, Olodumare and Oshanla cooperate to bring forth a new type of being. When the Orisha returned to Orun, the invisible world, it became the responsibility of these their human children to continue the ceremonies and sacrifices they began. Although the Orisha are powerful beings, they are not all-powerful, and depend on their followers to continue their existence by continuing their worship. Like all beings, the Orisha require continued nourishment. Their worshippers provide for their continued sustenance through the sacrifice of plants and animals. Without these offering and sacrifices, without worship, the Orisha would cease to exist.

In exchange for these offerings the Orisha provide for their worshippers. As nodes of power and the owners of ashé, the Orisha can provide health, wealth, children, and guidance. According to the understandings developed in Cuba, each person is born as the special child of one or more Orisha. If a person becomes involved in the religion, he or she can discover their patron Orisha and, if they decide to become initiated as priests, they will be initiated as priest of that Orisha. It is this Orisha that is said to "own their head."

## ANCESTORS

As people live out their natural life span, they die and become members of the *egun* (Yr. the ancestors). The egun exist at another, different level of power from either the Orisha or humans. Although they no longer exist in the visible world, they continue to have an interest in the affairs of their descendants. Within the family, the ancestors assume an important place in religious activity. Among the Yoruba, while it is the Orisha who are concerned with the destinies of individual practitioners, it is the ancestors, the egun, who watch over the moral and social order of the society and one's adherence to public norms.[9]

Not all of a family's ancestors are considered egun. Those who died young without fulfilling their destiny and those who were evil and cruel may be respected as members of the family, but are not accorded the veneration given to the egun as the honored ancestors. In Yorubaland, the most important ancestors may also become part of the *Egungun*, or masked dancers, that visit the towns in yearly celebrations. Members of the family are initiated into the Egungun society, construct a costume for the ancestor, and dance as one of the masqueraders during the yearly celebrations. Although the Egungun society didn't survive in Cuba, members of some American Orisha communities have returned to Nigeria, received the appropriate initiations, and revived the Egungun ceremonies in the United States. Even without a formal Egungun society, the respect for the dead remained strong in the Americas. Every ceremony and ritual begins with an invocation of the egun, and every priest and many other devotees have small shrines to their personal egun in the homes.

Among the Yoruba, reincarnation is considered a positive experience instead of a punishment for past lives. The ancestors are believed to be reborn into their own family lineage, and often children are considered to embody the spirit of a grandparent. Thus, the dead are always part of the family, and may be seen to return in the faces and mannerisms of their descendants. After a period of rest and relaxation in the good heaven (*orun rere*), most people are reborn into the lives and families of their children. Those who have been cruel or wicked, who are guilty of murder, assault, theft, slander, the use of magic for evil purpose, or those who have harmed other people are not allowed to reincarnate. Instead, they are sent to *orun bururu*, that is, the bad heaven or the heaven of the potsherds. The metaphor here is that just as a broken pot cannot be repaired, these people can never be restored to the living. They are discarded just as one discards broken pottery.

People stand at the center of the Yoruba cosmological system. Only people can provide worship to the Orisha and it is for their human children that the Orisha act in the visible world. Through a process of reincarnation, people return again and again to the visible world to enjoy the pleasures found there. Two proverbs exemplify the Yoruba viewpoint. One says that Aiye is the marketplace while Orun is home. The other says life in heaven (Orun) cannot be pleasant, otherwise people would not live so long and come back so quickly. Together these proverbs suggest a deep appreciation of the visible world. In a culture without television, computers, and the personal entertainment center, home is where you go to eat and sleep and refresh yourself. The marketplace is where the action is. It is in the market that one meets friends and enemies, gains power and authority, and makes one's name in the community. While home is necessary, the marketplace is where people want to be; while heaven provides a welcome respite from the challenges of earth, it soon becomes boring and one quickly returns. This suggests a view of life as generally a positive and cherished experience. Rather than a vale of tears one must endure or a place of suffering one hopes to escape, life in the visible world is seen as generally good and welcome. Regardless of what one thinks about what happens in that space between death and rebirth, it is the life that we are living now that is most important. Everyone wants to live a full, happy, and productive life, and, as we will see, when suffering comes into this cosmological system, there are physical, emotional, and spiritual remedies, rituals intended to bring one back into balance with one's destiny of a long and productive life, good health, and the happiness of family and friends.

## THE NATURAL WORLD

At the lowest level of power, but still of vital importance to the cosmos, are animals, plants, what some people might call "inanimate" objects like rocks, the wind, dirt, water, honey, and manufactured items like iron, food, and the like. Just as these can be used to feed, clothe, protect, and serve the needs of people, all of these contain levels of ashé that can be used by human beings for the benefit of the visible and invisible worlds. Everything contains ashé and everything is or can be associated with an Orisha or the egun. Through ritualized attention these objects become either repositories for religious energy or the contributors of their ashé for the benefit of others.

These objects and their uses are neither idealized nor demonized. Consequently, there is no custom of ascetic practice within the Orisha traditions. Although each priest has a set of requirements and prohibitions that may impose a certain level of spiritual discipline on him or her, there are few universal requirements or prohibitions. While some priests may be forbidden to drink alcohol, eat pork, or wear certain colors or styles of clothing, there is no food or drink that is universally prohibited or required, no color or style of clothing that is universally prohibited or required. Nothing in the visible world either natural or manufactured is considered evil in and of itself. Similarly, although certain activities may be forbidden to certain priests on a temporary or permanent basis, there is no human activity that is absolutely forbidden. Thus, although devotees may be required to forgo sexual activity, for example, for short periods of time, sexual activity in general is not forbidden. Not only may priests be married or single, there is no group within the tradition that is equivalent to the monks, nuns, and priests of other traditions who are expected to forgo marriage in the service of the religious community.

## CONCEPT OF MULTIPLE SOULS AND WHAT THAT MEANS

One question that often comes up in discussions of Yoruba cosmology is whether the dead really become egun, spirits that continue to be concerned about the lives of their descendants, or if they leave the invisible world to reincarnate in those very descendants. It doesn't seem as though a single spirit can be both in heaven watching over the family and reborn into one of his or her grandchildren. The two ideas seem mutually exclusive. Not everyone agrees on how this can happen, but probably the best explanation comes from the work of William Bascom, an anthropologist who studied the Yoruba people in the early- to mid-twentieth century.[10] He suggests that even then, after more than a century of Christian missionary activity and much longer Muslim influence, the Yoruba people still believed in multiple souls. According to his research, the Yoruba people generally identify three separate souls in human beings. The first is the breath, known as *emi*. The breath provides one's vital force; it gives life and makes it possible for us to work. In one creation story, after Obatala has molded the bodies of human beings, Olodumare moves among them, animating them with his *emi*, the breath of life. Each new child is similarly animated by the breath of Olodumare. According the Yoruba philosopher Segun Gbadegesin, since the breath of Olodumare animates everyone, we are all children of Olodumare and worthy of protection from harm.[11]

The second soul that Bascom's informants identified was *ojiji*, the shadow, which has no function but to follow one around throughout one's life. The third and most important soul is *eleda* or *olori*, which he identifies as the ancestral guardian soul. Eleda resides in the head and is associated with one's destiny; *olori* actually means the "owner of ori or destiny." Gbadegesin identifies the *ori* itself as the guardian spirit of the person and the most important of a person's souls, since the ori bears the person's complete destiny. As I will discuss further in "Destiny, Divination, and Sacrifice," ori is also considered to be one's person deity, the only Orisha that will follow one anywhere, and the one who can accept or reject the services of the other Orisha.

In some parts of Yorubaland they say that it is the breath (emi) of the witch that travels at night and causes harm to others; in other places they attribute this activity to the shadow, which is free to roam in the dark of night. It is also the breath or the shadow that remains in heaven when one is reincarnated. This is the part of the ancestor that is honored in the Egungun rituals and who is venerated at the ancestral shrine. Some people also believe that there is a portion of a person that remains in the *orun* throughout one's life. The heavenly counterpart does in the invisible world exactly the same things that one is doing in the visible world. Some people call this heavenly counterpart the *eleda*. Upon death one's souls are reunited with all of one's ancestral souls before taking on a new body, a new life, and a new destiny. Although not everyone is reincarnated, all living people are the reincarnation of some ancestor.

Although this explanation presents some logical problems, it continues to influence the thoughts of contemporary practitioners of Orisha religion. Devotees have attempted to solve some of the logical dilemmas by appealing to the reincarnation theories of Asia. Some devotees who invoke these ideas think that reincarnation provides a way for the soul to spiritually progress until it becomes an Orisha or other highly evolved spirit. Although there are Orisha who had human lives before becoming Orisha (Shango is perhaps the best known) the idea that one can or should spiritually evolve so as to escape the pains and pleasure of the visible world is contrary to the Yoruba cosmological viewpoint.

## WITCHCRAFT AND THEODICY

The lives of the Yoruba people and Orisha worshippers are not that different from the lives of people around the world. Babies are born and old people die, some people are wildly successful while others are miserable failures, accidents happen, children inexplicably sicken and die, a horrible natural or man-made disaster catches people unaware, sweeping away the good and kind along with the evil and cruel. Scholars use the term *theodicy* for the study of how people answer the questions that arise from these life experiences. Questions like: Why do good people suffer while the wicked prosper? Why do innocent children suffer and die? Why does the whirlwind destroy one house and leave its neighbor standing? Why, in any catastrophe, are some destroyed while others survive? And most basically, Why me? Why must *I* suffer? Why do *my* children sicken and die? Why can't *I* find the path in life I deserve?

Yoruba ideas of destiny, which I will discuss at length in "Destiny, Divination, and Sacrifice," provides some answers, but Orisha mythology suggests two additional types of beings whose activities help to answer these questions. These are the *aje* and the *ajogun*. The ajogun, or warlords, are all of the forces of nature that challenge the balance of the cosmos. The most prominent among these forces are *iku* (death), *arun* (disease), *ofo* (loss), *egba* (paralysis), *oran* (literally, big trouble), *epe* (curse), *ewon* (imprisonment), and *ese* (a generalized name for all other human afflictions).[12] Although some devotees describe the ajogun as dark forces that work in opposition to the Orisha who are light forces, the Yoruba understanding of the cosmos isn't dualistic—that is, they do not ascribe absolute good or evil, light or dark, to any visible or invisible forces. Although no one wants to meet the ajogun, often devotees describe situations in which the forces of disease, loss, and other afflictions are used to nudge individuals back onto the path of their best destiny. Iku is spoken of in the mythology as the divine bailiff; the collector of the debt cannot go unpaid. According to these stories, Iku has been commissioned by Olodumare to release one's spirit so that it can return to Orun. Iku is not an evil force but rather the enforcer of the final agreement in one's destiny. Although Iku cannot be avoided as all must die, through propitiation of Orisha and egun people believe that they can be protected against the worst of these forces and not face premature death and the other afflictions.

Much of the work of Orisha priests involves helping others avoid the ajo-gun and have a long, healthy, and fulfilling life. Sometimes, however, it is necessary for one to face the challenge of the ajogun in order to fully manifest his or her destiny. Although no one wants to meet these forces, sometimes their challenge is necessary to keep one on the path of one's best and highest destiny. Many people have had the experience of being challenged by and overcoming the ajogun. Although the challenge was difficult, they often report that their lives were happier, their characters better, and their destinies clearer than before.

The aje or witchcraft power can also affect the length and quality of one's life. Contemporary notions of witchcraft in American Orisha traditions draw on both African and European notions of witchcraft. In many African cultures including the Yoruba, witchcraft serves to explain not only why bad things happen to good people, but also why it appears that some people are more successful than others with similar circumstances. The Yoruba word *aje* is often translated as "witch" or "witchcraft," however, among the Yoruba, aje is not so much a role or personal characteristic as a special ability that one has. Thus, rather than saying one *is* a witch, it is more accurate to say that one *has* witchcraft power, power that can be used for good or ill depending on the character of the person possessing it. Anyone could be born with this power, and it is assumed that powerful and successful people not only have this power, but that they have learned to use it to their advantage. Being in the right place at the right time, what we may call good luck, is perceived as having strong aje. Similarly, being at the wrong place at the wrong time, bad luck, is either attributed to a lack of aje or the effect of someone with stronger aje working against you.

Although anyone can have (and use) witchcraft power, and its power can be used for good as well as evil, there is still an extremely negative stereotype of witchcraft among the Yoruba. Berry Hallen and J.O. Sodipo, who have written the most extensive analysis of the concept of witchcraft among the Yoruba, say that aje refers to "[a] person who is anti-social and deliberately and destructively malevolent towards other members of his community..." Although anyone might have this power, generally the aje are thought to be women who belong to their own clubs that meet together at night. These women are thought to be capable of killing others, even their own children.[13] Among the Yoruba, to name something is to call it into presence, so those with this power are more generally referred to as *eleye* (literally, "owner of birds") and *awon iya wa* or *iyami* ("our mothers"). One of the implications of this terminology is that those who are witches, "our mothers," by night are also our mothers (and sisters, aunts, cousins, wives, and co-wives, etc.) during the day. In some part of Yorubaland there are even festivals to honor and appease those with aje so that they might work positive witchcraft for the benefit of their sons and daughters, their grandchildren, and society as a whole.

Although the owners of aje are generally thought of as malevolent, the power itself is not considered inherently good or evil. All powerful people, including kings and priests, wealthy market women, and male and female titleholders, are assumed to have strong aje. Most of the Orisha are also said to be strong witches, and many of the female Orisha are said to be leaders of their own witchcraft societies.

Although witchcraft power among the Yoruba has an ambiguous quality in that it can be used for good or ill, in European thought, witchcraft has a much more sinister reputation. During the height of the European witch hunt that lasted from the twelfth to nineteenth centuries, witches were thought to be those who had turned their back on civil society and succumbed to the temptations of Satan. People thought that their pact with the devil gave them extraordinary powers that allowed them to act against their neighbors, causing crippling and painful illness or death, sexual impotence, frigidity or barrenness; unpredictable climatic or meteorological changes, crop failure and loss of livestock; and involuntary actions, rapid personality changes and loss of friends. Although both men and women were persecuted for witchcraft, stereotypically, a witch was an old, unattractive, and disliked woman, often either a widow or spinster who was living outside normal (male) social control. Unlike the owners of aje who may have been born with witchcraft substance, European witches were seen as morally depraved persons who chose their depravity. Many of those accused and executed for witchcraft were local healers who depended on both medical and magical knowledge in their work. Such knowledge could be used for both beneficial and detrimental purpose—the power to cure assumes the power to kill, as cursing and removing curses are two sides of the same coin. Thus these magical workers were both loved and feared in their communities. As the Inquisition progressed, these magical powers became more and more associated with the demonic forces. This fear was used by religious and secular authorities against their victims.

The Spanish Inquisition, however, presents a unique case. Although Spanish villages had their own healers known as *curanderos*, in Spain (and later in its New World colonies) the focus of inquisitors' investigations were not witchcraft but "heresy." With the *Reconquista* (the Reconquest that drove the last of the Muslims off the Iberian Peninsula) and uniting of the kingdoms of Isabella and Ferdinand in 1492, Spain turned its energies to the creation of a Catholic nation and the elimination of Muslim and Jewish influences. Issues of ancestral and religious purity dominated Spanish thought. *Limpieza de sangre* (Sp. purity of blood) began as a way of distinguishing between those whose ancestors had "always" been Christians and those whose ancestors had been Jewish or Muslim or had been disciplined by the Inquisition for some offense. Relatively few people suffered death for witchcraft under the Spanish Inquisition, and there were no executions for witchcraft in the colonies of New Spain (the Americas). Religious activity, rather than witchcraft, seems to have been the focus of the Spanish Inquisition in both Spain and her colonies. Thus, witches and the practices associated with them were less likely to be recognized and punished by the Spanish Inquisition than in other parts of Europe. This does not mean that witchcraft was unknown or that witchcraft accusations could not be used to demonize certain classes of people, merely that it was less common than in other European countries and colonies.[14]

Contemporary Orisha practitioners combine these ideas about witchcraft in interesting ways. On the one hand (and in line with African sensibilities), all of the Orisha, and by extension all of their priests, are understood to be imbued with the ability to subtly affect the visible and invisible world, to use "magic" to change lives and fortunes, and to control natural phenomena. On the other hand (expressing a European understanding), witchcraft is perceived as an essentially malevolent force used by others. Seldom is someone directly accused of witchcraft. However, vague notions of witchcraft being used against devotees is common both in divination sessions and in everyday conversation. This idea that witchcraft is everywhere is very African, as is the notion that the perceptive person must guard himself or herself against the witchcraft of others. Many strive to develop an arsenal of tools and powers to control the ever-present witch forces. Moreover, in modern Orisha traditions, the Orisha themselves are seen as powerful "witches" who can be invoked against the witchcraft of others. Although no one would admit doing witchcraft against another, positive magic for healing, for wealth, for the love of another, and for all the good things of life, are an essential part of the religion, and many casual conversations among practitioners include discussions of "recipes." These are spells, generally based on a form of sympathetic magic, designed to enhance the life of oneself or one's client.

## HEALTH AND SICKNESS

Many people first come to the Orisha religion in search of physical, emotional, or interpersonal healing. Through divination and ebo (Yr. sacrifice), the priest attempts to nudge the individual's life back into the best manifestation of their destiny. Magic performed for the betterment of oneself or one's family is seldom perceived of as evil or as the work of witchcraft. However, devotees believe that malevolent forces permeate the environment and may harm those who are weak or unprotected. Often, an on-going regiment of offerings, spiritual baths, and other minor rituals are prescribed to strengthen one's ashé and to protect one from ever-present bad luck. When plagued by interpersonal, job, or love problems, divination can discover the cause and recommend a cure. Although it is not uncommon for clients to want to know the person from whom their bad luck emanates, such information is seldom forthcoming unless a direct question is asked. For the most part, the identity of the "witch" is unimportant; rather, securing the good will and protection of one's ancestors, spiritual guides, or the Orisha is enough to overturn malevolent forces whether they have a spiritual or material origin.

Because the Orisha cosmological system places great importance on a good life in the visible world, devotees are encouraged use all available healing traditions. Devotees are encouraged to combine religious rituals with biomedicine, and good results can be expected when rituals are performed to enhance and strengthen the work of one's medical team. A modern scientific worldview doesn't allow for any of these activities to be effective. Although research has shown that prayer in conjunction with conventional medicine enhances healing, the types of activities performed by *santeros* in the course of their healing work are generally discounted, and practitioners may be prosecuted for fraudulent behavior. However, hearsay evidence provided by clients often suggests that they find these activities beneficial.

It is often helpful in analyzing these types of situations to distinguish between the concepts of healing and curing. As generally understood, "cure" refers to the compete restoration of health and recovery from whatever disease plagues the patient. Although it is possible that a ritual might affect such a restoration to complete health, cures are understood to operate at the level of the physical and to be the providence of biomedicine with its reliance on sophisticated drugs, diagnostic tests, and machines. Healing, on the other hand, implies a restoration to wholeness that has a wider range of implications.[15] While a cure can only be claimed when the patient has been returned to some assumed ideal human condition free of disease and its complications, healing ranges over the whole physical, psychological, and spiritual landscape in an attempt to bring the patient into a balanced relationship with himself and his environment. A client may be considered healed when he makes peace with his physical, mental, or spiritual condition, even though a cure has not been effected. Thus, a visit to a santero is unlikely to cure one of AIDS, for example, although the healing rituals might enable one to live a full and rich life in spite (or, perhaps even because) of the disease.

# The Orisha and Their Mythology

Whether we think of the cosmos in terms of Olodumare, the great God, or in terms of the workings of ashé, it is Orisha who form the major focus of devotees' beliefs and practices. Every ritual involves the invocation of one or more Orisha. Every prayer and every offering is offered to a specific Orisha. Yoruba mythology suggests that there are an infinite number of Orisha, however, American practitioners commonly recognize about 16 major Orisha. Although individual practitioners may name additional Orisha, these 16 form the major focus of contemporary American practice. They are Eshu/ Eleggua, Ochosi, Ogun, Osun, Obatala, Shango, Yemaya, Oshun, Oya, Obba, Olokun, Agayu, the Ibeji, Babalu Aye, Inle along with Abata, and Orula/Orunmila.

Devotees discover the Orisha from their personal interactions with these sacred beings and through their stories. The stories have never been collected into a single document, nor could they be. Rather, devotees learn about the Orisha by listening to their elders tell this story or that as part of an explanation about why things are the way that they are or why things are done in a particular way, as part of a divination session, or to pass the time. Often, different Orisha are the protagonists in the retelling of similar stories: perhaps it was Odduduwa who climbed down the golden chain to create the earth or Oya who convinced Obba to cut off her ear. As I tell the stories below, know that these are only the stories I've chosen to tell at this time, the ones I think can lead to an understanding of the nature of the Orisha.[1]

## CREATION

Long ago, after the energy of the universe had recognized itself as Olodumare and after the power of Olodumare had been distributed among the Orisha, Olodumare called in one of Olodumare's favorite sons, Obatala, for a visit. Obatala's name is formed from the words "oba," which means ruler, and "ala," which refers to white cloth. His name is generally translated as "ruler of the white cloth." He is the head of all the Orisha, the wise old man whose white clothes represent all that is holy and pure and good. Olodumare pointed to a watery ball hanging in the sky and told Obatala that he should make it into a habitable world. Leaving Olodumare's palace Obatala was unsure of how to proceed, so he went to the home of his friend Orula. Orula was a diviner who gave good advice based on his reading of the past, present, and future. He advised Obatala to collect all the gold that he could find and then to ask Ogun, the blacksmith, to construct a golden chain. While Ogun was working on the chain, the two friends gathered together a five-toed hen, a chameleon, a shell of dirt, and a palm nut. When all was ready, they hung the chain and Obatala climbed down toward the watery planet below. When he reached the end of the golden chain, he spilled the dirt onto the water and then dropped the five-toed hen on to it. Immediately she began to scratch around, spreading the earth in all directions. To test the firmness of the earth, he dropped down the chameleon whose delicate tread proved that the newly formed ground was solid. Finally, Obatala dropped the palm nut onto the earth. It sprouted immediately and grew into a fine palm tree that reached to the end of the golden chain. Obatala dropped from the golden chain to the top of the palm tree and from there to the solid ground below. He surveyed his handiwork and saw a fine combination of earth, sea, and sky, a beautiful new land. Although Olodumare is the great god, the personification of all the ashé of the cosmos, it is Obatala who is credited with being the creator of the earth and its inhabitants.

Sometime later Obatala and a contingent of the Orisha returned to the earth to explore what had been created. There must have been other seeds mixed into the dirt Obatala used to create the solid ground. As they climbed down the golden chain and the palm tree, they saw that an impenetrable forest had grown up. It extended from the base of the tree as far as the eye could see. Taking his beautiful silver sword Obataba began hacking at the undergrowth. However, the soft metal of the sword was soon bent and nicked with little affect on the bush surrounding them. Shango, the young king, stepped forward with his trademark double-headed axe, called an *oshe*. He began to hack at the underbrush, but with little effect. Realizing that Obatala's sword and Shango's oshe were more ceremonial than utilitarian, Ogun, the blacksmith, stepped forward. The machete that he swung was neither as finely wrought as Obatala's sword nor as beautifully carved as Shango's oshe. Although it was plain, even ugly, it was well made with a razor-sharp edge.

**Orisha Correspondences**

| Orisha | Yoruba | Spanish | Saint | Colors | Number | Force of Nature | Icons |
|---|---|---|---|---|---|---|---|
| Babaluaiye | Òbalúàyé or Sòpònà | Babalú-Ayé | St. Lazarus | purple, black, light blue | 13,17 | small pox, AIDS, infectious diseases, skin eruptions | beans, dog, crutches, popcorn, |
| Eleggua | Èsù-Elegbára | Elegguá | Niña de Atocha, Lonely Spirit of Purgatory, St. Anthony of Padua | black & red, or black & white | 3 | roads, chance, messenger | sugar cane, guava, candy, rum, hooked staff |
| Ibeji | Ibeji or meji | Jimugas | Sts. Cosmo & Damien | red & white, blue & white | 2, 4, 8 | doubling, wealth, children, play | twin dolls |
| Inle (and Abata) | Erinlè, Àbátàn | Inlé, Abatán | Archangel Raphael | green | 7 | fisherman, healing | fish, snake |
| Obatala | Òbàtálá | Obatalá | Our Lady of Mercy (Señora de las Mercedes), Jesus Christ, St. Joseph, St. Sebastian | white | 8, 16 | purity, wisdom, coolness, creation, older man | eggs, meringue, pears, rice pudding, doves, white fly whisk |

Orisha Correspondences (continued)

| Orisha | Yoruba | Spanish | Saint | Colors | Number | Force of Nature | Icons |
|---|---|---|---|---|---|---|---|
| Obba | Òbà | Oba | St. Clare, St. Kathleen of Sienna | dusty pink, coral, and burgundy | 8 | navigation, commerce, teaching & learning, matrimony, stability | dove, feather pen, sword, book, earring, mask, |
| Ochosi | Òsóòsì or Ososi | Ochosí | St. Norbert, St. Hurbert | blue & yellow, violet | 2, 7 | hunter, bow and arrow, justice | anisette, deer, police |
| Ogun | Ògún | Ogún | St. Peter | green & black, or green & white | 3 | iron, work, technology, railroad, car, warrior | honey dew melon, aguardiente (cane liquor), iron, dog |
| Olokun | Olókun or Olóòkun | Olokun, Olocun | | dark blue | 4, 7 | deep ocean, mystery, Middle Passage | shells, mask, mermaid, snake |
| Orula | Òrúnmìlà | Orunlá | St. Francis of Assisi | yellow & green | 16 | divination | Tray of Ifá, palm nuts |
| Osain | Osain | Osaín | St. Sylvester, St. Joseph, St. John the Baptist, St. Anthony the Abbott | none | 7, 21 | forest, herbs | Gourd, herbs |

| Orisha | Yoruba | Spanish | Saint | Colors | Number | Force of Nature | Icons |
|---|---|---|---|---|---|---|---|
| Oshun | Òsun | Ochún | Virgen de la Caridad del Cobre, (Virgin of Charity of Cobre) | yellow | 5, 10, 15 | sweet water (river), female sexuality, young woman | pumpkin, honey, orange, fan, gold, brass |
| Oya | Òya | Oyá | Our Lady of Candlemas, St. Teresa of Avila, Little Flower | maroon/ nine colors | 9 | wind, death, cemetery | eggplant, chocolate, black fly whisk |
| Shango | Sàngó | Changó | St. Barbara | red & white | 6,12 | lightning, male sexuality, power, passion, force, balance, young man | bananas, corn, okra, horse, oshé, pilón |
| Yemaya | Yemoja | Yemayá | Our Lady of Regla | blue & white or crystal | 7 | ocean, fish, maternity, moon, stars, mature woman | watermelon, brown sugar, molasses, fan, mermaid |

Soon it proved sturdy enough to stand up to the thick weeds and bushes blocking their way. Ogun opened the way through the wilderness so the others could explore. Metaphorically, devotees also say that Ogun is the one who can open the way when our lives become overgrown and we are blocked from our own best destiny.

Perhaps then, perhaps later, Olodumare commissioned a group of Orisha to bring civilization to this new world. He sent 17 Orisha, 16 male Orisha and Oshun, the youngest and most beautiful of the female Orisha. Each of the 16 brought their special talents to the task of making the earth habitable. Ogun was soon at work clearing the undergrowth and creating tools for the others at his blacksmith forge. Orisha Oko, the Orisha of the farm, was laying out the fields and planting the first crops. Obatala and Shango were working together to construct the first towns and establish the political and social systems. Working together, each of the male Orisha were given their own sacred site and a place in the building efforts. However, they all ignored the young woman who had been sent with them. She couldn't forge or plow or build, so they thought she was useless. It seemed as though all she did was sing and preen, so they ignored her and refused to give her a site to make her own sacred grove. Not being one to cause trouble directly, Oshun stayed out of the way of the other Orisha. She bathed in the beautiful rivers and sat on their banks, combing her hair and looking at herself in their still waters.

Soon the Orisha discovered that their building efforts were not going well. What was planted died. What was built fell down. In spite of all their best efforts, nothing was succeeding. Finally, they decided to return to Olodumare to ask why they were having so much trouble. Leaving Oshun sitting by the side of the river, the other 16 returned to the palace of the great god.

"Father," they said, "we have done as you asked and are trying to bring civilization to the new world you gave us. But nothing is going right. What we plant dies. What we build falls down. Nothing that we have done has endured."

Olodumare survey the assembled Orisha.

"Where is Oshun? Where is the young woman I sent with you?"

The Orisha all spoke at once.

"She is useless." "She can't plow." "She can't plant." "She can't build." "All she does is bathe and comb her hair."

"We left her behind," they exclaimed in unison.

"What!" Olodumare exploded. "Each of you has a role in the creation of a habitable world. Oshun, too, has a role. Without her power, nothing you do will succeed. She is the matrix of life, the architect of civilization. You must include her in your work."

"Now you have insulted her, a powerful Orisha in her own right. You must go back to the earth and beg her to help you. You must give her gifts and offerings to make up for your bad behavior. You must pay whatever price she asks for her help, for without her your efforts can not succeed."

On their way back to the earth, each Orisha thought of what he could offer to the beautiful young Oshun. One by one they approached her at the side of the river. Soon the contrite Orisha and their pile of gifts surrounded her.

Oshun accepted their gifts but she demanded more. She reminded them that she is the leader of the *aje*, the powerful beings that can cure and kill in the dead of night. Not only must they recognize her powers, but in the future, men must also recognize the special power of women, their power to create and their power to destroy. They must initiate women into all levels of society and welcome them into their all their deliberations.

When the other Orisha agreed to her terms, Oshun began to work with them. The mother of civilization added her special power to the power of the other Orisha, and soon the earth was flourishing with new growth, the town had beautiful new buildings, and all had been prepared for the most important creation of all, that of human beings.

Again Olodumare summoned Obatala. "Now you must form human beings to live upon the earth. When you are finished, I will come and blow the breath of life into the beings you created."

Obatala went the edge of the river, where fine clay and mud provided the perfect materials for the construction of human beings. He began early in the morning, shaping arms and legs, head and torso, fingers and toes. As the sun rose higher in the sky he became thirsty, so he began to sip some of the palm wine he had brought with him. Palm wine is made from the natural fermentation of the sap of the palm tree. When it is first tapped, the sap is sweet and mildly intoxicating, but as the day progresses it becomes stronger and more sour. At first Obatala took only small sips of the mildly intoxicating wine, but as the day progressed he drank more and more. At first his drinking had no effect on his creative efforts, but as the day progressed and he became more and more inebriated, his hands became more and more clumsy and the perfection of the early morning was compromised. In his semi-drunken state, Obatala didn't notice that some of the arms and legs were too long or too short, that the heads were malformed, that the fingers and toes were twisted. At the end of the day, having finished with his task, he returned to the village, and in the dark of night the wind that was the breath of Olodumare blew over the riverbank, animating the bodies Obatala had created. When he returned the next day to see his living handiwork, Obatala soon realized that not all of the people were as perfectly formed as he'd intended. Immediately he realized what had happened. Instantly remorseful, he swore never to touch alcohol again. But the damage had already been done and even today some of the children shaped by Obatala in their mother's wombs are less than perfectly formed. Such children are believed to be under Obatala's special protection. Because priests of Obatala are prone to his weaknesses, they also must abstain from alcohol and all intoxicants. It is important that they maintain a cool and clear head throughout their lives.

In these stories we begin to understand the characteristics of the Orisha and their worshippers. All of the Orisha have strengths and weakness. Their weaknesses are often an exaggeration of their strengths. Obatala, the ruler of white cloth, is the creator deity who formed both the earth and the human beings who inhabit it. He is considered to be the oldest and wisest of the Orisha. But he can be arrogant and thoughtless, prone to what we would today call addictive behavior. Many devotees will say that his priests also tend toward arrogance, thoughtlessness, and addictions. Similarly, the priests of Oshun embody her special enjoyment of all the good things of life. They can often be recognized by their love of beautiful things and their flirty and flighty behavior. However, they are easily slighted, and since their *aje* power is especially strong, one must be wary of offending them.

## Eshu/Eleggua

There are many stories told about Eleggua, who is often known as Eshu in Africa. Eleggua is a trickster deity who is often the provocateur in the stories told about other Orisha. As a trickster, it is his responsibility to see that everyone else does as they should, and fulfills their promises. He watches everything and can often be found testing one's sincerity. He is the great friend of Orula the diviner, and his face is often found on Orula's divination board. He not only helps Orula during the divination process but also see to it that whatever rituals and ceremonies Orula prescribed are completed in an appropriate and timely manner. His own powers of divination are very strong, and olorisha (Orisha priests) who have not been initiated as priests of Orula most often use the shells of Eleggua for divination for themselves and others.

One of the best-known stories from the Yoruba mythology concerns two young boys who are best of friends from childhood. As young men, they go together for a divination session. There they are told that they must sacrifice together to cement their friendship. Laughing as the young often do at their elders, they neglected the sacrifice, firm in the belief that their friendship would endure forever.

However, Eleggua provokes an argument between them that causes them to draw weapons against each other. In some stories they kill each other, while in others they are stopped before their argument reaches its tragic conclusion. In any case, it is Eleggua who triggers the situation that exposes the shallowness of the boys' friendship. Often, devotees suggest that temptations to lie, cheat, steal, or in some other way act outside social mores and one's own public nature are tests of one character by Eleggua, who delights in exposing the flaws and weaknesses in even the most highly respected people.

Eleggua exposes other weaknesses of character as well. Once, Obatala, the great and wise Orisha, wanted to go on a journey to visit his friend and fellow king Shango. In accordance with Yoruba custom, first he visited Orula, the diviner. Orula told him that it was not a good time for a journey and that he should delay his departure. Obatala, however, already made his plans and proceeded on his journey in spite of Orula's warning. He felt comforted that his badge of office, his trademark white clothes, would protect him from any misfortune.

Eleggua, of course, must show Obatala the errors of this line of thought. Three times along his way Obatala meets with trouble. Once, in an effort to help a fellow traveler, he is drenched in bright red palm oil. Even with the best of today's cleaning products, it's almost impossible to remove the stain of palm oil—his clothes are ruined. After changing clothes and continuing on his way, again his clothes are ruined. In an effort to help a child, he falls into a creek and is splattered with mud and debris. Finally, he spies Shango's horse outside the village. Realizing that the horse must have escaped from its grooms, he captures it and rides it the rest of the way to the gate of Shango's village. The guards, seeing not the grand Orisha Obatala, but a disheveled old man riding the king's horse throw him into jail where he languishes until, much later, Shango, warned by his own diviners that the world is out of balance due to the old man in his prison, finds and releases him.

Here again we see Eleggua testing Obatala's character. In this case, he exposes his arrogance and disregard for the advice of others. In addition, Obatala languishes in jail and Shango's world it thrown out of order because Obatala is too proud, too confident in the honor due him to protest and work for his own release. This story contains many warnings, not only for the children of Obatala, who tend to have the same personality strengths and weaknesses of their father, but also all those who tend to disregard good advice or who are overly confident in their own reputations and the correctness of their actions. Three times Obatala is penalized for doing the right thing at the wrong time.

In spite of the fact that early missionaries to Yorubaland chose the name of Eshu as the name of the devil in their translation of the Bible, and in spite of his tendency to provoke both the Orisha and human beings, Eleggua is not an evil character. When one resists the temptation toward evil, obeys the moral law, and fulfills the promises made, it is he who sees to it that the tools that one needs to make the best possible life are available when they are needed. Often, in the divination text, one finds the very the things that are required to offer as sacrifice are waiting when one needs them to deal with an unforeseen problem or dilemma.

## ORULA/ORUNMILA

Although the babalawo, the priests of Orula, claim that he was present from the beginning of creation and thus knows the past, present, and future of both the Orisha and human beings, there are many stories told of how Orula, whose name in Yorubaland is Orunmila, came to be the diviner of the Orisha. In one story, when Olodumare was distributing attributes to all the Orisha, he gave divination to Shango, and the drum and dance to Orula. However, Shango, the great ladies man, would rather be dancing and flirting than sitting at home listening to people's problems and perfecting his divination skills. Orula, on the other hand, was shy and retiring. He hated going to parties, and although he was a good enough dancer, he didn't like showing off his dancing techniques. One day the two Orisha were talking and realized that they'd be happier with each other's gifts. When they approached Olodumare with their proposal, Olodumare agreed that Shango was certainly an excellent dancer and would be a good patron of dancing and drumming, and that Orula would be a great diviner. However, before they could exchange gifts, Olodumare decreed that they must each prove their worthiness in a public display. They agree that they would do so on the next market day. In preparation, Orula went to his good friend Eleggua.

"How can I prove my worthiness, without my divination tools?" he complained.

Eleggua, who has his own ways of knowing what is to happen, had heard Olodumare tell his servants how to prepare the test for Orula.

"Tomorrow, when Olodumare asks you which side of the field he had planted in yams, look for me. I will be standing on the opposite side of the field."

The next day, Shango easily proved himself to be the best dancer and the most skilled drummer among the Orisha. When it came time for Orula to prove himself, Olodumare took him to a newly planted field.

"Which side of this field did I have planted in yams?" Olodumare asked.

While Orula considered his answer, he looked for his friend Eleggua. When he spied him, he went to the other side of the field, dug into the newly cultivated earth and pulled up the seed yam. Everyone cheered and Olodumare confirmed Orula as the owner of divination.

It is said that in the beginning, Orula use cowry shells to determine the cause and solution for the problems that were brought to him. At the time, he was married to either Yemaya or Oshun—different people tell the story differently—and through observation and intelligence his wife learned the secrets of the shells. One day, when Orula was away, his wife began divining on her own. The mythology says that she read the shells with exquisite aptitude and was able to mark the most effective *ebo* (sacrifice) to solve her clients' problems. The long line waiting their turn outside her door certainly attested to her skill. Orula, however, was enraged when he returned and discovered that his wife had appropriated his power. From that moment he eschewed the use of the shells and developed a different divination system, one that only men could read. However, Yemaya or Oshun took the divination shells and shared this oracle with all of the other Orisha. Thus, today all of the Orisha speak through the shells, except Orula, who speaks to his priests, the babalawo, only through the Table of Ifá.

Divination is very important among both the Yoruba and their American descendents. Orula is the quintessential diviner, and the highest form of divination belongs to his priests, the babalawo. However, Eleggua and the other Orisha, speaking through the cowry shells, also speak to their devotees. All Orisha priests in the Americas can learn one or the other of these divination techniques and help their clients learn the best ways to fulfill their personal destinies.

## THE WARRIORS: OGUN, OCHOSI, AND OSUN

Ogun is the blacksmith Orisha. Metalworking was very important and highly developed among the pre-colonial Yoruba people. The blacksmith's shop created the tools needed by both farmers and warriors, and was seen as a place of great power and mystery where rocks from the earth were turned into useful tools.

According to some stories, Obatala and Yemaya were the first parents who gave life to many of the Orisha. One of their children was Ogun, who as a young man sexually abused his mother. When he is found out (through the spying of Eleggua), he is so remorseful that he curses himself to work day and night without a break for the good of society. Because of this, Ogun is the patron of work and workers, as well as technology, all sorts of metalworkers, and those who use their tools, including soldiers, policemen, surgeons, jewelers, and in today's world, those who work with computers, especially the hardware. Even today, devotees notice that Ogun's priests tend toward seriousness and a strong work ethic. As the embodiment of the strong, silent type, his priests, both male and female, are hard workers who prefer doing to talking.

One day Ogun became angry with the other Orisha, left his forge, and went into the forest. Without his constant making and refurbishing of their tools, the work of the village ground to a halt. Each of the Orisha went into the forest and, using their special gifts, tried to get him to return to his forge. Ochosi and Shango, warrior Orisha, tried to force him back to work. Eleggua tried his powers of persuasion. Everyone tried but none could convince Ogun to leave the forest. Finally, Oshun, the youngest and most beautiful of the Orisha, spoke up. The other Orisha laughed at her suggestion that she, a delicate young woman, could do what none of them were able to accomplish, but finally they decided they had no other options.

Oshun, rather than gathering together weapons, dressed in her finest wrapper, put some of her sweetest honey in a bowl, and went to the river deep in the forest. There she set her clothing aside and went into the water to bathe. Singing to herself she lovingly washed every curve of her luscious body. As she expected, soon she was being watched. After drying herself she surprised Ogun in his hiding place, smeared his lips with her luscious honey, and lead him back to the village, where the other Orisha greeted him joyfully and apologized for their earlier disagreement. Thus Oshun proved once again that force is not always the best method of persuasion, that sometimes the sweetness of honey can overcome the strongest and most defiant.

Ogun is an interesting Orisha. Although he co-habits with several Orisha and maintains a lifelong desire for Oshun, he never has an enduring relationship and never has a family. Instead, he works day and night, never taking a rest to enjoy himself or to develop relationships. As a consequence, he is quite productive but incredibly lonely. Because he is the patron with both constructive and destructive metals he is associated with all forms of killing and violence. At one time, Ogun was the king of the city of Ire. When the city was attacked, the people called out to their king to come and help them fight. As a true warrior, Ogun rushed to defend his people. Swinging his mighty machete right and left, he mowed down the invaders like so much grass. However, his bloodlust was not quenched by the deaths of the intruders, and he turned and began attacking his own people. Soon, not only were all the enemy soldiers laying on the battlefield, but also all of the people of Ire as well. When there was no one left to attack, Ogun awoke as if from a dream and realized what he had done. At that moment, he renounced his kingship and retired to the forest, leaving behind the tools and techniques of the blacksmith and the warrior so the people would be able to defend themselves in the future. Ogun's bloodlust is legendary, and this story reminds us that once violence is unleashed, it is often hard to control. But Ogun's energy is not only about uncontrolled violence; it is also the energy of violence in the service of the common good. This includes the violence that is a necessary part of the work of surgeons, policemen, and soldiers. The scalpel is also a metal tool designed to draw blood and cause exquisite pain all in the service of health and well-being.

In the United States and Cuba, the Orisha Ochosi lives together with Ogun. Ochosi (also known as Oshosi or Ososi) is the hunter Orisha, who is often represented by a deer or deer antlers. Like Ogun, Ochosi lives at the boundary between the town and the bush, and is comfortable in the forest where he hunts. In the mythology, he is often referred to as a "left-handed sorcerer" because he is able to freely move between the visible and invisible world, using the power of the plants and animals he discovers in the forest to work for the benefit of his devotees.

Although Ogun may be more closely associated with the administration of justice in Yorubaland, in the Americas it is Ochosi that is invoked when one is having legal problems. Devotees associate him so closely with the justice system that they identify the jail as one of his places of power. They can often be heard praying, "Ochosi, please live in my home so I do not have to live in yours (the jailhouse)." However, you must be sure that you are in the right before involving Ochosi in your problems with the law, as he will punish the wrongdoer, whoever that may be. In one well-known story, Obatala asked Ochosi to bring him some birds for a feast he was planning. Ochosi went out the next morning and bagged two beautiful Guinea fowl. Leaving them at his home on the edge of the forest, he continued hunting. While he was gone, his mother stopped by for a visit and, seeing the birds, decided to take one for herself, feeling assured that her son would not mind. When he returned, Ochosi was enraged that someone would dare to steal from him. Shooting an arrow into the air he commanded it to find the thief. Only when he heard his mother's cry did Ochosi realize what had happened. Devotees say that Ochosi's justice is as swift and sure as his arrow, and that he does not hesitate to punish even his own mother for bad behavior.

When the ashé of Ogun and Ochosi are combined, they form (together with Eleggua and Osun) the Orisha group known as the Warriors (*Los Guerreros*). Placed near the front door of the devotee's home, they protect against any forces that might be arrayed against him or her, but they also provide the first steps in the development of the devotee's destiny. Spiritually, Ogun "opens the way," removing obstacles and clearing away blockages, while Ochosi as the master tracker points the way to one's best spiritual, emotional, and physical fulfillment. Working together, they guard against evil forces while moving the devotee forward along the path of his or her chosen destiny.

Also included in the set of Orisha known as the Warriors is the shadowy Orisha Osun. The icon of Osun received as part of the Warrior initiation consists of a metal rooster standing atop a closed cup with bells hanging from it lip. Osun is a sentry whose job it is to warn the devotee of impending danger. His icon should be place on a shelf at or above the head of the devotee where he can watch the comings and goings of the household. If his icon should tip over, it is a sign of some deadly danger that the devotee should immediately investigate through divination.

## SHANGO

In many stories, Oshun is the wife of Shango, the great king of the city and kingdom of Oyo. Shango was a human king, who is often listed as the fourth king of Oyo. As king, he was famous for conquering all of the surrounding territory and for his love of the magical arts. Once he acquired a new magical potion that could pull lightning from the sky. Going to the top of a nearby hill, he began to experiment. Unfortunately, his aim was bad and he accidentally struck his own palace, killing many of his own wives, children, and attendants. Remorseful, he left the city and went into the forest, where, according to some accounts, he hung himself; according to other accounts he did not hang but sunk into the ground to arise as a great Orisha. Regardless, thunder and lightning are still the special emblems of the kingly Shango, who is swift to punish transgressions against the social order, such as lying, cheating, and theft.

There are many stories told of the great Shango. He is often described as a great womanizer who easily wins the heart of any woman he desires. As the embodiment of masculine sexuality, he works with his counterpart Oshun to bring men and women together in the greatest act of creation, the making of new human beings. In one of his stories, he is the husband to three of the most beautiful of the female Orisha: Obba, Oshun, and Oya. Obba is said to be his first wife, who taught him many of the martial arts he employs as an empire-builder. She is also credited with bringing navigation and other practical arts to the Yoruba people. Oshun, as the most beautiful and sensual of the Orisha, however, was his favorite partner, and many an evening found him ensconced in her quarters. If Oshun was his favorite bed partner, Oya was the one who often accompanied him on his military assaults. Oya is the patron of the whirlwind, as well as the guardian of the gates of the cemetery. She shares the power of lightning with Shango, and is often seen together with her husband in thunderstorms.

Shango is generally remembered for the abuses of his power as king and as the great playboy who has innumerable sexual liaisons. In Yorubaland his mythology has incorporated that of Jakuta an earlier thunder deity who was known as "the Wrath" of Olodumare.[2] Consequently, in spite of his personal failings, Shango is also said to punish lying, stealing, poisoning, and other offences against the common good with the swiftness of lightning.

Twins hold a special place in the cultures of West Africa. Twins are considered special beings infused with their own type of ashé. In some societies, they are considered to be dangerous, an aberration or excess of fertility, and they are left in the forest to die. It appears that, at one time, the Yoruba people also disposed of any twins who were born. However, according to the mythology, one day one of Shango's wives gave birth to twins, and the great king could not bring himself to abandon them to die. So he decreed that from that day forward all twins were under his special protection and should be honored as especially auspicious beings. From that day forward, twins (*ibeji*) were welcomed into Yoruba families and celebrated by the community. They were considered to be filled with ashé, and were thought to bring special blessings and prosperity to the family.

If one or both twins should die in childhood, the parents would commission a small statue to be carved in honor of the dead twin. Regardless of the age at which the child died, the statues would be in the form of a fully formed adult, complete with the genitals appropriate to the child's sex. The statue would be bathed and fed and fussed over along with the living twin. If both twins died, or when the living twin grew up, the ibeji statues would be placed in the family shrine, where they would be venerated and propitiated so that they would continue to bring good luck to the family.

Within Orisha mythology, the Ibeji are universally acknowledged to be the children of Shango; however, the name of their mother is a mystery. Although both Oya and Oshun have been named as possible mothers, the twins' primary associations are with Shango and Yemaya. According to the stories, Yemaya found them on her doorstep one morning with a note indicating their paternity. With Shango's permission, she raised them as if they were her own, loving them fiercely and spoiling them as one should spoil such special children. Among the Yoruba, twins are considered to be "powerful spirits" who are capable of bringing riches to those who honor them, and misfortune to those who don't. Mothers of twins worship them every five days, that is, once during each Yoruba week. They go to the market, dance in their honor, and receive money for their dancing. This is one of the ways twins bring riches to their mothers. Although the Ibeji are the only Orisha that are always described as children, they are considered to be powerful and able to provide for their devotees.

Although only families with twins venerated the Ibeji in Yorubaland, in the Americas this veneration of twins was extended to include the entire community. When devotees receive the Ibeji, they also receive two dolls dressed up in costumes reminiscent of the Twins' heritage as the children of Shango and Yemaya. Although living twins may come in any combination of male and female, the Ibeji are always dressed as a male and a female, with the male in the red and white of Shango and the female in the blue and white of Yemaya. As Orisha, the Ibeji bring good luck and balance to the lives of their devotees.

## THE LADIES: YEMAYA, OSHUN, OBBA, AND OYA

The four major female Orisha, Yemaya, Oshun, Oya, and Obba, are all associated with rivers in Nigeria. Although all have a relationship with the different male Orisha, they all have a special association with Shango. In the mythology, Obba is his first or legitimate wife, while Oshun and Oya are either secondary wives (in Africa) or mistresses (in the Americas). Yemaya is said to be either his actual or his adoptive mother. But these Orisha do not get their power and authority from their association with Shango or any other male Orisha; rather, they are fully independent Orisha, rulers of their individual domains. Except for Obba, who remains faithful to her husband Shango, all of the others form and dissolve relationships according to their own desires.

Although Yemaya is associated with her own river in Nigeria (the Ògùn river, not be confused with the name of the Orisha Ògún), in the Americas she has become the patron of the ocean, the source and goal of all rivers. As the great mother of the Yoruba pantheon, she represents all that is female, "cool," subdued, peaceful, and soft, the antithesis and the antidote to the "hot," volatile, violent, tough, and destructive power of men. As the ocean, she represents that which nurtures physical, psychological, and spiritual growth; she is the soothing and comforting sense of the transcendent many people find at the ocean. As the mother of the Orisha, Yemaya is the primal mother who not only births but also protects her offspring and the children of others. Yemaya is the mother, adopted mother, or foster mother of almost all of the Orisha. As mother, she is both nurturing and demanding. Devotees say that one can hide from the wrath of the other Orisha in her skirts, but that nothing can protect you from her wrath.

A story told of the *Ibeji* exemplifies both sides of Yemaya's maternal aspect. One day, she gave a party in honor the Ibeji, inviting all of the Orisha. However, an argument ensued when Shango, who had been drinking, began to eat the bananas given to the children. Even though Shango was her natural son, Yemaya, defending the rights of the children against the greed of their father, banished him from the party and cursed him in her anger. Here we see the ways in which Yemaya as mother both defends and disciplines her children. As youngsters, the Ibeji must be protected and shielded from the behavior of adults; as a grown man, Shango must be disciplined when his behavior is unacceptable, particularly when that unacceptable behavior is aimed at children. Thus we see that Yemaya is imagined to be both a beneficent and a stern mother. Like the ocean, she can be both beautiful and terrible, blessing and punishing in turn.

Obba (sometimes written as Oba) is often said to represent the good but abused wife. As Shango's first or legitimate wife, she should receive the respect both of her husband and her co-wives. However, as often happens, in mythology Shango finds his other wives (or his mistresses) more appealing. In her best-known story, Obba attempts to regain her husband's favor by magic. After discussing her plight with either Oshun or Oya (both are named by devotees), she is advised to flavor Shango's favorite stew with her own ear. Not considering the source of this disgusting advice (how likely is it that a co-wife or mistress would be interested in helping one gain more of the husband's attention?), Obba prepared the stew and added the fateful ingredient. When Shango came to dinner, he noticed that his wife was distracted and her head tie was disheveled and bloodied. When he found her ear in his stew, he questioned her. As the story unfolded, she saw the horror in his eyes and realized that she had lost everything. Although she would always remain Shango's first wife, she left his palace that evening and went to live in the solitude of the cemetery, where she is remembered as the bitter and unhappy wife, while her earlier accomplishments are often overlooked. As with the embittered wives of other mythologies, Obba is the champion of loyal wives and all women in unfortunate relationships. But Obba is more than the abandoned wife; it is also said that she taught the Yoruba people the techniques of navigation, warfare, and metallurgy, as well as the housewifely arts. Some say she taught her husband Shango how to become a great swordsman, and fought at his side until she was supplanted by Oya. She is considered to be the most learned of the Orisha, and it is common to find a quill pen and a book among her offerings.

As the goddess of all flowing rivers, Oshun exhibits their qualities. She is vivacious, fresh, quick, lively, the most beautiful of the Orisha.[3] Her lush figure and sensuous hips embody the divine spark of erotic life. Her name is related to the word for "source," and she is associated with basic concerns and the sources of life itself.[4] As the beautiful woman who reveals the wisdom of pleasure, she is graced by her priests with rich gifts: silks and perfumes, sweet foods flavored with her own honey (and in the New World, sugar), jewelry, coral, amber, and all the red metals (copper, brass, and gold, although in the New World copper is usually associated with Oya).[5] She is especially partial to champagne, the pale yellow drink that represents fine or even extravagant living. She is the lithe young woman in the full bloom of her womanhood. Thus, in the New World, Oshun is considered to be the young, sexual woman, juxtaposed to Yemaya's more maternal form.

In some of the myths, she is considered to be the youngest or one of the youngest Orisha. But even though she is young, she is not without power. As we saw in the creation story above, if she is ignored, the creative work of the other Orisha fails. While Ogun may provide technology and the other Orisha other goods, without the blessings of Oshun, one cannot develop civilization, the enjoyment of all the good things in life. In the Americas, her special provenance is female sexuality, the conception and bearing of children, and by extension the conception and implementation of other creative activities.

Although Oya is considered to be one of Shango's wives, like all of the female Orisha she is a powerful force in her own right. Best known in the Americas as the ruler of the whirlwind and the cemetery, she controls powerful forces of nature as well as ruling the spirits of the dead. In the mythology, she is also known for calling up the forces of the dead to use as her army. They are especially effective against her husband Shango, who is unusually afraid of the dead. In one story, to punish him for an infraction of an agreement between them, she stations her minions around his compound to prevent him from leaving. They are instructed to allow anyone else to enter and leave the compound but to detain the king. When Oshun learns of his fate, she hurries to his compound. There she devises a plan whereby she dresses him in her wrapper and cuts off her own beautiful hair to create a makeshift wig. Dressed in a clumsy imitation of a woman and clinging to Oshun's arm, Shango is able to escape the wrath of Oya.

As the owner of the cemetery and the leader of the *egun*, Oya is important in the funeral rituals of Orisha religion. It is she who takes the dying person's last breath, and she who conducts their spirit to the invisible world where they will be able to review the manifestation of their destiny and prepare for the next incarnation. It is generally her priests who conduct the traditional funeral rites.

In spite of any disagreement they may have with each other, Shango and Oya are especially powerful when they work together. Both have control of lightning and love to fight together. Like the wind rushing before a terrible storm, Oya often precedes her husband into battle, wreaking her own havoc as her tornado-force winds destroy all in her path. Shango follows behind, carried along by the thunder, lightning, and raging rain.

Although Oya is a great warrior, she is also a loving mother. One of her praise names, *Yansan*, means "mother of nine," which refers both to the nine tributaries to her river in Nigeria and to her own fertility and procreative prowess. All of the female Orisha have warrior aspects, and these do not detract from their maternal characteristics. Culturally, Yoruba women are expected to not only keep a home for their husbands and children, but also to help support their families. Many women make and sell food or crafts in the marketplace, and work as small-time traders, buying in one village to sell in another. Although men generally control the long-distance trade, it is women who control the local markets. Oya is generally recognized as the leader of the market women, and her devotees are usually credited with being exceptionally savvy business people. This association of Oya with the market-place and the fact that all female Orisha have both maternal and martial aspects present potent images of self-determination and self-protection to contemporary women

## OLOKUN: OWNER OF THE OCEAN

Olokun, whose name means "owner of the ocean," is one of the most mysterious of the Orisha. Generally, Orisha worshippers in the Americas agree that Olokun is the Orisha associated with the ocean and its riches. However, there is much disagreement on the details of that association. In Yorubaland, there were two major Olokun shrines. One set of shrines located along the coastal areas of Benin identified Olokun as the deity of wealth and fertility who was the first son of the supreme deity. However, a major shrine to Olokun in Ile-Ifè identifies her as a female Orisha associated with the bead industry. Henry John Drewal and John Mason suggest that this inland shrine may have been developed during the fifteenth-century expansion between Ifè and Benin when overseas trading became a source of Ifè's wealth.[6] It appears that priests from both areas were brought to Cuba, as there have developed two major Olokun lineages, one that views the Orisha as male and one that views the Orisha as female. One of the ways that devotees discount this discrepancy is by quoting the divination verse associated with Olokun that says, "No one knows what lies at the bottom of the sea." In either case, Olokun is associated with the treasures that are hidden at the bottom of the ocean, or those that come mysteriously from over the seas. In the contemporary view, as the depths of the ocean, Olokun is associated with the subconscious and all that lies below the surface of our personalities.

Because both Yemaya and Olokun are associated with the ocean in the Americas, Yemaya is often said to be its upper reaches while Olokun is its depths. Some say that the two are merely aspects of the same Orisha force, or that one (generally Yemaya) is the spouse to the other (Olokun in his male aspect). The ocean depths and the Orisha associated with it have special importance for African American devotees because of the many victims of the Middle Passage whose burial at sea sent them to the arms of Olokun.

## ORISHA OF HEALING

All Orisha provide physical, emotional and spiritual healing to their devotees, but there are several Orisha who are especially associated with healing. These include Inle and Abata, most commonly known as the fisherman and his wife or brother, Osain, the Orisha of the plants of the forest, and Babaluaye, the smallpox god, and the family of Orisha that are associated with him.

## INLE AND ABATA

Inle (Erinle in Yorubaland) was the original Orisha of medicine, healing, and protection against witchcraft. He is the fisherman Orisha who has strong associations with the other forest Orisha, Ogun and Ochosi. According to some stories, Inle lives on land half of the year and in the water the other half, attesting to his powers of transformation and his expertise with the resources of both locations. As an herbalist and healer, he knows secrets of the forest and the river and can bring the powers of both to his healing work. Because the forest is associated with men and rivers with women, some say he is male half of the year and female the other half. This ability to move between the domains of men and women has lead some devotees to suggest that he is also the patron of gay men and lesbians. Inle is especially close to Ochosi, the hunter deity who, it is said, he drug away with him into the forest when Ochosi was a young child. As hunters, Inle and Ochosi live in the forest, hunting and providing for the people of the town but not living with them. Although it is said that Ochosi lives with his brother Ogun, the blacksmith, he maintains an especially close relationship with Inle. All three of these Orisha are considered hunters who live at the boundaries of human society. Because, traditionally, the Yoruba view disease as a lack of balance in one's physical, emotional, and spiritual life, Inle's ability to move between the spheres of forest and water means he can not only draw on both sources of power but also that he can balance those powers in his patients.

In one story, Yemaya sees the beautiful young man, Inle, falls in love with him, and takes him with her to her palace at the bottom of the river. There she shows him all her riches and tells him all her secrets. When her passion cools, she cuts out his tongue before returning him to the forest, so he cannot tell what he has seen and learned. In the Americas, Inle is mute and cannot speak in divination or possession, but allows his former lover, Yemaya, to speak for him.

In some communities in Cuba and the United States, the vessel of Inle is presented with a second vessel containing the icons of his wife Abata, whose name means "forest pond" or "swamp."

## Osain (Osanyin)

Although Inle continues to be honored as a healer and herbalist, the forest and all the herbs and plants that live there have become the special providence of Osain, the Orisha of Plants. It is said that Osain is not from Yorubaland, but was of "Mandingo" origins.[7] This suggests that his worship was brought to the Yoruba people by way of trade with the neighbors. Osain is not the only Orisha to have "foreign" origins. From their earliest history, it appears that the Yoruba were willing to incorporate deities from other regions. Some say that both Shango and Oya have roots among the Nupe of what is now northern Nigeria.

Traditionally, Osain is represented by a staff surmounted by a bird. In the mythology, it is said that Osain, like the staff or a tree, has one leg, one arm, one eye, one big ear that is deaf, and one tiny ear that can hear the softest sound. He has neither mother nor father, but grew like a tree in the middle of the forest. He is not linked romantically with any other Orisha, but lives alone in the forest, tending his plants and guarding them from those who would take them without the proper respect. As the owner of all the plants, he has the power to cure and to kill, and his herbs and the priests that collect them are an essential part of all rituals.

Although Osain owns all of the herbs and plants, it is said that he was made to share them with the other Orisha. Consequently, all of the Orisha have certain herbs and plants that are especially associated with them. Ideally, a priest of Osain should collect all of the plant materials used in Orisha rituals. In actuality, many devotees are knowledgeable enough to help collect the most common plants materials used for the rituals of initiation and healing.

## Babaluaye

When Desi Arnez sang "Babalu. Babalu. Babalu Aye. Babalu Aye…" in the 1950s comedy *I Love Lucy*, few in the audience realized that he was invoking one of the most powerful of the Orisha. The mythology tells us that Babaluaye (Father, Lord of the World) is the praise name for the Orisha known as Sopona, the god of smallpox who can both heal and inflict his trademark disease. By extension he has become associated with all skin ailments, especially those that cause boils or rashes, all infectious diseases, and, in the late twentieth and early twenty-first centuries, with the disease of AIDS. In precolonial Yorubaland, those who had survived smallpox became the priests of Sopona. They were responsible for carrying the bodies of those who had died of the disease into the bush for burial. They also claimed everything that the patient used before he or she died, and swept the home of the deceased with their trademark brooms. It was claimed they used these items, which still carried the smallpox germ, to spread the disease themselves. However, we also know that they were able to develop an early form of inoculation that could protect those inoculated from this dreadful disease. Although they were criticized for appropriating all of the belongings of those who died, they were probably responsible for curtailing the spread of the disease.[8]

According to the mythology, Babalu left Yorubaland in disgrace and traveled west to the land of the Fon people. There he was welcomed as a great king and given the respect he was denied in his homeland. It is suggested that the worship of Babalu came to Cuba not by way of the Yoruba people, but through their neighbors, the Fon, who established the kingdom of Dahomey in what is now Benin. Although his name and many of his roads or avatars are from the Yoruba language, most of the songs and ceremonies for him can be traced back to Dahomey, and are in the language of the Fon people. Babaluaye is generally presented with his own family of Orisha, including his mother, Nana Baruku, and his own Eshu, Afra.

In the Americas, Babaluaye (Obaluaye in Brazil) became associated with Saint Lazarus, the leper mentioned by Christ in the parable of Lazarus and the rich man in the Gospel of Luke (16:19-31). Because, according to the Yoruba worldview, to name something is to call it into presence, Sopona is seldom named directly, and in the Americas he is called not by this name but by a praise name, Babaluaye. Among Cuban and American devotees, this prohibition is often further extended by using the name of the Catholic saint rather than that of the Orisha. Thus, you'll often see Saint Lazarus included in lists of Orisha. Perhaps by this association or perhaps with the increased efficiency of modern medicine, the image of Babalu in the Americas has softened somewhat, although his name is still spoken with respect.

# Destiny, Divination, and Sacrifice

In 1993, the United States Supreme Court agreed to review the case of the *Church of Lucumí Babalu Aye, Inc. vs. Hialeah.* According to court records, the city of Hialeah, a suburb of Miami, had passed a series of ordinances that made it illegal "to unnecessarily kill, torment, torture, or mutilate an animal in a public or private ritual or ceremony not for the primary purpose of food consumption." Since the city allowed the killing of animal for a host of other reasons "'even if you're tired of taking care of them,' as long as the purpose was not sacrifice," these ordinances appeared to be an effort to suppress the Church of the Lucumí Babalu Aye, a local Santería congregation. The congregation decided to fight the ordinances as a violation of their First Amendment right to freedom of religion. In its ruling, the Supreme Court found for the church and overthrew the ordinances restricting this essential part of their religious practice.[1]

The idea of sacrifice, particularly blood sacrifice, is one of the most difficult parts of this religious tradition for newcomers. In this chapter I discuss the place of sacrifice in the tradition, placing it within the context of devotees' understanding of destiny and divination. I will begin with an analysis of the Yoruba and Lucumí understandings of an open destiny. Then I will look at the different divination techniques devotees use to determine one's destiny. Finally, I will consider the ways in which one can modify it and the practices, including sacrifice, for softening a difficult destiny and enhancing a fortunate one.

## Destiny

Many people believe that everyone is born with a destiny or purpose for their lives, such that one of the goals of living is to discover and begin to live in a way that reflects that purpose. The Yoruba say that before we are born, each of us kneels in front of the great god Olodumare and chooses or is given a destiny for this lifetime. This destiny includes our intelligence, competence, personal limitations, and capacity to defend ourselves. In some of the stories, Olodumare gives to each of us our individual destiny, but in others, we choose it from among an array of destinies laid before us. In some stories, we can negotiate the major milestones of our lives with Olodumare, but in others, we must choose more or less blindly, as a destiny may be beautiful on the outside but full of worms, or it may be ugly on the outside but solid and neat within. In many ways, choosing a destiny is like choosing a lottery number or a lifelong spouse. We have full freedom of choice but not full knowledge of the future. Everyone, even those who negotiate the framework of their destiny, must embrace the Tree of Forgetfulness before they begin their journey to the visible realm. So all of us are born ignorant of our destinies.

One's destiny forms the general outlines of one's life path. Destiny determines when and to whom one will be born, when and how one will die, and the broad sweep of one's life. However, the Yoruba do not believe in a strong, unalterable destiny. Rather, they understand that individual actions can modify one's destiny for better or worse. If one has chosen a difficult destiny, one can soften it and enhance the possibility of enacting the best possible scenario within that destiny. On the other hand, if one has chosen a fortunate destiny but refuses to engage his or her legs (industry) and brain (intellect) in the manifestation of that destiny, it will remain dormant. Character, industry, sacrifice, and dynamism are all required to manifest the success encased in the most fortunate destiny. In addition, others can also affect one's destiny. The hostility and misconduct of both visible and invisible beings can work against one, thwarting the best of destinies.

Just as many Americans believe that intelligence resides in their head and feelings in their heart, the Yoruba assign aspects of themselves to different parts of their bodies. They use the word *ori* to refer both to the outer, physical head and to the spiritual or inner head that is the bearer of their personal destiny. Ori is also considered to be one's personal divinity, the one Orisha that never abandons one. It is said that your Ori will accompany you, even to the ends of the earth. Ori, the bearer of one's destiny, is believed to be the key to one's success or failure in life. Indeed, a proverb says that if your Ori is against you, there is no question of success, but if your Ori is with you, there is no question of failure.

Each individual worships his or her own Ori, making offerings and propitiating it in order that one follows one's best and most fulfilling destiny.

Among the Yoruba, a container studded with cowry shells called an *ibori* represents Ori. In Cuba and the United States, devotees make offerings directly to their inner heads through the ritual called the *rogation*. During the rogation, the priest places ground coconut meat and other ingredients on the outer head of the devotee in order to cool and bless their inner head, their Ori. The rogation strengthens the Ori, bringing the person into balance with their destiny.

Orisha devotees in the Americas also believe that, along with the outlines of one's lifetime, one's destiny includes a pact with one (or more) Orisha who will serve as one's guardians and, should one be called to the priesthood, will serve as one's primary Orisha, the Orisha that is said to "own one's head." The relationship between them and their guardian Orisha is described in terms of familial relationships. Everyone is understood to be the child of an Orisha. And just as one exhibits certain characteristics inherited from one's natural parents, many people also exhibits the characteristics—both positive and negative—associated with the Orisha that owns their head. By understanding the foibles of the different Orisha, one can not only recognize one's own strengths and weaknesses but also those of the people one meets in daily life. Understanding one's destiny means understanding that it is through the interaction between one's will, one's head, and one's Orisha that one can manifest the fullness of one's personal destiny

Although the association with an Orisha is not solidified until the time of initiation, there is much theorizing among devotees about the identity of this Orisha, and many solicit knowledge of "their" Orisha in anticipation of eventual initiation. Outside of formal divination, it is common to hypothesize about a person's Orisha based on a correlation between the person's personality and the known characteristics of the Orisha. While there does not appear to be any *necessary* relationship between the personality of the individual and the Orisha guardian, it is commonly assumed that the individual will exhibit those characteristics associated with their patron, and will be subject to the personality idiosyncrasies detailed in the mythology. Even someone without children will begin to look for maternal feelings after being identified with Yemaya, for example. Or someone who has a problem controlling their temper or sexuality may attribute their failings to their association with Shango, the great womanizer among the Orisha. Practitioners will dig into the mythology in order to explain certain types of behaviors. For example, a priest of Ochosi might find an explanation for her own problems with her mother in the story of Ochosi accidentally killing his mother because he thought she was a thief.

Devotees are apt to explain or excuse certain behaviors as the manifestation of that Orisha energy. This is especially easy in those cases where a priest exemplifies the characteristics of the Orisha. This becomes a problem in the community when a priest chooses to explain unacceptable behavior in this manner. Priests of Shango are especially noted for doing this. Shango, the arrogant manly Orisha with hundreds of wives and a quick temper, is often used to provide an excuse for his priests to exhibit the worst of these characteristics. "I can't be faithful to my wife; I'm a son of Shango, after all." However, older priests who see this behavior as the excuse it is will often counter with the reply "but you are *not* Shango". In this way they tell the young priest that, outside of the controlled environment of the possession event, he is still expected to be in control of his own behavior and is expected to follow the general norms of the community, *not* the example of the mythological corpus.

## MORALS AND ETHICS (GOOD CHARACTER)

Because there are few absolutes within the Yoruba cosmology, Orisha traditions are often considered to be non-ethical or amoral. The worldview of Orisha devotees values the maintenance of balance within one's life, one's family, one's community, and the world at large, the fulfillment of each person's highest and best destiny. Ethical judgments rest on four pillars: *iwe pele* (Yr. generous character), *ori* (Yr. personal destiny), the Orisha, especially the Orisha of one's head, and the individual's personal *ewe* (Yr. prohibitions).

The actions and behaviors of iwe pele are conventional ethical conduct, those actions and behaviors associated with the outstanding members of the community, the role models one looks to and aspires to emulate. As Robert Ferris Thompson explains it, iwe pele describes the gentle generosity of a person who lives according to customs of the traditional way of life. He suggest that a person's good character is seen in the degree to which one lives "generously and discreetly, exhibiting grace under pressure" such that, through everyday appearance and actions, one becomes noble, the classical good person, one who obeys and upholds the general ethical standards of the community.[2] The universal ethical goal is to achieve a generous or gentle character within the confines of one's destiny. Destiny is important, but it only provides the limits within which one must work. One's character (along with one's industry and intellect) determines whether one achieves all that is possible within one's destiny. At the same time, destiny affects character, since what constitutes good character (*iwa rara*) is partially dependent upon the destiny that one has chosen. The destiny of a warrior or a physician may require actions that bring pain or death to others. Such actions would be abhorrent in general but expected and required for the members of these groups. In smaller actions as well, one's destiny may put one at odds with the general standards of behavior. One's destiny may lead one away from the traditional profession of one's family or even away from one's home community under the dictates of one's *ori*. In this way, Yoruba culture and its descendent cultures encourage both conformity to community standards and individuality.

Many religions identify certain activities as either obligatory or prohibited. Certain foods (for example, pork or beef) may be forbidden, while other activities (praying, attending services, or tithing) may be required. Within the Orisha traditions in the United States, both obligatory and prohibited activities are gathered together under the heading of *ewe*, prohibitions. Unlike other traditions, there are few, if any, general ewe. Rather, each individual receives specific ewe during divination sessions. Sometimes the ewe is limited by time or place (wear white clothes for seven days, avoid meat during a trip out of town); other times the ewe is life-long. This is particularly true of those ewe received as part of initiations and other major divinations. Ewes may restrict or require numerous different activities. Many people have food restrictions, specific foods they should avoid or certain types of foods or even foods of a particular color. Others may be required to avoid certain colors of clothing (black and red are common), certain clothing styles (no fringe, no holes whether as part of the design or not, no stripes or polka dots or plaids), or, conversely, to wear certain clothing styles or colors (white is common). Some people are told to avoid certain situations, including crowds, groups of three, cemeteries, hospitals, bars, and the like. Some ewe are positive obligations: always keep your head covered, sleep on white sheets, always give something to a beggar.

The ewe that devotees receive may be divided into three types: allergies, *ebo*, and character-formation.[3] Many times, devotees are told to refrain from eating foods that they already know cause them physical problems. Since allergic reactions depend on repeated encounters with the allergen, it may also be that some food ewe, by restricting access, prevent a low-level reaction or forestall the development of a more severe reaction.

Other ewe, by restricting the casual performance of an activity by the devotee, serve as strong ebo, or offerings, in times of great need. Many ewe are tied to the stories and characteristics of the Orisha, and are described as enhancing the close relationship between the devotee and the Orisha. By limiting the performance of an activity by ewe, the devotee is given a powerful way to connect with the Orisha when desperate illness or another catastrophic event threatens them.

Ewe may also be a source of character formation. Every destiny contains certain strengths and weaknesses. While divination can point out these traits, ewe helps to fortify one's character and avoid the situations that work against one's best destiny. Children of Obatala, for example, often have what we call addictive personalities. Consequently, they are often forbidden to drink alcohol or indulge in other mind-altering drugs. Whether their sensitivity to alcohol is an allergy or a character issue, the ewe, by prohibiting the activity, works toward the fulfillment of the devotee's destiny by helping him avoid what would be for him an unhealthy situation.

At this juncture it is important to reiterate that there are no universal ewe. While drinking alcohol, eating pork, or wearing striped clothing may be forbidden to some devotees, they are not universally forbidden. Most children of Obatala don't drink, while most children of Oshun do not eat pumpkin, but neither alcohol nor pumpkins are forbidden to everyone. There is no one-size-fits-all solution here; instead, each person's prohibitions are specific to them based on their needs, and as those need change, the requirements placed on the devotee may change as well.

Honoring one's ewe can also be a type of ascetic practice. Broadly defined, asceticism is the performance of certainly bodily practices in the service of a higher order. The Orisha traditions have no general philosophy of asceticism. There are no general requirements for fasting or abstaining from certain goods or activities. There are no stories of heroic predecessors who fasted in the desert or sat in prolonged meditation. Indeed, in this tradition it seems as though the deities enjoy eating and drinking as much as their human children. Maintaining one's ewe is not about denial, but about spiritual practice, about protection and devotion. The overriding purpose of these practices is to maintain and strengthen one's contact with the spiritual (the Orisha, one's ancestors, or one's Ori). In this way, these practices can be a form of asceticism. While they may be protective, they also serve as a constant reminder of the commitment devotees have made to their destinies and their Orisha. These choices may be as subtle as choosing roast beef instead of ham, the cherry pie instead of the pumpkin, or not buying clothing with fringes. But each decision to honor one's ewe serves as a reminder of one's relationship with the Orisha and strengthens one's commitment to the religion.

## DIVINATION

The idea that everyone has a destiny that is forgotten in the birth process leads to the practice of divination to determine not only the fundamental contours of one's destiny, but also the ways in which that destiny is unfolding at the present time and how one might bring out the best possible destiny given their current circumstances. Through divination, one is able to remember the agreement made between one's Ori and Olodumare, and to make the life choices that bring one into harmony with that agreement. As we move through life we must make choices that enhance certain inherent skills and abilities while neglecting others. Choosing a particular school may require that I move to a new town far away from family and friends; time spent studying can't be spent perfecting my free throw. Taking a certain job, committing to a spouse, having or not having children all cut me off from other possible opportunities. Divination, as well as familiarity with my guardian deity, can help verify that my choices are in harmony with my best possible destiny. If it seems as though I have wandered away from my best destiny, divination provides ways for me to return to the path chosen by my Ori so that I can live in harmony with myself, my family, the community, and ultimately the world.

Divination also provides a method for communication between the invisible and the visible worlds. Many people come to Santería in a last-ditch effort to solve some personal or familial problem. In Hispanic communities, it is common to combine western-style medical treatment with spiritual baths and other treatments recommended by various types of divination, and even those who do not generally participate in Orisha rituals will visit a santero or a babalawo for a consultation when they encounter serious situations that appear intractable by other methods. People in other communities who are familiar with Orisha religion may also call upon practitioners when they encounter difficult situations.

Although priests may use many different divinatory techniques when working with clients, only three forms of divination are used to contact the Orisha directly: coconut divination, *diloggun*, which uses cowry shells, and *Ifa*, which is the special tool of the babalawo. All three forms of divination are used to communicate with specific invisible beings. Coconut divination can be used to talk to one's ancestors or an Orisha. In diloggun, one addresses a specific Orisha, although within the divination session itself other Orisha and sometime the spirits of the dead also speak. Ifa addresses only Orula (Orunmila) who speaks for the other Orisha and even Olodumare.

Divination with coconut pieces, sometimes called "throwing cocos" or "*obi* divination," is the simplest form of divination used in Orisha

**Cowry shells used for diloggun-style divination.**

communities. Although in the hands of an experienced practitioner it can resolve complex situations, normally it is used to answer straightforward questions and to confirm ritual actions. When the pieces of coconut meat that have not had the dark outside rind removed are dropped on the ground, they fall in one of five dark/light patterns (all white, or one, two, three, or four dark sides showing). Each combination is read as "yes," "no," or "throw again." By asking a series of yes/no questions, a person can determine the will and pleasure of the Orisha or *egun* consulted and discern a plan of action. Coconut divination is also used at strategic points in ritual to determine that the Orisha or egun are happy and satisfied with the ritual to that point, and if not, what needs to be done to achieve such satisfaction. It can also be used to get quick answers from the ancestors or the Orisha outside the context of other rituals.

Although traditionally coco divination is performed with fresh coconut, some priests make permanent divination pieces by using four cowry shells or four pieces of coconut shell. Sometimes, cowries are glued to the coconut shells to identify two pieces as male and two as female, lending an additional level of complexity to the divination process. Practitioners of this form of coco divination say that it more closely replicates the method of throwing four kola pieces used among the Yoruba in Africa. Although it appears simple and is easy to learn, in the hands of a talented diviner coco divination can provide sophisticated solutions to difficult problems. However, if someone is having severe problems or if they require a more detailed answer, priests will often choose one of the more complex divination systems.

*Diloggun* is a divinatory technique that uses cowry shells to communicate directly with an Orisha. As part of their initiation, each priest is given a set of small seashells for each of the Orisha he or she receives. These shells can be used to talk directly to that Orisha. Cowry shells have an opening that resembles the human mouth. When the rounded back is removed, the shells have two flat surfaces so that when dropped, they fall in a heads or tails configuration. Although there are more shells in each set, only 16 shells are used for a divination session. Each session begins by a double throw that determines the *odu* or divination verse that guides the session. There are 256 possible odu (16x16), each of which has one or more proverbs and a set of stories associated with it. The Orisha whose shells are used for the divination session is considered the main speaker, but other Orisha, even the *egun*, may also speak to the inquirer.

Every fully-crowned priest may use the shells to talk to the Orisha, however, only a few spend the time and effort to learn all the proverbs and stories necessary to a skilled interpreter of the fall of the shells. Most santeros use the services of a divination specialist called an *itelero* or *oriate*. Although both men and women learn to read the shells, the majority of diviners are men.

Each divination session begins with prayers to the Orisha said by the diviner in their language, Yoruba. At the end of the prayers, the diviner proclaims, "Orisha reo," which means "It is the Orisha who speaks." The inquirer and any others in attendance respond, "Adacha," which means "With their blessing." They thereby acknowledge that what will be said comes not from the diviner, but from the Orisha through the diviner. At the end of every divination session, the oriate determines what further action on the part of the inquirer will be necessary to secure the good luck exemplified by the session or to rebuff the bad luck. Often, the inquirer will be required to participate in further rituals or make some offering to the Orisha.

## IFA

The third type of divination used in Orisha religion is called *Ifa*. Although all priests can learn to read the shells, only a man who has been initiated into the priesthood of Orula can perform this type of divination. Orula, who is so closely associated with his style of divination that he is sometimes also called Ifa, is the Orisha whose primary gift is divination. Although some practitioners believe that diloggun is based on Ifa, both the mythology and scholars agree that diloggun is the older divination method.[4]

The priest of Orula, called a *babalawo* (father of mystery), has two different ways to perform Ifa. He can "beat" a set of 16 palm nuts, transferring them from hand to hand and leaving only one or two in the first hand. Based on the number left in his hand he marks one or two slashes in the dust scattered on a round divination board known as the Tray of Ifa. Eight marks are required to produce one of 256 possible *odu Ifa*. Like the odu of diloggun, each odu Ifa has a set of proverbs and stories associated with it. Through the interpretation of the odu, the babalawo can diagnose the client's problem and recommend a solution that reinforces a fortunate destiny or softens a difficult one. Because beating the nuts is such a laborious process, babalawo have developed a faster way to generate the odu using a chain with eight nuts or other tokens that can fall in a heads or tails configuration. With a single throw of the chain, the babalawo can determine the entire odu and proceed with the divination session.

According to the mythology, Orula was present at the creation of the world, and he is also present when each person chooses his or her destiny. Thus, he knows each person's past, present, and future, and how their destiny fits into that of the world as a whole. Consequently, the divination performed by his priests is believed to be the highest and most accurate of all the divination methods. Oriate do not generally interpret when the 14, 15, or 16 shells fall mouth up at the beginning of a divination session, preferring to refer these cases to a babalawo. Some Orisha communities use babalawo for all their divination needs, except for those cases (generally as part of initiation ceremonies) where cowry divination is required. These communities can be referred to as babalawo- or Ifa-centered houses. In other communities, an oriate is the principal diviner. These may be called oriate-centered houses. This overlap of function leads to some conflict, as the babalawo and oriate in an area compete for divination clients. Some babalawo say that the oriate have appropriated rituals—for example, determining which Orisha owns a client's head—that belong to the work of the babalawo. Some oriate, on the other hand, say that babalawo have an inflated view of their own importance and claim for themselves privileges that are not supported by traditional practice. In addition, some babalawo have begun performing divinations during initiations, formerly the exclusive prerogative of the oriate.

Because they are the keepers of the most sophisticated divination system, the babalawo are often referred to as the high priests of the religion. This, however, is a misrepresentation of their place within the religious hierarchy. While only babalawo can perform Ifa divination, they play a much smaller role in initiation rituals, including the kariocha ceremony that initiates new priests into the worship of all the Orisha except Orula. Only a babalawo can initiate another man (all babalawo are men) into the priesthood of Orula. Similarly, only an Orisha priest, under the guidance of an oriate, can initiate someone, man or woman, into the priesthood of the other Orisha. Some practitioners have even argued that, rather than calling the role of babalawo the most important in the religion, that honor should be accorded to the iyalocha and babalocha (godmothers and godfathers), who initiate others into the religion and continue the work of the Orisha.

Traditionally, if a man is shown by divination to be a potential babalawo, he must choose between serving as a priest of Orula or as a priest of the other Orisha. He cannot do both. Although initiation as a priest of Ifa doesn't require any other Orisha initiations, many babalawo are fully crowned priests of an Orisha before being initiated as a babalawo. However, once he serves as a godparent in any ritual, a man is precluded from being initiated as a babalawo. If he has already been initiated as an Orisha priest when he becomes a babalawo, a man must abstain from participating in any Orisha ritual except in his capacity as a babalawo. He may not engage in diloggun divination, give necklaces, or adimu Orisha or initiate anyone as priest of the Orisha.[5] While a babalawo who is also a priest of another Orisha may worship his Orisha in private, he may not act as an Orisha priest for any other person.

Some Americans have found the rules surrounding the priesthood of Ifa difficult to accept. As a consequence, we are seeing two important innovations in the United States and elsewhere. Some babalawo are giving themselves permission to participate more fully in the life of the Orisha communities. They not only attend Orisha initiations in their official capacity as babalawo, but also fully participate in those rituals. Some have even gone so far as to initiate godchildren, giving necklaces and even serving as the godparent at a kariocha.

A second innovation that is becoming widespread is the pursuit of Ifa initiations by women. As I will discuss in "Religious Rituals," both men and women can be put under the protection of Orula by receiving the "Hand of Orula," however, traditionally, only men are initiated as priests of Orula. One way for women to participate in the rituals of Ifa is as an *apetebi* or consort of a babalawo. Although the apetebi, who play an important part in rituals conducted by babalawo, have traditionally been the wives or daughters of a babalawo, other women can also be initiated into this important role. As the Ifa priesthood has grown and strengthened in the United States, many women without familial associations with a babalawo have been initiated as an apetebi. Although their work is vital to that of the babalawo, they are still considered to be the subordinate to him. In the last several decades, many American women, who have watched their sisters in other religious traditions fight for full equality, begun to ask for and receive initiations as priests of Ifa. Called *iyanifa* (mother of Ifa), these women learn to read Ifa and perform most (but not all) of the rituals of the babalawo. Although the initiation of women as iyanifa is not unique to the United States (Chief 'Fáróunbí Àìná Mosúnmólá Adéwálé-Samadhi, who goes by "Chief FAMA," is a contemporary Yoruba woman who has been initiated to Ifa), the priesthood of Ifa has been male-dominated in Cuba and the United States until recently, and both the roles of apetebi and iyanifa continue to be controversial in the wider Orisha community.

## SACRIFICE

Often the course of action recommended by either diloggun or Ifa requires the inquirer to perform a cleansing or healing ritual, or to make a sacrifice in order to bring their life back onto the path of their best destiny. Sometimes these sacrifices are simple: one might be asked to offer natural or manufactured goods to an Orisha or enact a simple ritual. However, if the problem is serious, the inquirer might be asked to participate in a complex ritual or an initiation, or to offer the blood of one or more animals to the Orisha.

Along with possession trance, animal sacrifice is among the most controversial aspects of Santería practice. People who have no qualms about using or eating animal products or killing small animals for sport or because they are perceived as vermin become incensed at the idea of killing in a ritual context. However, sacrifice, the giving of natural and manufactured items to the deities, is an important part of most religious traditions. Through sacrifice, one restores the positive processes in one's life and acquires general well-being. Within Santería, one gives to the Orisha and the ancestors what they need and want in the expectation that they in turn will give what one needs or wants. This is not viewed as "bribing" or "buying off" the Orisha; rather, it is the mutual exchange of ashé necessary to maintain the balance of the cosmos. Although you might give presents to your friends and family in order to win them over to your position on an issue or cause, you more commonly exchange presents as a way of showing your love and strengthening your relationships. So it is within Santería. Devotees give so that they may enhance the mutually satisfying relationship they have with the Orisha.

Although the idea of sacrifice is difficult for Americans, blood sacrifice is only a small part of the larger idea that is embedded in the Yoruba word *ebo*. In its more general form, sacrifice is the relinquishment of something precious for a particular purpose. In many traditional cultures including the Yoruba, no one would come to a deity, an elder, or other prominent person without some sort of gift, no matter how small or simple. That tradition continues among contemporary Orisha devotees. No one would approach the Orisha in either petition or thanksgiving without some sort of offering. Orisha religion both among the Yoruba and in the Americas is focused on the preservation and continuation of life. Devotees depend on the Orisha for their prosperity and good health. They understand that gift giving, both at the time of requests for assistance and in thanksgiving for assistance rendered, helps to solidify the connection between themselves and the Orisha.

Many types of items are offered to the Orisha. Just like people, the Orisha have certain items and food they like to receive as offerings. Every thing in nature, every manufactured object, and many types of raw and cooked foods can be associated with an Orisha and offered to that Orisha. Devotees offer money, fruit, cloth, liquor, candy, palm oil, knives, mats, deer antlers, seashells, honey, and molasses. Every Orisha is also associated with a particular number based on their stories in the divination texts of diloggun and Ifa, and many are also associated with a geographic locale. Thus, a devotee might be instructed to perform a simple ritual for Oshun using five (her sacred number) oranges (a golden fruit) on the banks of a river (the geographical location associated with her). Or someone may be asked to give three small knives to his own or his godparent's Ogun, the patron of iron and all weapons and tools. Usually, such offerings are made by the devotees of the Orisha based on the recommendations of a diviner or a godparent. Sometimes, the required offering is the blood of an animal, typically a bird, a chicken, or a dove, for example, or a larger animal, like a goat or a small ram.

When one's life is at stake or a new priest is being born into the life of service to the Orisha, the sacrifice includes the blood of animals. All types of sacrifice, but particularly animal sacrifice, serve to remind the participants of the delicate balance of the universe. As principally city-dwellers, many of us forget that something must die—be it a cow or a chicken or a carrot—to make our lives possible. We have become unconscious of the trees that died to give us this book, the cow, the wheat, the tomato, the potato, etc., that died for our cheeseburger and fries. When our grandparents wanted chicken for Sunday dinner, they went out into the yard, chose a chicken, killed it, plucked it, and cooked it; we, on the other hand, pick up a daintily wrapped package from the supermarket. Santeros value the lives of animals, but they value the lives of humans more. When Orisha religion requires the sacrifice of an animal, it is offered with respect, then it is killed quickly and with as little pain as possible. Santeros understand what the animal has given and are grateful.

In many instances, only the blood, which contains the life force of the animal, is given to the Orisha, while the meat is cooked and eaten by the ritual participants. In large rituals, for example an initiation where many animals are sacrificed, an important part of the ritual is the effort to clean, cook, and serve the carcasses of the sacrificed animals. In these cases, the sacrifice is in the form of a feast that enables the Orisha and their followers to share in the ashé of the ritual. But not all sacrificed animals are eaten. If the animal is sacrificed as part of a ritual cleansing, it is believed to have absorbed the problems, dangers, and bad luck of the person being cleansed. In such a case the body is disposed of without being eaten. Although the body might be thrown into the trash, often it is discarded at a location associated with the Orisha to whom the offering was made. Thus, offerings to Ochosi might be discarded at a courthouse or jail, those to Ogun near a railroad track, those to Oshun in a river, stream, or canal. One of the arguments presented by the city of Hialeah against the CLBA was that the discarding of such animal carcasses was a public health hazard. This practice of discarding animals throughout the city has presented problems to officials not only in Hialeah and Miami, but also in New York, Los Angeles, and other cities with a concentration of Santería practitioners.

Another problem often presented when sacrifice is discussed is whether or not it is a cruel and inhumane practice. The ASPCA (American Society for the Prevention of Cruelty to Animals) suggests that Santería sacrifice is less humane than that used in licensed slaughterhouses. They say that animals die slowly and painfully, and that they are often kept in filthy and inhumane conditions before the ceremony. However, santeros contend that their methods are no more cruel than other types of legal slaughter, that the animals are killed quickly and cleanly, that they are generally eaten, and that the animals used are ordinary fowl and four-legged animals commonly available pre-slaughtered in the grocery store.

American discomfort with the idea of sacrifice has been exhibited by the passage and enforcement of laws designed to limit to eliminative the practice. In the early 1990s, the city of Hialeah, Florida, passed a series of ordinances which appeared to be designed to suppress the religious practices of the Church of the Lucumí Babalu Aye (CLBA), a local Santería congregation. Unlike other Orisha communities that have been persecuted for their sacrificial practices, the leaders of CLBA decided to fight the ordinances as a violation of their First Amendment right to freedom of religion. Ernesto Pichardo, one of the founders of the Santería church, said, "Animal sacrifice is an integral part of our faith. It is like our holy meal." At the hearing before the Supreme Court, Douglas Laycock, a law professor at the University of Texas, said, "The only way to show that sacrifice is 'unnecessary' to the Santeria followers is to prove that Santeria is a false religion." However, the legitimacy of Santería as a religion was never questioned as part of the hearing. In the Court opinion overthrowing the city's ordinances, Justice Kennedy, quoting an earlier ruling (*Thomas v. Review Act of Indiana Employment Security Div.* [1981]), said "Although the practice of animal sacrifice may seem abhorrent to some 'religious belief need not be acceptable, logical, consistent, or comprehensible to others in order to merit First Amendment protection.'"[6]

Another reason blood sacrifice is offensive to many American is its association with primitive, frenzied, or irrational behavior. Some nineteenth- and early twentieth-century theorists of the history of religion suggested that it was born out of the inherent violence in early human society. According to one view, religion was used to redirect the violent tendencies of our early ancestors away from the primary social group by focusing them onto a scapegoat, whose murder helped to unify the community and decrease violence within the community. As human communities moved from a more primitive to a more civilized society, ritualized violence was replaced first by religious ecstasy and then by rational law and more contemplative forms of mysticism. In its simplest form, this theory suggests that primitive religions engaged in wild irrational practices including bloody sacrifice, but that more highly developed religions practiced a more restrained ritual form epitomized by the highly ritualized and symbolic form of Christian sacrifice. To engage in actual rather then symbolic sacrifice, then, is an indication that a tradition is primitive and irrational, a less-than-fully-developed spiritual system.[7]

Another way of viewing sacrifice uses a metaphor not of scapegoating and murder, but of animal domestication and gift-giving. Animal sacrifice is most commonly found in agrarian or pastoral societies. When members of these societies are asked why they sacrifice, they rarely talk of using sacrifice to enforce group solidarity or identify a scapegoat, but rather, they describe sacrifice in terms of gift-giving and pollution removal. In agrarian and pastoral societies, breeders, like sacrificers, are concerned with selective killing, and choose their animals according to certain physical and behavioral characteristics. While the breeder may cull from the herd or flock the animal with the least desirable traits, the sacrificer chooses the most perfect animal (for example, the unblemished lamb of the Hebrew Bible) for presentation to the deity.[8]

Listening to santeros talk about their sacrificial tradition, we can see that they exemplify this view of sacrifice. They speak of "feeding" the Orisha or "giving" an animal to an Orisha. Sacrifice is seen as part of an exchange of ashé between the visible and invisible worlds that revivifies both the giver and the recipient. The rituals themselves are not frenzied or irrational events, but controlled performances that balance the heat of blood with cool water, songs, and prayers. Animals are dispatched in an efficient and orderly fashion that is designed to please and vivify the Orisha. Because sacrificial animals are often prepared and cooked for the community, the sacrificial arena includes not only the area designed to hold the animals until the sacrificing priest is ready for them and the actual sacrificial site, but also spaces set aside to convert the raw carcasses into a feast. In these spaces, devotees skin goats and sheep, pluck chickens, and separate those parts of sacrificed animals destined for presentation back to the Orisha from the meat and the offal. Finally, the kitchen staff must prepare and cook designated portions for the Orisha, and the meat for the santeros and their guests. All of this activity, some sacred and some more mundane, belies any characterization of this activity as wild or frenzied.

In it ruling, the Supreme Court upheld CLBA's basic right to perform the sacrifices required by their religion. In addition, the court suggested to the city of Hialeah that, if there was a problem with the dumping of the animal remains, they would have to find a way to regulate the "disposal of organic garbage" (Greenhouse 1993, p. 9.) that does not unnecessarily burden the practitioners of Orisha religion. This is one of the issues that practitioners will need to take into account as the religion expands and moves into the mainstream of society. Just as communities cannot unduly burden practitioners, practitioners will need to find a way to continue their practices without unduly burdening the surrounding community. As the religion grows and becomes more visible, we can expect to see some sort of compromise between practitioners and officials that allows santeros to practice their religion while participating as respected members of the larger community.

# Life, Death, and the Afterlife

Orisha devotees' ideas about life, death, and the afterlife are among the most syncretistic element of the tradition, as they combine ideas from African, European, and Asian worldviews. According to Yoruba cosmology, human beings exist in a continuing cycle of movement between the visible and the invisible worlds. People are born and they live according to the destinies they chose in heaven. When they die they are judged on how well they performed, and, after some period of rest and rejuvenation, they are reborn, generally into the children of their offspring. Heaven, or the invisible world, may be peaceful and pleasant, but people seem to prefer life in the rough and tumble visible world as it appears that they are reborn within years (sometimes even months) of their deaths. A theory of multiple souls explains how, even though one's ancestors have chosen to be reborn relatively soon after their deaths, they also continue to reside in the invisible world where they watch over the families of their descendents and offer advice and counsel to them.

European Christian cosmology also postulates spirits of the dead, both family and non-family members, who can provide advice and counsel to the living. In Catholic Christianity these dead guardians include both the saints canonized by the Church and others that individuals may hold in special esteem. Although the saints may be considered especially powerful spirits, one's own relatives are also honored and venerated. Because the dead are not reborn, those who died in a partially sinful state are said to reside in state of punishment known as Purgatory. Here, souls are cleansed of their sins so that they can eventually be allowed into heavenly bliss. While the saints can aid the living, the living can help speed the souls of the dead to eventual entrance into heaven by their prayers and other offerings.

Asian worldviews provide another way in which the souls of human beings could become purified and spiritually advanced. Through the mechanism of reincarnation, a spirit is repeatedly born and reborn, their situations improving or deteriorating according to their actions in each lifetime based on the laws of *karma*. Unlike the Yoruba, who believe that they are always reborn as human beings generally into their own family or lineage, in many Asian traditions one may be reborn not only as a human being, but as any type of animal, including an insect. In some Buddhist traditions, one might also be reborn into non-earthly realms of either pleasure or suffering. But even those reborn into the so-called Heavens or Hells eventually die and are again reborn. In some traditions one might eventually become so spiritually elevated as to be able to avoid reincarnation into this world of suffering altogether. Those who are more spiritually advanced can help those at a lower level of advancement move to a higher plane both during life and after death. One's spiritual guides may include not only a living guru or teacher, but also otherworldly beings that have reached the highest spiritual levels.

Although these worldviews are philosophically incompatible, ideas from each have been incorporated into contemporary devotees' worldviews. Contemporary Santería practice commonly encompasses several different traditions, including the Egungun traditions of West African, Christian and Asian ideas, and the Spiritist traditions of the Caribbean. Practitioners in the Orisha traditions often say that the dead give birth to the deities. Among other things, this saying suggests that religious practice always begins with the veneration of one's religious and blood ancestors. This chapter will describe these precedent traditions and explore some of the ways practitioners have used them to develop their own techniques to honor the dead.

## ANCESTOR VENERATION

Ancestors, those blood relatives who have died and passed on to the invisible world, are extremely important to the peoples of Western Africa. Among many groups including the Yoruba, the ancestors are thought to continue to be concerned about the lives of their descendents after their deaths. Ancestors watch over their children and their children's children, rejoicing when things are going welling and unhappy when they are not. Because they continue to live in the invisible world, Yoruba ancestors can provide guidance to their family members through dreams and divination and through the institution known as *Egungun*. The Egungun are masquerade dancers who visit the towns and villages during special ceremonies and festivals. Dancing through the streets, they bless and chastise their descendents. The Egungun "mask" is a full-body costume that conceals the identity of the dancer from observers. When an Egungun speaks, it is believed to be the voice of their dead ancestor that listeners hear. The Egungun not only bless and counsel the people, they also serve as an important part of Yoruba society. They are the moral voice of the town, working to ensure that everyone from the youngest child to the king acts according to the moral and ethical code of the community. The Egungun masqueraders and their helpers belong to a secret society that constructs and maintains the costumes and supports the dancers during their appearances. Being a member of the Egungun Society is a great privilege reserved for the most highly-respected members of the community.

We know from the historical record that there was a revival of the Egungun Society in Cuba during the late nineteenth and early twentieth century. However, several factors seem to have worked against the continuation of the Egungun on the island. Constructing, maintaining, and presenting the Egungun masks is expensive, requiring the support from the most well-to-do and most highly-placed members of the society. Moreover, since the ancestors and their human representatives were not part of the colonial government that ruled the island, their words did not have the authority in Cuba that they had had in their homeland. For these reasons and perhaps others, the Egungun Society died out in Cuba.

Among the Yoruba in precolonial times (and often still today), the dead were buried within the compounds of their families. Often a room or portion of a room above the burial site was designated as a shrine where one could honor the ancestors. Just as many Americans today visit the cemeteries where their loved ones are buried and leave flowers and other tokens of respect, the Yoruba visited the family shrine. There they could tell their ancestors about the doings of the family and leave small offerings, perhaps a plate of food, some palm wine, or pieces of kolonut.

When the Yoruba were taken to the Americas, they didn't forget to continue to honor their ancestors. Although they could no longer bury their dead beneath their homes, they often constructed small shrines in the house where they could continue to communicate with their loved ones. There they could leave plates of food, glasses of water or rum, or other offerings. Because the dead were buried in the earth, if not directly below the shrine, the offerings could be set on the floor just as they had been back home. Even though the Egungun Society no longer performed their community festivals and danced in the streets, people continued to build personal shrines for the family dead, the *egun*, in their homes.

In the meantime, another way of communicating with the dead was coming to the Caribbean. *Espiritismo* (Spiritism), the practices of speaking with the dead based on the work of Allan Kardec, was brought to Cuba in the 1950s. Kardec, who was born in France as H. Leon Denizard Rivail in 1804, was trained as a scientist and mathematician.[1] In 1850 he began to investigate the phenomenon of "table turning" that was sweeping though Europe with the intention of discrediting it. Table turning involved a group of people who gathered around a table in an effort to communicate with disembodied spirits. When the spirits were present the table would move, sometimes raising into the air or spinning rapidly. Although he was a natural skeptic, Rivail soon became convinced of the reality of this phenomenon and began a systemic investigation. As he would later say, "It is a most curious thing! My conversations with the invisible intelligences have completely revolutionized my ideas and convictions. The instructions thus transmitted constitute an entirely new theory of human life, duty, and destiny, that appears to me to be perfectly rational and coherent, admirably lucid and consoling, and intensely interesting."[2] After two year of investigation he decided, with the approval of the spirits, to write a book describing the information he had gathered from these conversations under the nom de plume of Allan Kardec. Soon he was the center of an organization of mediums from around the world that were continuing and extending his research.

The Spiritist movement added to the European worldview another group of spirits one might turn to for guidance and counsel. Neither saints recognized by the Church nor family members, these were highly evolved spirits who choose to work for the spiritual elevation of those still on the earth plane. Although these spirits may be individuals with personal names and histories, in the Caribbean they often became members of a band known collectively for their common characteristics: the Sailors (all those who died at sea), Gypsies, Kongoes (Africans of any ethnic group), Madams (fine Afro-Creole or mulatto ladies), and the like. When Espiritismo moved to the United States with Puerto Ricans and other peoples from the Caribbean, many of these spirits again become individualized, although they maintain their stereotypic designations, so that American spiritists have a Sailor, a Gypsy, a Kongo or a Madam among their spirit guides.

Originally embraced by the Cuban middle class who wanted scientific proofs that the living could communicate with the dead, in Cuba Kardec's techniques was soon embraced by all levels of Cuban society, and evolved into four different systems of practice. Professor Armand Andres Bermudez calls these Scientific Spiritism (*Espiritismo del Mesa*), Spiritualism of Charity (*Espiritismo de Caridad*), Spiritism of the Chain (*Espiritismo de Cordon*), and Mixed or Crossed Spiritism (*Espiritismo Cruzado*).[3] Although Orisha devotees may participate in any of these forms of Spiritism, American and Cuban devotees who practice Spiritism most commonly engage in a form of Espiritismo Cruzado. In this form of Espiritismo, Afro-Cubans created their own methods for speaking with dead by mixing Kardec's techniques with elements from Yoruba and Bantu religious practices. Through these rituals, they were able to communicate with elevated spirits who they believe had the power to aid them on their spiritual journey. Espiritismo Cruzado provides a vehicle whereby both European and African methods and cosmological ideas can be integrated, along with elements from other cultures, into a single system of practice that allows the living to speak and interact with the dead.

Because Espiritismo has no initiatory hierarchy, individuals may choose the practices and rituals that provide what they feel they need for their own spiritual development.

Orisha devotees in the United States maintain several traditions for communicating with their ancestors and other spirits that can be traced back to Spiritist traditions developed in nineteenth- and early twentieth-century Cuba. In addition, some communities have reestablished the Egungun ceremonies that didn't survive in Cuba. From the Yoruba tradition of maintaining ancestor shrines in their homes, contemporary Americans continue the practice of setting up and maintaining egun shrines where they can honor their ancestors. Although it is a separate tradition, many santeros are also practitioners of the Kongo-based tradition of Palo Monte, which provides another way for practitioners to communicate and work with the spirits of the dead. From Kardecian Spiritism they have adapted the white table ritual to a home shrine known as a *bovada* where they can connect with their spirit guides and helpers. In addition, many participate in the *Misa Espiritual* where they can both develop their mediumistic skills and work with experienced mediums to communicate with these spirits directly. The rest of this chapter will describe these rituals and traditions.[4]

## THE EGUN SHRINE

The contemporary Egun Shrine is modeled on the home shrines the Yoruba people built in their family compounds. The shrines are placed near the ground in order to be close to the family members buried in the earth. Contemporary practitioners often place their Egun shrines in bathroom or kitchen cabinets where the shrine, following Yoruba traditions, can be close to the ground and close to the running water that is believed to be the conduit between the land of the living and that of the dead. Cabinets provide the added advantage of privacy. Since, as santeros are quick to say, everyone has ancestors, new devotees are encouraged to construct Egun shrines even before they receive other religious initiations. The area is dedicated by drawing a circle similar to a Kongoese cosmogram[5] on the walls and floor of the cabinet. Often this circle is drawn so that half is on the wall and half on the floor, representing the intersection of the world of the living above, and that of the dead below. Nine X's are drawn along the circumference of the circle, invoking again the shrine as a type of crossroads. Nine is the number of Oya, the ruler of the dead and the Mother of the Egun. Among the objects typically found on these shrines is a stick known as *Opa Egun* or the Staff of the Ancestors decorated with ribbons and bells reminiscent of the costumes of the Egungun masquerades, candles, glasses of water, cigars, food and drink, and other things the ancestors may have enjoyed while alive. Many people also include photos or other tokens of particular ancestors. During the meals following rituals and at other times according to their personal preferences,

**Egun Shrine with food and drink offerings.**

devotees prepare plates of food for the ancestors and place them on these shrines. Although some devotees say that one should only honor blood relatives at these shrines, many people include others, including adopted family members and influential mentors and teachers. Additionally, initiated devotees often also include tokens honoring their religious ancestors—that is, the deceased godparents and other priests in their religious lineage—at these shrines.

Just as other people may pray for and to their ancestors in graveyards and cemeteries, devotees honor their ancestors at these Egun Shrines, speaking to their ancestors on a weekly or even daily basis, sharing their hopes and dreams along with the news of their lives and that of their families. Although prayer and meditation are common activities at these shrines, devotees can also use coconut divination to speak directly to their ancestors and get their guidance for their lives.

Santeros say, "Sin Muerto no Hay Santo," that is, without the dead there are no Orisha. This saying has several meanings. On one level, there is an understanding that many of the Orisha are deified ancestors. The Orisha are people who lived in the mythical past who have been elevated to the position of deities. From another point of view this saying suggests that since this is an initiatory tradition, one cannot come to the Orisha and their worship cannot be maintained without those who passed on the traditions to their children and godchildren. Without the ancestors who initiated the living, the traditions would not have survived; without the dead, the Orisha would have no worshippers. Additionally, the saying reminds devotees that the Egun are always the first honored at any ritual. Before any other ceremony can take place, the devotees stand before the Egun Shrine to ask the blessings and co-operation of the ancestors on their actions.

## THE BOVEDA

Although most of the Spiritist literature only speaks of the group rituals, many Spiritist practitioners, called *espiritistas,* set up a Spiritist shrine, known as a *boveda,* in their homes. The shrine modeled after the altar table used in the *misa blanca,* or white mass of the Espiritismo del Mesa, consists of glasses of water, a white candle, and a rosary or cross which are placed together on a table or bureau covered with a white cloth. Generally, there is an odd number of water glasses, five, seven or nine (all of which are significant numbers for santero-espiritistas), however, instead of a set number, many espiritistas place a glass of water for each of their spirit guides and guardians. Some people will also include glasses of water for their ancestral dead, although Kardec himself discouraged his followers from attempting to contact their recently dead family members, and many people feel that the Egun shrine is a more appro-priate venue for such communication. In general, natural materials—for example, wood and glass rather than plastic—are preferred for these items, because they are seen as closer to the natural world. When it is first set up and periodically when it needs to be refreshed, the boveda is sprinkled with Holy Water from a Catholic Church and *Florida Water,* a kind of cologne commonly available in *botanicas* and markets serving the Hispanic community.

Although fresh flowers may be included on a boveda for special occasions, many people include a bouquet of artificial flowers on their altars. Other tokens representative of or requested by the spirits may also be included on the display, including statuettes, dolls, perfumes, cups, bowls, and the like. Although a strict Kardecian view of the spirit world suggests that material offerings are not appropriate since spirits exist on a non-material plane, many devotees leave coffee, rum, cigars, and food offerings on their bovedas. This is just one example of the spillover between strictly Spiritist practices and Yoruba-based egun practices. As sites of communications between the physi-cal and spiritual worlds, the boveda is used by espiritistas to pray and meditate in an effort to maintain connections with their spirit guides. These spirit guides are not generally deceased family members, but instead are highly evolved spiritual beings that have chosen to work with the devotee for their mutual spiritual elevation.

One of the rituals commonly performed at the boveda is a series of prayers for the recently dead. In line with Catholic theology, is it believed that the prayers of the living can smooth the path of the dead as they make their way

Boveda (Spiritist shrine) in devotee's home.

to God to receive His final judgment. Every evening for nine days the espiritista places a glass of cool fresh water and burns a white, unscented candle in front of the boveda while praying that the spirit may receive light, spiritual elevation, and clarity. The first evening, the water and candle are placed on the floor in front of the boveda. On each subsequent evening, the water and candle are raised slightly higher by placing them on short stools, piles of books, or the like. On the final day, the water and candle should be on a bookcase or cabinet above the head of the espiritista. Nine is a significant number in both Yoruba and Catholic practice. Among the Yoruba, nine is the number associated with the Orisha Oya, who, among other attributes, is the owner of the cemetery that rules the spirits of the dead. Among Catholics, a *novena* is a special nine-day prayer cycle based on Greek and Roman mortuary customs. According to the *Catholic Encyclopedia*, novenas may be conducted for any number of reasons, including prayers for the dead.[6] This ritual draws on all these influences to give devotees a way to grieve and offer spiritual aid for those who have died.

This is only one of many private rituals that may be conducted by the espiritista in front of this shrine. Because it is a home altar, the rituals and prayers performed by the owner of the shrine are only limited by the desires of the espiritista and his or her spirit guides.

## THE MISA ESPIRITUAL

Although many followers of Kardec's Spiritist system construct bovedas in their homes in order to have a site for interaction with their spirit guides and helpers, most also participate in the ritual known as *Misa Espiritismo* or the Spiritist Mass. The *misa* is a form of Espiritismo Cruzado that incorporates Yoruba and Bantu (often called Kongo) elements into the Kardecian mediumistic ceremony. The purpose of the ceremony is to raise both spirits and human beings to a higher spiritual level through communication and interaction. During the ceremony, spirits may speak to the assembled congregation through the bodies of experienced mediums in a type of altered consciousness called possession trance. Mediums may also hear, see, or feel the presence of spirits.

Before the ceremony begins, an altar table is prepared with glasses of water, flowers, and candles arranged on a white cloth. Rum, cigars, coffee, Florida Water, and other things that the spirit guides of the congregation enjoy are prepared and placed on the table. The participants sit in a semicircle in front of the boveda. After a special cleansing ceremony, they begin the ritual by reading prayers from Kardec's *Book of Prayers*, which is available in both English and Spanish versions.[7] They may also add other songs and prayers, many of which have been passed down through spiritist circles since the 1900s. In African American communities, devotes often sing Spirituals and

**Altar table being prepared for a Misa Blanca ritual.**

songs from Protestant Christian traditions. After praying and singing for some time, they call upon the spirits to join them in the ritual.

Although some of the members of any group participating in a misa are more experienced or skillful in spirit communication than others, at the misa everyone is said to be equal. Anyone who hears, sees, feels, or becomes possessed by a spirit is encouraged to declare it. Although some groups may follow a set format, often the misa is open-ended, guided by the desires and leadership of the spirits. The more experienced mediums will attempt to discern the true nature of the spirits participating in the misa, testing them to make sure the spirit is beneficial to the members and is not trying to trick or disrupt the ceremony. Disruptive or unruly spirits are dismissed while benevolent spirits are encouraged to share in the proceedings. Often, spirits mount or possess one of the members so they may speak and act more directly. These spirits may cleanse the human participants or give advice to individuals or to the congregation as a whole. The spirit guides of participants are identified either directly through possession or through the discernment of the more experienced mediums. The spirit guide or guardian of one of the participants might speak directly to its human counterpart, giving advice or asking for offerings or tokens to be placed up on individual's home boveda. Many spirits enjoy being embodied, albeit temporarily, smoking the cigars and drinking the rum or coffee or other drinks provided.

According to Espiritismo philosophy, these guardian spirits are spiritually elevated by this participation in the mundane world and by the guidance they provide to the human participants. However, some less pure spirits may also attend the misa in an effort to be cleansed and released from lingering impurities. These impurities are thought to tie spirits to the physical world and prevent their full release into the world of the dead. The healing activities performed by the elevated spirits on the living participants in the rituals as well as the healing provided by the living for these less elevated spirits both fulfill the ideals of Espritismo de Caridad, the spiritualism of charity or good works.

## PALO MONTE

When the bulk of the Yoruba arrived in Cuba, they were met by people from the Kongo basin of central Africa. People from that area had been part of the slave trade from the sixteenth century. The Kingdom of Kongo grew out of chiefdoms that were established as early as the 1200s.[8] By the time Portuguese traders arrived along the coast in 1483, it had been in existence for about a century and a half. Recognizing the Kingdom as sovereign nation, the Portuguese established the same types of economic, religious, and political alliances as they had with the emerging sovereign nations of Europe. The two nations exchanged diplomats as well as trade goods and the Kongolese aristocracy accepted Christianity, making it the official religion of the state. As early as 1510, the Portuguese were buying captives from the Kongolese nobility and selling them elsewhere along the West African coast. With the discovery of Brazil and the demand for labor to work the mines and plantations in South America, the African slave trade was born. People from Central Africa, who spoke a number of Bantu languages, were brought to Cuba in the 1500s, and there is evidence that they continued to arrive until the end of the 1800s. Although in absolute numbers there were fewer Bantu-speakers brought to Cuba over the course of the slave trade than Yoruba-speaking peoples who only began to arrive in great numbers in the mid-1800s, the Bantu peoples had a long and influential presence on the island. The contemporary religions of Palo Monte, Palo Mayombe, Kimbisa, and others generalized under the umbrella of *Regla de Congo* are based on the religious traditions of these peoples.

Although initially there was animosity between the Kongolese and Yoruba peoples in Cuba, eventually they intermarried and initiated each other into their religious traditions. Today it is very common for Orisha devotees to also be initiates into one of these traditions. These practitioners, called *palero* (*palera* if female), work with extremely powerful spirits of the dead called *nfumbi*, using as a sacred site a cauldron similar to Ogun's pot called a *prenda* in Spanish or *nganga* in the Kongoese language of Bakongo. While the contents of Ogun's cauldron are his iron implements, a prenda contains a variety of natural materials including sticks from the forest. Hence the term "palo," "stick" in Spanish, in the name of many of these traditions. Although the beings who are believed to inhabit these pots are not deities but highly developed human beings, they are considered to be powerful spirits who can work for and with their devotees. Because Palo works with spirits that are considered to be lower in the cosmological hierarchy than Orisha, many Orisha priests insist that if one is going to be initiated as a palero or a palera, that initiation must precede one's kariocha or initiation as a priest of the Orisha. It is said that one cannot put another initiation on top of the "crown" that is kariocha.

Many practitioners of the Palo traditions insist that they only use the power of their prenda spirits for good. However, within the larger religious worldview that encompasses these traditions, there is a moral hierarchy that places the Orisha at one end and the nfumbi at the other to suggest that the Orisha exemplify the highest moral position whose power cannot be used for malevolent purposes, while the nfumbi are strong and quick to act but always morally suspect. Without their own intrinsic moral code, the nfumbi are seen as dependent on the ethical code their human priests who can use their powers in both positive and negative ways. In this scheme the espiritismo spirits are generally considered to be morally upright, but less powerful than either the Orisha or the nfumbi. Those who work with all three types of spirits can choose which set of spirits are appropriate for the spiritual work that they want to do.[9] Many devotees would suggest, however, that this is not an entirely accurate portrayal of these spirits, as there is a range of characteristics within each of these categories that precludes absolute statements of relative power and morality.

## CONCLUSION

Together these traditions provide a variety of ways for contemporary practitioners to stay in communication with both their personal dead and with elevated spirits who are interested in guiding their spiritual development. Although practitioners attempt to keep their veneration of egun, nfumbi, Kardecian spirits, and Orisha separate, constructing separate shrines for each group, often ideas and practices appropriate for one group will find their way into the ideas and practices of another group. For example, even though Kardecian spirits are thought to be highly evolved and beyond material needs and pleasures, one often finds the rum and cigars more commonly offered to egun and Orisha on their shrines. Similarly, even though many think that the egun shrine should be limited to blood and religious ancestors, one often finds tokens of the spirit guides identified during Spiritist masses included on them. The Yoruba didn't think in terms of dark and light spirits, yet many contemporary devotees have incorporated a dualistic thought pattern from the surrounding culture, and identify some spirits as "dark" spirits who are morally suspect if not absolutely evil, and others as "light" spirits who are inherently ethical. Often these light spirits are described as less powerful than their dark counterparts in the same way that "good" people are less able to use absolute power to enforce their will than those with a weaker morality. There are certain devotees who view the practice of Palo Monte as a way of using these strong dark spirits to act malevolently toward perceived enemies. Many devotees are espiritistas who work with the highly elevated spirits of the Espiritismo tradition, palaros who work with the Kongolese nfumbi, and santeros who worship and work with the Yoruba Orisha. Within the overlapping cosmologies, those who practice some or all of these traditions have many different types of spirits they can call on for help for themselves, their families, and their clients.

In spite of this complex view of the organization of the invisible world, there is little discussion within these communities of one's own future place among these beings. Practice is much more focused on the fulfillment of one's destiny in the here-and-now than worries about the afterlife. There seems to be little theological speculation about what happens when one dies and the actual working out of one's reincarnation. Many practitioners, when questioned, end up using the metaphors and images of the larger Christian society (with some invocation of Asian and Yoruba concepts to help explain ideas of reincarnation) to articulate their understandings of these issues. This is consistent with a religious tradition that is more concerned about the way that one lives and worships than faith statements or proclamations of beliefs. The dead and other spirits of the invisible world are important, but how individuals make the transition after death seems to be little discussed.

# Religious Rituals

Santería and its sister religions are religions of practice rather than belief. One does not come to these traditions through the recitation of creeds or other statements of belief, but through the participation in rituals of initiation. Some rituals are public and open to whoever should be invited to attend. Others are completely private, closed to those without the appropriate levels of initiation. In this chapter, I will look at the public face of the major rituals of the religion. I will describe what an outsider might expect to see and do, and how to act in an appropriate way. I will also describe some common rituals that newcomers might participate in and explain what they can expect. Every tradition has certain behaviors that are considered good etiquette for those participating in their ceremonies. At the end of this chapter, I have included a short guide outlining how one should behave in order to exhibit good manners at these events.

Although much of what happens in many of these rituals takes place out of view, there is still much for us to consider. In this chapter, I will discuss the ceremonies of divination and healing and blessing rituals. I will also describe what a visitor might expect to see and do at a religious birthday party and at a drumming ceremony. In conjunction with my discussion of drumming rituals, I will discuss the most important aspect of these rituals, the possession of participants by the Orisha. Possession trance is one of the more difficult aspects of these traditions for newcomers to understand. Possession involves the incarnation of an Orisha in the body of a priest for the purpose of communication between the deity and the congregation. This is an important aspect of the practice of all the Orisha traditions, as it allows direct, face-to-face interaction with the deities. Although many people are not completely comfortable with the idea of possession, in this chapter, I will explain what is happening, why it is an important part of the religion, and how one should act if she should come into the presence of a possessed person.

Finally, at the end of the chapter I will include a short summary of Santería ritual etiquette and what might be expected of visitors at different types of rituals.

Since initiations are such a major portion of this tradition, I have given them their own separate chapter.

## DIVINATION RITUALS

For many people, one of their first encounters with these religions is through a divination session. Perhaps they're having problems and someone suggests a visit to a santero or babalawo. Perhaps they're just curious. In any case, the diviner is prepared to speak on their behalf to the Orisha and to communicate the Orisha's recommendations for their lives.

Among Orisha worshippers, divination isn't fortune telling, but rather, a way to communicate directly with the Orisha in order to get their advise and help in manifesting the best possible life within their destiny. As discussed in "Destiny, Divination and Sacrifice," these traditions provide several forms of divination. Many practitioners communicate with the invisible world through the medium of cards, crystal balls, glasses of water, and the like. These are not Yoruba divination forms, but rather, draw upon Western, European, Christian, and New Age traditions. Many *espiritistas* (spiritualists) use these methods to communicate with the *egun* and other spiritual beings, and talented mediums are credited with accurate portrayals of the past, present, and future actions of their clients. In addition to describing the clients' lives and actions, these practitioners will often prescribe small rituals and ceremonies that the clients need to perform in order to protect themselves from harmful forces or to bring forward the desired changes in their lives. However, it is the Yoruba divination forms that are most important to these religions, and those they will look at more deeply.

## DILOGGUN

All fully-crowned Orisha priests are entitled to perform cowry-shell divination, although many are not proficient and defer to a specially trained divination priest known as an *itelero* or *oriate*. Priests receive a set of 18 to 21 cowry shells dedicated to each Orisha as part of the initiation ceremony. The rounded back portion of the shells are removed, leaving the natural opening, called the mouth, and the back, which is often called the stomach. When dropped, the shells fall in either a "heads (mouth)" or "tails (stomach)" position. The diviner uses a numeric system based on the number of shells that fall "mouth" up. Two such throws result in an *odu* that the diviner can tie to a set of proverbs and stories that provide the basis for the divination session.

The session begins with prayers to the Orisha and the proclamation "Orisha reo," that is, "It is the Orisha who speaks," to remind the inquirer that the diviner is only the mouthpiece of the Orisha. Once the itelero determines the basic numbers for the session, he goes on to determine whether this *odu* comes with *ire*, good luck, or *osogbo*, bad luck, and from what source the good or bad luck emanates. Finally, he determines what might be necessary to secure the good luck or soften the bad. It is at this point that the skills of the itelero come to the fore as he attempts to determine the will of the Orisha in the current situation through close observation of the fall of the shells and the responses to his questions.

The client can also interject questions and suggestions into the session, subject to verification by the itelero and his shells. Although the client usually brings a problem or question to the reading, often the italero will discover other things going on in the person's life that are either more significant then the presenting problem or are making the presenting problem worse. In conversation with the Orisha, itelero attempts to not only determine the problem or problems keeping the client from fulfilling their best destiny, but also to determine what might be done to overcome these problems and move the client toward a better life. Usually, the solution requires the cooperation of one or more Orisha. The result of the session is often an offering or ritual to tie the good fortune or soften the bad. The offering or ritual may be something as simple as taking oranges to Oshun at the river or abstaining from certain activities for a set period. However, if the problem is substantial, the requirements might be more demanding. In severe or life-threatening cases, the client might be asked to undergo certain initiations, even initiation into the priesthood.

It is up to the client to determine whether and to what extent he or she will fulfill the requirements demanded by the divination session. Good diviners talk to new clients before the session, outlining possible outcomes and preparing the client for the demands that might be imposed upon him or her. Even so, when they get together, itelero talk about clients who refuse to take the advice presented or who go to multiple diviners, "shopping" for the answer they want.

## IFA

Another type of divination is called Ifa. Whereas any fully-crowned Orisha priest can learn to read the shells, only members of the fraternity of Orula, the babalawo, can read Ifa. There are two different ways to perform Ifa: with palm nuts or with a chain called *opele*. When a babalawo "beats the nuts," he swiftly transfers a set of 16 palm nuts from one hand to the other. If, when he grabs the nuts, two are left behind, he makes a single mark (I) in the dust scattered on the Tray of Ifa. If only one is left, he makes a double mark (II). If three or more are left, he makes no mark. He continues beating the nuts until he has eight marks in two columns. Based on the configuration of the eight marks he has generated one of a possible 256 *odu*. Each odu, like the numbers generated by the oriate, has proverbs and stories associated with it. Based on the odu, the babalawo can diagnose the client's problem and recommend a solution. The opele has eight nuts or other tokens strung so that they can fall in a heads/tails configuration. When the babalawo throws the chain, he can generate the eight marks of an odu in a single motion. The opele is faster and more convenient, but "beating the nuts" is considered more precise and is used when a more significant reading is demanded, for example, in determining the reading of the year for the community or marking the head of a devotee. Although the proverbs and stories associated with the odu Ifa are similar to the proverbs and stories used in diloggun, Ifa is considered a more sophisticated divination system; as devotees say, Ifa is the highest form of divination.

The odu Ifa are the closest thing the Orisha traditions have to a scripture. Stories of the Orisha, along with other stories, animal fables, parables, and proverbs are embedded in them. These stories, tales, and proverbs form the basis of the religious tradition, tell why and how the world came to be as it is, and tell how model individuals in the past—human, Orisha, and animal —dealt with the problems of every life and either succeeded or failed to live up to their destiny. Yoruba children hear the stories and learn the proverbs while they are growing up. Since the Yoruba had an oral culture until they were colonized by the British, these stories were not written down until anthropologists and others began collecting them. Americans who come to the Orisha as adults use these written accounts to learn more about the culture that forms the basis of their new religious tradition. In many communities, newcomers to the religion begin to learn about the tradition through the study of Ifa, its stories and its proverbs.

Some Orisha communities use babalawo for all their divination needs except for those cases (generally as part of initiation ceremonies) where cowry divination is required. In other communities, an oriate is the principle diviner. Because oriate do not generally interpret numbers beginning with 14, 15, and 16 "mouths up" and because some problems require the more sophisticated divination system, an oriate will refer those cases to a babalawo.

Like the diloggun divination performed by an oriate, Ifa divination can determine what is causing problems in the client's life and how to move him or her toward a more fulfilling life. The babalawo may prescribe any number of rituals and ceremonies that he can perform himself, or he may send the client to an olorisha (santero/a) for initiation into the worship of one of the Orisha. Often, the babalawo has, among his own godchildren, Orisha priests that can perform the ceremonies that are reserved to them, for example, the Necklaces initiation or the priesthood initiation.

Because they are the keepers of the most sophisticated divination system, babalawo sometimes are referred to as the "high priests" of the religion. This is a misrepresentation of their place within the religious hierarchy. It is true that divination is an important part of the religion, but there are other important elements as well, including the initiation of new priests and the mounting of priests by the Orisha during possession trance. Babalawo must not become possessed by any spiritual entity, including the Orisha and spirits. Possession belongs to the Orisha priests (olorisha) who have been prepared by their initiation to provide a vehicle for the Orisha of their head to speak to a gathering of devotees during a drumming ceremony. Not all olorisha become possessed by the Orisha, but all of those who become possessed are olorisha.

Although a babalawo with appropriate initiations may observe the *kariocha* ceremony that initiates new priests into the worship of the Orisha, he cannot participate in or perform the primary rituals of the initiation—these rituals are the special provinces of the oriate. A babalawo can only initiate other men into the fellowship of Orula, He cannot initiate anyone into the worship of any of the other Orisha. In fact, although many communities use a babalawo for some secondary portions of the initiation ceremony, his services are not required at all. It is possible (and the standard in many communities) for an oriate to perform the entire ceremony without the assistance of a babalawo.

Both babalawo who perform the highest form of divination and olorisha who willingly to undergo possession for the good of the community are important members of the religion, but by some accounts the most important roles in the religion, the "high priests" if you will, are those of the iyalocha and babalocha, that is, the priests who are willing and able to initiate others into the religion and continue the tradition into another generation. Without these priests who are willing to initiate and train others, the tradition would die.

## Roots Reading (Oro Idile)

A new type of divination that has been developed by the babalawo associated with Oyotunji Village is the Roots Reading (Yr. oro idile). Using Ifa, these babalawo trace the ancestry of their African Americans clients, identify the two or three African ethnic groups that make up each one's ancestry, and determine which group is dominant for each individual. The diviner tells the client whether his spirit comes from his mother's or his father's family and what deities his family worshipped. Since each individual is believed to be the reincarnation of an ancestral spirit, the diviner also provides insight into the social, political, emotional, ethical, medical, and financial issues the client bring from his forebears into this lifetime. For African Americans who can't trace their family line beyond slavery time, the Roots Reading provides a way to map the questioner's heritage, bestow insight into the client's spiritual heritage and answer the basic question, where did I come from? Who are my people? How does my ancestral past inform my present and my future? Through these readings, clients can gain an identity that looks past the shame of slavery to regain the honor of association with the great West African empires of Oyo, Dahomey, and others. Not surprisingly, the majority of those receiving a roots reading are told that they come from noble and well-respected Ifa-worshipping families.[1]

## READING OF THE YEAR

The babalawo of large Orisha communities get together on the first day of the New Year to determine the so-called "letter of the year" (Sp. *letra del ano*), the Ifa odu that rules the coming year. Included in the divination are predictions for the year, the ruling Orisha, a flag to fly during the year, and the recommended ebo and sacrifices members of the community should perform. Today, major readings of the year are done in Cuba, Miami, New York, Ile-Ife and other locations in Nigeria and the U.S. Each group of diviners reads for the members of their community, although several claim their reading is for all of Cuba, or all of the U.S., or even the whole world. Since there is no worldwide or even countrywide authority for Orisha religion, the predictions and suggestions of any one babalawo or group of babalawo only apply to their own community. In spite of this, many groups publish their predictions on the net, and many devotees anxiously await such publications. It is also common for local communities to get together to produce a special divination for the New Year for themselves. These sessions are rarely published beyond the confines of the local group. Because all divination is personal, many Orisha priests discourage their godchildren from following the recommendations of the general divinations, preferring that they follow their own recommendations and those of local diviners. New devotees and those not associated with a local community are also discouraged from following these readings, as many of the recommendations require rituals and offerings that can only be performed by qualified priests.

## HEALING AND BLESSING RITUALS

Much ritual activity is involved in rituals of healing and blessing. Common examples include various types of spiritual baths one can do at home known as *Limpieza* (Sp. cleansing), the head blessing commonly called *Rogación* (Sp. petition), and a more intense cleansing known as *Rompimiento* (Sp. breaking). Each of these rituals is a type of sympathetic magic where, by performing certain actions on a person's body, one intends to have similar effects on their spirit.

## LIMPIEZA (BATHS AND CLEANSINGS)

Spiritual baths and other types of spiritual cleansings are often recommended as ways for devotees to remove negative influences from their lives and to return to the path of their destiny. One may be cleansed with almost any natural and many manufactured goods including the leaves of plants, fruit, flowers, candy, cooked and raw food, meat, cloth, and, of course, water. Although the cleansing item might be rubbed directly on the body, more commonly it is waved through the air about six inches away. Movement begins at the top of the head, and with long sweeping motions, the negative energies or spirits surrounding the person are brought down and away from the body. If done in conjunction with a Spiritual Mass (*misa espiritual*) the sweep motion might move the energies toward the table where they are spiritually absorbed. After they have been used for a limpieza, the cleansing materials must be disposed of by depositing them into an appropriate natural location (forest, ocean, cross-roads) or the garbage in a remote location. Sometimes the limpieza is combined with blood sacrifice. In that case the individual is cleansed with the animal before it is killed. If the primary purpose of the ritual is the removal of evil or malevolent forces, the animal's carcass is disposed of and not eaten. However, if the principal purpose of the ritual is not cleansing, the animal is generally butchered and the meat served to the participants.

Bathing in a combination of water and other materials is another way devotees remove negative influences from their lives and move toward a more positive destiny. The bath, usually performed by the devotee in the privacy of his or her own home, may entail dousing oneself with the herbal infusion known as *omiero* or some other spiritually charged liquid, or immersing in an enhanced bathwater. Omiero is the herbal liquid made potent by specific Santería rituals. Omiero is most commonly produced during initiation rituals where it is used to wash and spiritually cleanse the initiate. Portions of the omiero left at the end of the ritual may be distributed to the initiate and other participants and used for other occasions. When recommending a limpieza bath, a priest might give a client a container of omiero with which to cleanse himself.

Another form of limpieza involves introducing materials into one's bath water. The so-called "white bath" is one example. In this ritual, one is counseled to bathe in water to which a combination of calming white materials have been added. These materials might include milk, *cascaria* (a white chalky material made from crushed eggshells), coco butter, the cologne known as *Florida Water*, and white flowers. After bathing in the mixture, the devotees may be advised to either air dry or dry with a white towel and to sleep in a white night shirt on white (rather than colored) sheets. The white bath, by invoking both the ruler of whiteness, Obatala, and images of purity and spiritual advancement, is believed to calm emotional and spiritual agitation and bring on feelings of tranquility. Other ingredients might be used to invoke other Orisha and to encourage other emotional and spiritual states.

### ROMPIMIENTO (TEARING AWAY)

Sometimes, negative energies, often described as "dark spirits," can't be simply washed off, but must torn away from the client. In these cases, the priest may perform the ritual known as *rompimiento* (Sp. breaking). In this ritual, the clothing of the clients is cut and torn from their bodies by the presiding priest(s) in an effort to break the connection between the client and the negativity that is afflicting them. Often, rompimiento is performed as a preliminary ritual before initiations and other major rituals. Because of privacy and modesty issues, at least one of the priests performing a rompimiento must be the same sex as the client. At the beginning of the ritual, all of the priests in attendance cut or tear a small piece from the client's clothing. Then priests of the opposite sex leave the room and the remainder of the ritual is performed by priest of the same sex, tearing away the rest of the client's clothing. After all of their clothes have been removed, the client's body is washed with omiero or another herbal mixture, and they are dressed in clean white clothing and presented to the remaining priests for any other rituals that may be required. Since this is a more intense ritual than the limpieza, it requires at least one priest in attendance (two if the primary priest is not of the same gender as the client). Perhaps it is important at this juncture to mention that Orisha worshipers in general are very conventional in their attitudes toward nudity and sexual propriety, and a newcomer should be suspicious of anyone claiming that one should engage in sexual activity with them as part of any kind of ritual.

### ROGACIÓN (PETITION)

The head is the most ritually important part of the human body, since it is the outward manifestation of the *ori*, the inner head (*ori-inu*) or destiny. In Cuba and the United States, devotees make offerings directly to their inner heads through the small ritual called the *rogación* (rogation in English). The word *rogación* comes from the Latin root *rogare*, to ask or to beg, which refers to a type of prayer of supplication. By blessing the outer head, the *rogación* cools and strengthens the inner head, bringing the person into balance with their destiny. During the rogation, a mixture of coconut meat and other ingredients is placed on strategic points of the client's body as well as on the top of his or her head. After divination determines that the Orisha are satisfied with the ritual, the client's head, still topped with coconut, is wrapped in white cloths. Although the *rogación* might be introductory to other rituals, the client is often asked to leave the coconut mixture in place overnight, disposing of it the next morning. Many people report feelings of peace and tranquility after receiving this ritual.

All of these rituals may be combined into a larger cleansing or healing ritual or as preparation for some other type of ritual. Thus, a rompimiento might be followed by a limpieza and a rogación in a single seamless ritual, or as preparatory for an initiation or other larger ritual. By spiritually cleansing the client, the priest prepares him or her to receive the ensuing ritual from a position of purity, clarity and calm.

## RELIGIOUS BIRTHDAY PARTIES

Every year on the anniversary of their initiation into the priesthood, Orisha priests celebrate by throwing a party for their Orisha, their religious family and friends. The priest will build an elaborate *trono* (Sp. throne) for his or her Orisha and invite family and friends to join in the celebration. The celebration will include dinner, many different desserts, and perhaps a drumming ritual as described in the next section. Although the birthday celebration encompasses an entire seven-day period, the party generally is celebrated on the actual anniversary of the priest's initiation. Because they are personal festivals, these parties are commonly held in the home of the celebrant, the priest whose initiation is being commemorated.

The Orisha *trono* that a santera constructs as part of this celebration, often with the help of her godparents, godchildren, and friends, can be as simple or elaborate as her taste and finances allow. *Tronos* may be slipped into a corner, or may expand to fill an entire room so that a visitor can only stand at the doorway. Frequently, a spare bedroom or other room is set aside for the Orisha. The ceiling and walls of the designated space are covered with panels of fabric. Although the floor is usually covered with a mat, fabric can also be used to complete the space. Reminiscent of the style of the apartments of eighteenth century Spanish royalty, the cloths form walls and a canopy that encloses the entire area. Each Orisha is placed on a pedestal or other riser and surrounded by sumptuous cloth in their colors. Other items associated with the Orisha may also be included on the display. Thus, Yemaya may have a model ship, Shango a hobbyhorse, and Ogun machetes. On the floor in front of the enthroned Orisha, a *plaza* (Sp. market place) includes a mat that will be used by the guests to prostrate themselves before the deities and the spread of sweet deserts, fruit, and other offerings cooked especially for the Orisha. Each Orisha is associated with particular fruits and sweet deserts that are believed to keep them "cool" and happy. By calling this space a "plaza," devotees invoke both the open-air markets that are often the sources of these gifts, the traditional markets of West Africa, many Spanish-speaking areas of the Americas, and the Yoruba proverb that says that "the invisible world (heaven) is home, the visible world (earth) is a market place." Once the altar has been constructed and the Orisha installed, the trono area becomes sacred

Trono for Yemaya with plaza of fruit and desserts. Orisha shown include (l-r, back) Oshun, Ochosi, Yemaya, Inle (front), Ibeji, Olokun (below yemaya) with Eleggua in front.

space. Only those who have been initiated can stand on the mat or beneath the canopy.

On the first day of the celebration, the actual anniversary of her initiation, the santera welcomes her religious family to her home. Each guest first greets the Orisha by prostrating herself on the mat placed in front of the throne area specifically for that purpose. Godchildren of the hostess generally leave the ritually prescribed gift of a plate with coconuts, candles, and money; others will leave offerings of money or other goods. Entertainment may include live drumming or recorded music of special Orisha melodies depending on the resources of the hostess. Each guest is served dinner as well as encouraged to share in the various desserts that have been prepared and presented to the Orisha. At the end of the evening, everyone receives a bag of fruit from the plaza and perhaps additional samples of the sweets, thus sharing in the *ashé* of the celebration. Members of the religious family who are unable to attend the main celebration often try to find time during the week to drop in, pay their respects to the Orisha, and congratulate the santera on another year *en ocha* (Lk. as an initiate of the Orisha).

These birthday parties are one of the ways newcomers are introduced to the religion of the Orisha. Although the preparation and presentation of the event is a ritual for the celebrating priest, for visitors this celebration has the more informal feel of a party. During this party, one can meet and talk to other initiates and priests, and be introduced to the Orisha in the finest presentation. It is quite common to find priests standing in front of the display, describing to a newcomer what they are observing, who each of the Orisha displayed are, and some of the symbolism represented by the colored cloths and other paraphernalia surrounding them.

## DRUMMING RITUALS

The Orisha Ritual Drumming party known as *tambor* (Spanish "drum") or *bembe* (Yoruba) is one of the most important rituals in the tradition. The primary purpose of these rituals is, through drumming, singing, and dancing, to entice one or more Orisha to leave their home in *Orun* (heaven) and join their devotees in *Aiye* (earth) through the process known as possession trance. During the possession event, individual members of the gathered community enter into an altered state of consciousness that involves becoming entranced and dominated by an Orisha. Possession trance not only allows gathered Orisha devotees to talk to their deities and other spiritual beings, but for those beings to talk back, to respond in a clearly tangible way.

Although several different types of drums may be used in these rituals, the most sacred are a set of consecrated or fundamental *bata* drums. The bata ensemble consists of three two-headed hourglass-shaped drums that are played resting horizontally on the drummer's lap. Fundamental drums have been imbued with the spirit of the Orisha of the drum known as Aña. The largest drum, the *iya* or mother drum, is the leader, calling for changes in the rhythms and songs played. The middle-sized drum, *itotele* (Yr. he who follows in rank), speaks with and to *iya* in a musical conversation. The smallest drum, *okonkolou* (he who is small/young), maintains the underlying beat of the complex syncopated rhythms. All together, the drums are able to reproduce the tonal Yoruba language in order to speak directly to the Orisha. In addition to the drummers, a singer known as the *akpwon* is also a part of the ensemble. The akpwon, who works as a master of ceremonies, leads the call and response singing of the assembled congregation and speaks even more directly to the Orisha both before and after they have chosen to embody in one of the priests.

The first set of songs is played directly for the Orisha. The drummers are seated directly in front of the trono constructed for the occasion and play "dry," that is, without any singing or dancing. Afterward, they move to the front of the larger space set up for the full drumming ceremony. If there are iyawo to be presented to the drums, they will be brought forward one by one by their godparents or other priests. Each will present a plate offering to the drums and dance for a few minutes. Although it is unusual for a iyawo to become fully possessed, many are touch by their Orisha during this ceremony and exhibit some of the characteristics of possession.

After all of the iyawo have been presented, the drumming ceremony proper begins. Beginning with the rhythms of Eleggua and ending with those of the Orisha in whose name the drumming is taking place, the drummers play for each Orisha in turn while the akpwon leads the crowd in the songs of the Orisha. As each Orisha's rhythm is played, the priests dedicated to that Orisha come forward to greet the drums and dance. Although it is unusual for someone to become possessed during this introductory ritual, it is common to see the early of signs of possession among these dancers. After all of the Orisha have been called and every priest has had a chance to salute the drums, the drummers begin again, now playing more aggressively, forcefully trying to invite, entice, or provoke the Orisha to presence. All of the priests dance, and as one or another begins to show the earliest signs of possession, the others clear a space around them and channels their energy, their *ashé*, toward them. While not restricting the movements of the dancer, everyone moves to protect her as she moves through the transition from devotee to Orisha. The fight for possession of the priest's body ends with the Orisha in control, prostrating in thanksgiving to the drums that enabled the transition.

Once the possession has been established, the embodied Orisha is removed to a back room and dressed in the finery appropriate to its station. Like all Santería rituals, drummings are celebrated in the name of a particular Orisha. In addition to hiring the drummers and a singer, the person commissioning the drum also hires a known medium of that Orisha to dance in the expectation that the focal Orisha will possess her. A costume is prepared so that the

Orisha may have appropriate clothing to wear during his or her visit. If other Orisha choose to join in the festivities, they are also costumed, although often not as elaborately as the focal Orisha.

After the Orisha has been properly clothed, he or she is returned to the main room where the drummers play the Orisha's special rhythms and the singer sings his or her praises. But the Orisha do more than dance for the assembled worshippers; moving among the crowd, he or she will bless individuals, providing advice and guidance, haranguing some, comforting others, and asking for votive offerings or long delayed rituals. As members of the congregation are approached, they offer to Orisha small bills, kisses, hugs, and prostrations. There may be small rituals within the ritual as the Orisha may provide special consultations or even healing ceremonies. The party continues and often multiple Orisha choose to join in the festivities.

The Orisha may leave their mediums at any moment, but as the rituals winds down, any Orisha that continues to possess his or her priest is taken to the back room where he or she may be encouraged to return to Aiye, releasing the body of the priest back to its own spirit. The Orisha finery is removed before the return of the priest so that she wakes up again in her own clothing.

After the Orisha have departed, the mediums have returned to themselves, and the drummers have stowed their drums, a meal is served to the gathered congregation. There is much talk, comparing this drum to others and the words and actions of these Orisha both to those at other drums but also to their known characteristics. The advice given and the requests made by the Orisha are recounted and evaluated. Although there is always the possibility that someone will attempt to fake possession, the akpwon and senior priests have ways of testing the authenticity of a possession and are willing to heap shame onto anyone attempting to deceive them, and generally the advice and guidance received at a drum is accepted as the authentic word of the Orisha. The uninitiated and newcomers are seldom approached by the Orisha, but should be prepared to greet the deities with small offerings and respectful conduct. Each participant leaves the drum ceremony having had a special encounter with the sacred.

## Possession Trance

Possession by spiritual beings is a worldwide phenomenon. Based on her investigation of possession phenomena, Ericka Bourguignon discovered some type of possession belief in 74% of the societies in her investigation pool of 488 cultures, and possession trance in 52% of those societies. While the highest incidence of possession phenomena were in the cultures of the Pacific Rim and the lowest were in North and South American Indian cultures, they were widespread among cultures of Eurasia, Africa, the circum-Mediterranean region, and among the descendents of Africa in the Americas.

Those societies in which trance is most frequently interpreted as spirit possession were in Africa and areas influenced by Africa. Worldwide, possession phenomena are more likely to be found in agricultural societies than among hunter/gatherers, while the possessed are more commonly women than men. And although Western observers have often associated this phenomenon with mental illness, in those societies where it is common, observers have developed ways to discriminate between possession phenomena and other types of altered states of consciousness and mental diseases.[2]

During the possession event, the personality of the priest leaves so that the personality of her primary Orisha may temporarily take control of her body in order to experience the material world, communicate with devotees, and provide insight into the consciousness of the divine. It is important that possessions take place within the drum ritual and in the presence of the Orisha community. The medium, the possessed person, experiences a "break" in consciousness, during which she leaves and another is incarnate in her body. Because there is no direct communication between the invading spirit and the departed "soul," others must be present to manage the process and to receive any communications and insights from the Orisha.

Several elements are necessary for a successful possession event. Orisha do not normally enter into persons unless called, and although participants are encouraged to communicate with their deities outside of the communal events, they do not normally engage in full trance possession outside of the protected communal environment of the drumming ritual. In the context of Santería, the Orisha are only allowed to invade the bodies of those whose initiations have prepared them to receive their sacred presence. If the uninitiated begin to exhibit signs of possession, they are removed from the environment of the sacred drums and called back into themselves.

In the Santería context, the possessed person has no memory of the presence of the Orisha and its actions and communications. The movement toward possession is characterized by temporary, often violent, physical changes. These are understood as the struggle between the human spirit and that of the Orisha for the possession of the physical body. Although possession is considered desirable and actually promoted by participation in the religion, the temporary absence of one's soul and the "vacating" of one's body are not easy. Once the possession is complete, the violence recedes and the possessed person exhibits the characteristics typical of the possessing Orisha. These changes alert the remaining members of the group to the presence of the embodied Orisha.

Embodied Orisha are free to use the bodies of their priests during the possession event. Although the Orisha primarily provide counsel and advice to their devotees, they often take advantage of their physicality to eat and drink, dance with and embrace their devotees. Although no alcohol or drugs are used to enable the possession event, it is common for the Orisha, especially the warrior Orisha, to drink from the rum provided for them. Other Orisha may prefer other foods: Oshun is usually given honey and Yemaya molasses. Eleggua may "steal" fruit or cakes from the trono, offering it to his devotees or eating it himself. It is obvious in their dancing and other activities that the Orisha enjoy their temporary bodies. This provides a subtle but clear lesson for the assembly. There is no firm separation between body and spirit and no understanding that the physical, material world is somehow secondary or unimportant. This world of Aiye is good, life is good (or should be good), and enjoyment of the pleasures of life are good as well.

## BASIC ETIQUETTE FOR NEWCOMERS

Although the rest of this book gives information about the beliefs and practices of Orisha worshippers, it might happen that one is invited to an event and needs a quick basic etiquette list. This section will help him prepare to attend a Santería ceremony and to act in an appropriate manner. Generally, someone who is part of the community will have invited him to the event. Although the following information should be helpful, he should also talk to his host or hostess about the event and what is considered good etiquette in that community.

### ATTIRE

In general, Orisha-worshipping communities are very conservative in respect to the attire worn to an event. As very dark or black clothing is completely inappropriate and some communities frown on bright reds, both men and women should wear white or very light colors. Men may wear slacks and an informal shirt with a collar, while women should generally wear a dress or skirt and blouse. Many communities frown on women wearing pants to ritual events. Although shorts, halters, and revealing attire is not appropriate, the clothing need not cover the arms and hems need not cover the knees. However, modesty is always in good taste. Open-toed shoes and simple jewelry are permissible. Those who have received the ceremony of Necklaces should wear their Orisha necklaces. Although head coverings are not required, many women will wear scarves or African-style head-ties called *gele*. If the community has a strongly African focus, bright afro-centric clothing including a caftan or dashiki is appropriate. African clothing for women may also include a *buba* (blouse), *iro* (wrapper), *gele* (head-gear), and *ipele* (shawl). African clothing for men may also include a *buba* (shirt), *sokoto* (pant), and *fila* (hat).

### RITUAL SPACE

Every major ritual will have an altar display (*trono*) erected in honor of one or more Orisha. While a trono is seldom built for minor rituals (a rogation for example), the Orisha will be displayed in either a public or private area of the home. Although a visitor should greet the presiding priest(s) and her hosts, she should also acknowledge the Orisha soon after entering the home or hall. Generally the presiding priest will escort her to the space in front of the trono or home altar. If she has any initiations, her godparent will show her how to greet the Orisha. Otherwise, she should crouch, kiss the tips of her fingers and touch them to the floor just in front of the mat or floor covering. If she's brought a gift of money for the Orisha (see below), she can drop it into the basket or bowl on the edge of the mat. If she brought another gift, she can present it to the presiding priest.

If a visitor wants to pray to the Orisha, she will need to lie down on the mat provided and shake a maraca or bell while praying silently or aloud. If she chooses to pray aloud, she should ask for the Orisha's blessings for the presiding priest in addition to any other requests she may have. She can always ask the presiding priest or her host or hostess to show her the proper form.

## THE RITUAL ITSELF

### Religious Birthday Party

The religious birthday party celebrates a priest's anniversary of initiation into the priesthood. Both initiates and non-initiates are invited to the birthday party. Since this is the least structured of the Orisha rituals, it is a good opportunity for a newcomer to meet priests and get to know the Orisha without making any religious commitments. There is a short divination ritual performed by the priest before the public events begin, so those who arrive early may be asked to sit in another location until the private rituals are concluded. After greeting the Orisha, everyone socializes with the other attendees. Visitors should be careful that they do not step on any mats that are around, and that they do not enter into the space of the trono, which is delineated by a mat on the floor and some sort of covering on the ceiling above. Guests should feel free to ask respectful questions of their host, the priest whose birthday is being celebrated, or others in attendance. Most Orisha devotees love to talk about the Orisha, and will be happy to answer questions. Guests should not be insulted, however, if devotees refuse to answer certain questions. Some things are not shared with the uninitiated.

A meal is generally served (see information below), followed by the serving of the desserts that are resting in front of the trono. Visitors should feel free to eat and drink anything that is presented to them—Orisha events are famous for their excellent food.

If there is drumming, singing, and dancing, visitors should feel free to join in any singing but should not dance unless encouraged to do so by their host or other initiated priests. The singing is generally in the Yoruba language, but follows a call and response format where the lead singer will begin by giving the participants the refrain. Visitors should listen carefully and join in with the other participants if they wish.

When guests are preparing to leave, the priest may hand them a bag with fruit from the trono and perhaps other tokens of the event. Courteous guests thank him or her for both the fruit and the party as a whole, and give him or her their best wishes for another year with the Orisha.

### Initiation Event

As part of the priestly initiation (known as Crowning or *Asiento*), one day is set aside to present the new priest to the wider community. Family and friends of the initiate, the *iyawo*, are invited to day-long open house known as the Middle Day (Sp. *Día de Media*). This is an extravagant event in which the iyawo is dressed up in finery keyed to his primary Orisha and presented to the community so that all may recognize his new status as priest and embodiment of the Orisha.

The Middle Day trono is decorated in the colors of the new priest's primary Orisha, and that is where you will find the iyawo. Guests may greet him or her as they would greet the Orisha at other events (kissing the tips of their fingers and touch them to the floor just in front of the mat or floor covering). Those who have brought a gift of money for the Orisha, can drop it into the basket or bowl on the edge of the mat. Personal gifts for the iyawo are not appropriate.

Guests should not step onto the mat or under the ceiling covering. They should not touch the iyawo or hand any item directly to him, instead they should give it to one of the priests in attendance or place it on the mat in front of the trono.

Although guests may talk to the iyawo, they should remember that he has just undergone an extremely rigorous initiation. Some iyawo are alert and enjoy conversation with those who have come to celebrate their Middle Day, while others are dreamy and seem to be in an altered state of consciousness. Guests should be respectful of the iyawo on this important spiritual day.

Generally, guests will be served a meal (see below) and there will be some drumming. Uninitiated guests may be asked to leave before the drumming begins, otherwise they should follow the recommendations below for participating in a Drumming Ritual.

### Drumming Rituals

Drumming rituals provide a way for devotees to honor the Orisha and for the Orisha to communicate directly with their worshippers. Drums are often large events with both the initiated and uninitiated in attendance. After greeting the host or hostess, visitors should greet the Orisha on the *trono* built in their honor as they would at other events (kiss the tips of their fingers and touch them to the floor just in front of the mat or floor covering). Those who have brought a gift of money for the Orisha can drop it into the basket or bowl on the edge of the mat.

Although the event may have a festive and informal feel, there are important protocols that should be observed. Normally, the non-initiated do not dance, although they may join in with the singing. Possession trance is an important part of the drumming ritual, and visitors should expect to see one or more participants become entranced. It is important that visitors stand well away from the open area in front of the drums and away from anyone who appears to be moving into an entranced state. After the possession has been accomplished, the individual is taken to a back room. When they return they are dressed in the colors and clothing appropriate to the Orisha they are embodying. Visitors should remember that, once entranced, the individual has become a living god and must be treated as such. If one is approached by an embodied Orisha, they should greet them respectfully. They should not touch or embrace them unless they are encouraged to do so. Anyone the Orisha speaks to should listen carefully, since they are receiving a message from the gods.

If a visitor begin to feel light-headed or "spacey," he should step outside, away from the drums. Usually a priest will notice his light-headedness and take charge of removing him from the influence of the drums until he can return to normal consciousness.

Drum parties are usually followed by a meal for the participants.

## MEALS

Generally, those rituals that are not themselves a meal (for example, the religious birthday) are followed by a meal served to all participants. Normally, babalawo are fed separately from the rest of the congregation. If there is limited seating at the dining table, it is reserved for priests. Non-priests, both members of the community and visitors, will be seated in other parts of the home or hall. Any babalawo are served first, then priests, then the rest of those attending. Visitors shouldn't sit at the table with the initiated unless invited to do so.

Guests seated at the table should be aware of certain protocols. The food will generally be served family style from bowls and platters on the table. Once a serving bowl or platter is set down, it is not lifted until the end of the meal when it is removed. Plates are brought to the serving pieces. Everyone should feel free to taste everything that is offered, but should remember that, in many communities, the desserts that will be served later hold pride of place. If one is seated at a table with one or more priests, she should remain seated until the most senior priest stands up or gives permission for others to leave the table. If she needs to leave sooner, she should ask permission of the seated priests who will defer to their most senior member.

# GIFTS

While many people bring gifts for the Orisha being honored in a ceremony, it is inappropriate to bring gifts specifically for the person who is the focus of the ritual. Generally, there will be basket or bowl in front of the altar display (*trono*) for money offerings. Although each Orisha has special things that they like, items such as cigars, rum (but not if the principle Orisha is Obatala), plain white candles, or flowers in the color of the Orisha are usually welcome. If a guest wants to bring some other sort of offering for the Orisha, she should ask her host what would be appropriate in light of the ritual and the principal Orisha being honored. At the end of the event, the presiding priest or priestess may give attendees food or trinkets from the trono as a memento of the event. It is quite appropriate for guests to eat any food items offered or to share them with others who were unable to attend the event. The fruit from a trono is generally extremely fresh and imbued with the ashé of the Orisha. If a visitor has Warriors or an adimu Orisha, he can put any trinkets he receive in his home altar space.

# Initiation Rituals

Because this in an initiatory religion, one's membership in a religious community is dependent upon the initiation rituals one has received. In this section, I will discuss five of these rituals: Necklaces, Warriors, Hand of Orula, Crowning, and Knife. Participation in each of these rituals requires a different level of participation in the religion, but each also has a public or semi-public portion that non-initiates may attend, and that is what I will be describing.

## NECKLACES

Among Santería practitioners and many other Orisha communities, the imposition of necklaces is often the first ritual undertaken by a new devotee. The ritual of Necklaces (also known by the Spanish name *Los Collares* or the Yoruba *Elekes*) brings the inquirer into a religious family and puts them under the authority and protection of a priest or priestess. The ritual involves a spiritual bath and the presentation of a set of brightly colored beaded necklaces. Most commonly, one receives five necklaces representative of the Orisha Eleggua, Obatala, Shango, Yemaya, and Oshun, however, some houses may present more or fewer necklaces. Each necklace is a single continuous strand of beads without clasps or fasteners that is long enough to slip over the head and hang down to just above the navel. The necklaces are made in the colors and numbers of the Orisha they represent: red and black for Eleggua, white for Obatala, red and white for Shango, blue and white or crystal for Yemaya, and yellow or gold for Oshun. The actually design of the necklaces are house-specific and may include additional accent colors.

**Necklaces for Eleggua, Obatala, Shango, Oshun, Yemaya (arranged clockwise from top around plate), ready for presentation.**

The ritual begins with a purification bath that strips the initiate of their old life and prepares them to receive the protection of the Orisha and their priest. The head, as the seat of the person's destiny, is the focus of special ritual attention as it is washed in cool healing water. The initiate is instructed to wear old clothes, which are ripped and cut from his or her body in the style of the *rompimiento* ritual, and to bring fresh white clothes to wear for the following ceremony.

After the initiate has been bathed, he or she is seated in front of the primary godparent's Orisha and presented with each of the necklaces. The Orisha associated with each necklace is briefly described, although often the initiate has already been learning about them and their attributes. Afterwards, the godparents will explain how to wear and care for the necklaces. They may be worn individually or in combination with each other. As each represents a specific Orisha, many people choose the Necklace associated with the Orisha whose power or support that feel that they need at the moment. The necklaces must never be worn while bathing, sleeping, or during sexual activity, and the necklace of Obatala must be removed before drinking or taking other types of recreational drugs. Because of their spiritual qualities, the initiate is told not to allow others to touch or handle their necklaces and to treat them respectfully when they are not being worn. After the private portion of the ritual, the godparents participate in a meal with the new initiate. Often, the initiate's family members as well as other godchildren of the godparents participate in this celebratory meal.

At the conclusion of this ritual, the new initiate has become a member of the religious household of the godparents. In some religious communities, he may be known as a godchild or as an *aleyo*, a Yoruba word that means a stranger or non-family member living in the family compound. In a religious sense, an aleyo is a devotee who has made a commitment to the Orisha but has not yet been fully initiated as a priest. In some communities, the term aleyo is used to designate anyone who participates in the ritual life of the community whether or not they have received any initiations. In other communities, it is reserved for those who have received Necklaces, and thus have declared themselves a devotee of the Orisha and have become someone's godchild.

Although the primary godparent has the major responsibility for the religious care and training of the aleyo, he is linked with both godparents, and both have responsibilities in his religious development. The aleyo's responsibilities are primarily to work with and listen to the primary godparent, but he is also a member of the religious household of the secondary godparent and may be expected to work with and learn from that godparent as well. Working with the godparents and their other godchildren is an important part of the aleyo's education in the religious tradition of the Orisha. Although some larger houses and communities may provide formal or informal classes for new godchildren and other seekers, for most people, their best learning opportunities happen in conjunction with working with and for the godparent as she pursues the life of an Orisha priest. Godchildren who are willing and able to work in the religious and secular household of the godparent learn about the religion both through doing work for the Orisha and through the conversation and informal teaching that naturally occurs. All rituals are communal affairs and require the effort of many people to complete them successfully. Although an aleyo is barred from participating in many portions of these rituals there is still much that he can do and learn in the process.

## WARRIORS

Often, the Warriors ritual (also call by the Spanish term *Los Guerreros*) is performed in conjunction with the Necklaces ritual in a single ceremony known as Warriors and Necklaces. In that case, after the initiate has received his or her Orisha necklaces and before the meal is eaten, he or she participates in the ritual that vivifies the icons of the warrior Orisha. In other cases, the Warriors are given in a separate ritual, independent of the Necklaces ritual. Whether these two rituals are done separately or together depends on the

**Icons for the Warrior Orisha, Eleggua (r) and Ogun (l), placed near the devotee's front door.**

circumstances of the initiate, the judgment of the godparents, and the traditions of the religious community.

The Orisha given in this ritual are Eleggua, the trickster Orisha who opens and closes all doors and is always the first Orisha propitiated in any rituals; Ogun, the blacksmith Orisha who opens the way by removing both physical and spiritual obstacles in the path of the devotee; Ochosi, the hunter Orisha who works with Ogun to find the devotee's best and highest destiny; and Osun, the protector Orisha who watches over the devotee and warns of impending danger. Eleggua, Ogun, and Ochosi will be placed near the front entryway of the devotee's home to protect him or her from destructive forces both physical and spiritual. In most communities, Osun will be placed on a shelf above the devotee's head. In some communities, however, Osun is placed on the floor with the other Warrior Orisha.

Traditionally, only male priests are allowed to make and present the Warriors to initiates. This means that if the primary godparent is a woman, she must solicit the help of another priest for this ritual. This is one of the reasons many female priests combine Warriors and Necklaces into a single ritual, although male priests may also present both Warriors and Necklaces in a single ritual. Since each ritual requires at least two priests to serve as godparents, the male priest can be the second godparent for Necklaces, and the female priest can be the second godparent for the presentation of the Warriors.

Several days or a week before the ritual, the initiate, often with the help of the godparent or another priest, will collect and bring to the godparent many

**Devotee's warriors, Ogun far left, Ochosi in dish with antlers, Eleggua to right of candle, next to house full of offerings.**

of the items that will be used in the construction of the icons of the warrior Orisha. Through divination, the godparent will ascertain which of these items are suitable and approved by the Orisha. After the divination session, the priest will put together the icons of the Orisha based not only on the tradition of his lineage, but also the requests of the Orisha as determined in the divination session.

If the Warriors are presented in a separate ceremony, the ritual will begin with a ritual bath similar to that undertaken at the beginning of the Necklaces ritual. After bathing, the initiate watches as the godparents vivify the icons of the Orisha with the life-giving blood of roosters and pigeons. This may be the first time the initiate participates in the sacrificial rituals that are so important to the practice of Orisha religions. In the same way that Catholics believe that the words of the priest said during the celebration of the Mass changes ordinary bread and wine into the real, actual body and blood of Christ, so Orisha devotees believe that these sacrificial rituals change the icons of the Orisha into the very Orisha themselves. So, when the initiate takes these objects home and places them at his front door, he has become an Orisha worshipper with the deities now living in his home. In some communities, the title *aborisha*, that is, an Orisha worshipper, is given to those who have undergone this ritual and received these Orisha.[1]

**Icon for Osun, the protector deity.**

Participation in this ritual carries with it certain responsibilities toward the Orisha who are installed in the worshipper's home. Although the space devoted to these Orisha may be simple, even hidden from view, the worshipper is expected to perform a weekly ritual there, offering the Orisha water, rum, cigar smoke, palm oil, and a mixture known as *pescado y jutia* (dried fish and rat). Some godparents will also teach these godchildren how to perform the simple coconut divination so that they can communicate directly with these Orisha.

It is also possible to receive the warriors from a babalawo. In that case, the icons are made slightly differently, and the rituals are also slightly different. Instead of Eleggua, babalawo give the Orisha Eshu (also known as Echu or Esu). There is some disagreement among priest about the relationship between Eleggua and Eshu. Some say that they are different Orisha, others that Eleggua is merely a path of Eshu, still others that they are two faces of the same Orisha. However, because the priesthood of Ifa has not been completely integrated into the Orisha traditions along with priesthoods of the other Orisha, Warriors received from a babalawo cannot be brought into the ritual of kariocha. Before the Orisha initiation, a devotee who received his original warriors from a babalawo will need to receive another set from an Orisha priest.

## ADIMU ORISHA

Sometimes, a devotee who has not received the priestly initiation discussed below is given a single Orisha to worship in their homes. As determined by divination, the worship of this Orisha may be deemed necessary for the devotee's physical or spiritual well-being, or a devotee may receive this Orisha while making preparations for a full priestly initiation. These are called *adimu Orisha* (Yr. Orisha that one embraces) or *santo lavado* (Sp. washed Orisha). Receiving one or more adimu Orisha doesn't make one an Orisha priest, but simply a worshipper of those Orisha. In a certain sense, the Warriors are a special type of adimu Orisha. Olokun and Obatala are commonly presented as adimu Orisha, although any Orisha may be given in this manner. Like the Warriors, the icons of these Orisha are blessed and fed the blood of certain animals, generally birds, so that they become the embodiment of Orisha themselves. While the ritual for each Orisha is different in its details, it generally follows the format described for the Warrior ceremony: the initiate is bathed and then watches as the icon of the Orisha is vivified by the blood of the sacrificial animals and certain other rituals unique to the particular Orisha are performed. After the ceremony, the aborisha must set up proper ritual space within his home and perform the ongoing ritual practices appropriate for that Orisha.

Orisha received after priestly initiation may also be referred to as adimu Orisha to distinguish them from the Orisha received as part of the priestly initiation. In many communities, Orisha received after initiation that are vivified with only the blood of birds and not with the blood of four-legged animals are also referred to as adimu Orisha. Since such a ritual is simpler and less expensive then the full ceremony required to receive an Orisha, many priests choose to receive subsequent Orisha in this manner. Even though there are certain limitations on the ceremonies that can be preformed for such Orisha, most priests do not find that to be an undue hardship, and it is always possible for priests to complete the rituals for these Orisha by feeding them the four-legged animals they require (usually these are one or more goats) and performing the *ita*, or special divination session that is always associated with the sacrifice of larger animals.

## RITUALS OF IFA

Any Orisha male priest can give their godchildren Warriors, and any priest male or female can give Necklaces and adimu Orisha, however, only priests of Orula, the babalawo, can put a devotee under the protection of Orula through a ceremony known as Hand of Ifa or Hand of Orula. Depending on the lineage, these ceremonies may be somewhat different for men and women. Within the Santería tradition, the ceremony for women is called *ikofa* or *cofa*, and the ceremony for men is called *abo faca* or *awofaka*. These ceremonies are similar to the rituals to receive an adimu Orisha in that one receives not only a beaded necklace and bracelet in the colors of Orula (yellow and green), but also a set (one hand) of the kola nuts that are his tools and icons. Because of a pact between Orula and Iku, the personification of death, the babalawo say that one cannot die prematurely while wearing the beaded bracelet one receives as part of these ceremonies. In addition, the *odu* that controls one's life and embodies one's destiny is revealed as part of this ritual. Knowing this odu and the proverbs and stories associated with it helps the devotee understand their destiny, the past, present, and future as it was given to them before they were born. Just as the priest or priests who give one Warriors and Necklaces become one's godparents and spiritual guides, after this ritual, the babalawo that has given one the Hand of Ifa becomes one's godparent in Ifa and another spiritual guide. Often, in houses lead by a babalawo, his wife is a fully crowned priest in the Orisha tradition. She can then perform all of the Orisha rituals—for example, the ceremony of Necklaces—for his godchildren. In this way, the babalawo and his wife become one's godfather and godmother for each other's godchildren without the necessity of calling on outside priests.

Receiving the Hand of Ifa makes one a worshipper of Ifa and Orula, but it does not make one a babalawo, a priest of Orula. That requires a special calling and a much more complex and intense initiation, commonly called Making Ifa. In the United States and Cuba, only straight men can make Ifa, that is, be initiated as *babalawo* (father of mystery); however, there are instances of gay men who have been initiated, and the practice of initiating women into a Ifa is becoming more common in some communities. Once one has received this initiation, one can begin to learn the odu and rituals associated with Ifa divination. The ritual itself is long and arduous, over a week long, with many tests of the initiate's firm intentions. It is the follow-up by training and practice in the arts of the diviner that makes one a babalawo. It takes years of work under the guidance of a senior babalawo for one to learn not only the 256 *odu* with all their symbols and stories, but also all the rituals one is called upon within the divination sessions to perform.

Although there may have been female Ifa priests in pre-colonial Africa, they were relatively rare. In the African context, the priesthood was often passed from father to son. The years of training were begun in early childhood and continued until the babalawo was a young man. It was easy for a father-son dyad to maintain such an intense training schedule. It would have been harder for a father-daughter dyad to complete her training, as young girls generally left the households of their fathers soon after puberty to join the households of their husbands, where their primary responsibility was to become a successful wife and mother. In Cuba, women's roles were often tightly circumscribed, and only men were allowed into the fraternity of the babalawo. There are important positions for women within the Ifa hierarchy, but the role of divination priest was limited to men, ideally heterosexual men.

In the United States, women's circumstances are very different. Many women have the training and education to be full participants in professions formerly limited to men. Thus, women within some Ifa communities feel as though they should also be able to become members of the highest ranks within those communities, and the leaders of those communities have agreed with them. So, women with the title of *iyanifa* (mother of Ifa) are beginning to appear. These women have full initiations as priests of Orula and diviners within the system of Ifa, although they are still excluded from the very highest ranks within that priesthood. Not all babalawo agree with the practice of initiating women, and this practice has caused dissention within the community of Ifa priests. However, it is likely that the practice will continue and eventually become a fully-accepted practice.

## MARKING THE HEAD

Before someone can be fully initiated as an Orisha priest, the identity of the Orisha that owns their head, the Orisha that has chosen to walk with them during this incarnation, needs to be determined. When one is initiated, he or she is initiated primarily as the priest of that Orisha. In the United States and Cuba, two different methods are used to determine who owns the head of a future priest. One method is performed by an oriate and uses the dilog-gun, the shells of the Orisha; the other is performed by a group of babalawo and uses the tools of Ifa. Although each set of diviners argues that their method is superior, both have been used successfully for many decades.

In communities in which the oriate is the primary divination specialist, a godparent will take her godchild to an oriate for a special type of reading where he determines which Orisha owns the godchild's head. In communities that use babalawo for divination, a group of babalawo will perform a ritual known by its Spanish name *plante* (to state or to establish) to determine the Orisha of the head. Often, the plante is performed as part of the Abo Faca or Kofa ceremony. Once this has been determined, it is said that the devotee is the "child" of that Orisha ,who is sometimes referred to as one's "guardian angel" (Sp. ángel guardián) or one's mother or father Orisha. From that day forward, the Orisha of the head is the most important member of the devotee's personal pantheon, and when it comes time for the devotee to be initiated, he will be initiate as a priest of that Orisha.

Because Orula, who speaks through Ifa, is said to have been present at creation and thus knows everyone's complete destiny, when a plante is properly done, the results cannot be changed or disputed. Even though it may be many years between the time of the divination session and the time the devotee is initiated, the results are fixed. A properly done plante requires at least three babalawo, one of whom does the actual divination, and the others who serve as witnesses; the devotee whose head is being read must be present, and he or she should also be represented by the godparent who will initiate him when the time comes. The alternative to having a set of babalawo mark the devotee's head with a plante is to have an oriate perform a special diloggun reading. Although this is similar to other diloggun readings, because the principle purpose of this reading is to determine what Orisha owns the devotee's head, it is somewhat more complex. Although this ritual only requires a single diviner along with the devotee and the godparent who will be initiating the devotee, additional witnesses should be involved.

The babalawo claim that only their determination of the guardian Orisha is accurate, however, oriate and priests of the other Orisha have been making that determination for most of the history of the religion in the Americas. Because once a plante has been performed it is never repeated, the Orisha determined by the babalawo is never called into question, although if one goes to a different godparent for initiation, that priest might require a confirmation divination. In the case of the determination made by an oriate, it sometimes happens that the divination is performed a second time with different results, and sometimes, when the final divination before initiation is performed, the identity of the Orisha changes. These changes are often written off as the incompetence of the original diviner, or, if there has been a long time between the original divination and the initiation event, santeros will say that the original Orisha got tired of waiting for the devotee.

Sometimes it also happens that the devotee is confused as to the type of divination that was performed. It is common for diviners, both babalawo and oriate, to tell the client that he or she is especially loved by an Orisha or that one or more Orisha are walking with him. Clients interpret these statements to mean that the named Orisha is the Orisha of his or her head, which may not be accurate. According to Orisha cosmology, an Orisha may be a special protector or guardian, either throughout one's life or during an especially trying period, without being the Orisha that made the pact with one's ori before birth. Even after initiation, priests will speak of certain Orisha as special protectors or guardians, even through these Orisha may not be the Orisha of their head. Devotees have many relationships with the different Orisha throughout their lives.

Although many people, both devotees and their godparents, are interested to know which Orisha owns one's head, elders often counsel against marking a devotee's head until initiation is about to happen. The primary reason for marking one's head is to determine the rituals that will be necessary to complete the initiation: which will be the primary Orisha, what secondary Orisha will be included, what additional or special ceremonies will be necessary? Some elders say that this divination also alerts the Orisha that a new priest is about to be made. If there is a long delay between the marking of the head and the actual initiation, they say that both the Orisha of the head and the others who would normally be expected to participate in the ritual may become unhappy and cause problems for the devotee. In addition, they say the information serves no real purpose before initiation.

## CROWNING

Perhaps the most important event in the life of an Orisha devotee is the initiation into the priesthood. Known variously as *crowning, asiento* (Spanish for "seat" or "contract"), and *kariocha* (Yoruba for "to place the Orisha in or on the head"), this ritual unites the head of the initiate with the energy of their primary Orisha in a ceremony that installs the Orisha into their inner head, so that the Orisha serves as a spiritual "crown" for the devotee. The initiation process itself is a series of ceremonies that begins before the initiation itself and encompass a yearlong novitiate period known as the *iyawoage*.

Although there is much for both the initiate and his or her godparents to do in preparation, the initiation event itself begins the day before the actual ceremony, when the initiate is brought to the initiation site, often the home of the primary godparent or space specially rented for the event. The initiate, who will be known simply as *iyawo* from this moment until he or she complete the iyawoage, is placed under the care of the primary godparent and the second godparent, known as the *yubona*. During that evening and most of the next day, the iyawo endures the rituals that transform him from an ordinary person into a priest of the Orisha. As part of these rituals, he is stripped of his identity and reborn into his new spiritual life; his body is washed and cleansed and his head is shaved in preparation for the reception of the Orisha he will worship throughout the rest of his life. At the same time, the icons of his primary Orisha and the set of five to seven other Orisha that he will receive are vivified with herbal liquid called *omiero* and the blood of the sacrificial animals.

The following day, he is presented to the community at large. Unlike the ceremonies of the previous day, which are only open to the priests participating in them, this Middle Day (*Día de Media*) celebration is open to the community as well as the family and friends of the iyawo. For this event, he is dressed as the embodiment of his primary Orisha in the finest clothes that he and his new ritual family can afford, and enthroned in the initiation ritual space. At this one event, all of the priests who come to visit honor him by prostrating themselves to him as the embodiment of the Orisha that has been seated on his head. After this day, the prostrations that form the greeting among santeros are always based on their ritual hierarchy, the younger (in initiation years) prostrating to their elders. On this day, the elders humble themselves before their youngest member. In addition to the presentation of the iyawo to the community, the Middle Day will include a feast for all those who visit, and perhaps a drumming ritual. Depending on the traditions of the community, the drumming portion of the ceremonies may be closed to those who have not achieved a certain level of initiation. In that case, the uninitiated will be asked to leave before the drummers begin.

The following day, the iyawo's initiation divination, called *Ita*, is read. This is the most powerful divination session of his life, as the newly-born Orisha speak directly to their new priest and tell his past, present, and future. During this divination session, the form of the iyawo's new life with the Orisha will be laid out together with the obligations and prohibitions (*ewe*) that will follow him throughout his life. There are few universal sets of laws followed by all Orisha initiates; instead, each Orisha priest has his own set of rules and requirements based on his destiny and the will of the Orisha he worships. One may not eat pork or eggs or the meat of certain sacrificial animals, another may be allowed to eat anything but be prohibited from engaging in certain activities or visiting certain types of locations, another may be required to engage in certain spiritual, religious, or other types of activities. One may be required to take additional initiations or receive additional *adimu Orisha*. Another may be prohibited from certain ritual activities. One may be required to welcome into his religious household all serious inquirers, while another may be barred from initiating any others. Each person's religious regulations are unique. All are for his protection and development, and for the manifestation of his best and highest destiny.

For a week, the iyawo remains sequestered in the ritual room with his new Orisha. He is pampered and fussed over by his godparents, especially his yubona and the other priests who attend to his physical, spiritual, and emotional needs. At the end of a week, the iyawo is ready to begin his re-integration into the outside world. He and his newborn Orisha return home, where the Orisha are given their own sacred space. Many priests dedicate a room in their homes as a chapel for their Orisha, however, some create a space for them in the public areas of the household, placing them prominently in the living, dining, or other area of their homes.

His return home is not, however, the end of the initiation process for the iyawo. He has only begun the yearlong process of becoming a priest known as the *iyawoage* or iyawo-period. During this time, often referred to as the Year of White, he lives surrounded by cool, peaceful white, and encumbered with an array of restrictions on his behavior. He must keep his head covered for at least three months, and must wear and carry only white: white clothes from the inside out, white shoes, white purse or billfold, white coat, white hat or head covering. He must eat on his own white dishes. He may not touch or be touched by anyone except his godparents and members of his immediate family. He many not visit bars, jails, cemeteries, hospitals, or other places of contamination. He must not drink alcohol or use illegal drugs. Nor must he use profane language or eat with a knife and fork. He may not drink intoxicating beverages or take any mind-altering drugs. Female iyawo may not wear makeup or curl, cut, or dye their hair. The only jewelry iyawo are only allowed to wear are their Santería necklaces and the bracelets given to them during the initiation ceremony. During the entire year, the iyawo loses his name and is addressed simply as "iyawo." These rules are designed to protect the iyawo, who is considered especially sensitive, from places and situations that are physically, emotionally, or spiritually dangerous. They teach the iyawo to remain cool, calm, and clear-headed, in control of himself and aware of his environment. They help him to solidify his understanding of himself as both the priest and the embodiment of his Orisha. His ongoing adherence to these rules helps to establish and maintain his commitment to his Orisha and the practices they demand.

Several other additional rituals are commonly performed during this period so that at the end of the year, the iyawo has participated in all of the rituals that allow him to be designated as a fully-crowned priest. Only one who has participated in all of these rituals may perform as a priest in the community. If, for whatever reason, he has not completed all of these rituals, even though he has completed his iyawoage, he is still a priest-in-waiting, unable to take his place among the priestly ranks until all of his ritual commitments have been fulfilled. He may not divine for others, dance in front of the drums, or participate in other initiation ceremonies until he completes the appropriate priestly rituals.

In any case, at the end of the year, on the anniversary of the day that the Orisha were place on his head, the iyawo constructs his first Birthday *Trono* and celebrates his first religious birthday, his first year "en santo." At the end of the week, on the anniversary of the day he returned home from the initiation site, he may lay aside his white clothes and, within the limits prescribed by his ita, resume his life and activities. He has completed his iyawoage and may stand before the Orisha and the community in his new role as Orisha priest.

## KNIFE

Many people consider the ritual known as *Pinaldo* (Knife or *Cachillo*) to be the completion of their Orisha initiation. With this ceremony, the priest is given the right to use a knife to sacrifice both two-legged and four-legged animals. Within Orisha cosmology, Ogun is the owner of the knife, and in Yorubaland, it appears that, generally, only his priests perform major sacrifices. However, in Cuba and the Americas, other priests are given the authority to perform all types of sacrifices through this ritual. In spite of the fact that generally only men actually perform the sacrifices that require the Knife initiation, both men and women can receive this ceremony, and properly-initiated women have been known to use the knife when a qualified man was not available. Some people suggest that one should receive the Knife after they have initiated a certain number of godchildren, or, alternatively, before they begin initiating godchildren. However, there are many priests who have initiated many godchildren but have not received this ceremony, and some others who have no godchildren who have received it. As part of their initiation into Ifa, babalawo receive a similar ceremony, called Wanaldo, that allows them to perform sacrifices, and priests working within babalawo-centered communities, use them to perform the *matanza* (Sp. sacrifice) associated with priestly initiation. Because this ritual is seen as a completion of the kariocha, for priests who have lost or severed the ties with their original godparents this ritual provides a new set of godparents that can guide their further spiritual development.

Most of this ritual is private and not open to those who have not already receive the ritual themselves, however, the uninitiated may be invited to auxiliary ceremonies such as a drumming performed in conjunction with the Knife ceremony.

# The Religious Family

Rather than proclaiming assent to a creed or belief system to become a worshiper of the Orisha, one comes to be a participant in this religion by undergoing the different initiatory rituals that introduce them into the tradition and deeper levels of knowledge. Such initiatory rituals require that the initiate place himself or herself under the spiritual protection and authority of a priest or priestess who is at a higher initiatory level. Within the Orisha traditions, the priest or priestess who performs one's initiations is called one's godfather or godmother (*padrino* or *madrina* in Spanish). The relationship that one has with one's godparents is especially important because these are the people who guide one's life, especially one's spiritual and religious life.

Among Orisha devotees in Yorubaland, parents and grandparents often pass the knowledge of these religious traditions from generation to generation, and many priestly orders belong to certain family lineages. However, when the Yoruba peoples were brought to the Americas as slaves, their family lines were broken and such a system could not be reconstructed. Instead, a different way of determining family lines was developed, with the lines based on initiation rather than birth. Even today, even if one's parents are Orisha devotees one must be born into a religious family through the initiations provided by its more senior members. This means that, rather than the more informal relationship of other types of religious congregations, everyone within a Santería household (often call by the Yoruba word for family or household, *ile*) is related through a complex hierarchy of initiation described in terms of kinship and family.

According to the Santería worldview, before one is born they kneel before Olodumare and choose a destiny for this life. Included in that destiny is not only when and where one is born, the identity of one's parents and family, where one will live and work, and where and when one will die, but also which of the many Orisha will be one's personal protectors during this lifetime. The relationship one has with these protector Orisha is also a familial one. Although these protectors are not formally identified until one is initiated into the priesthood, everyone, whether they know it or not, has at least two Orisha who watch over and protect them like parents because everyone is *omo-Orisha*, that is, a child of the Orisha. As one prepares for initiation (or often earlier) one's primary Orisha guardian is identified. This Orisha is said to own one's head or one's destiny. During the initiation process, a second Orisha of the opposite gender is named one's secondary Orisha. There, two parent Orisha form the basis of one's personal pantheon. Because of their protective functions, often these Orisha are known as one's "guardian angels" or (*ángel guardián* in Spanish).

An analysis of spiritual kinship or the religious family within Orisha traditions can focus on two different sets of relationships. One is the person-to-person relationship formed by the devotee and his or her godparents along with all of the other people in one's human religious family. The other is the relationship formed between the Orisha and their devotees, which are also described according to familial metaphors. In the rest of this chapter, I will describe both these two types of familial relations: that of the religious household headed by one's godparent and that of one Orisha family headed by one's guardian angel Orisha.

## THE RELIGIOUS HOUSEHOLD (*ILE ORISHA*)

In pre-colonial times (and often even today), Yoruba people lived together in family compounds that were headed by the most senior man and included several generations of his descendants. A typical family consisted of a man, his wives, and their children, along with his adult sons and their wives and children. In addition, members of the previous generations—for example, the senior man's mother and her co-wives—unmarried daughters, and their children and unrelated outsiders may have also lived within a family compound. While the compound as a whole, lead by the senior man or his elders, may have served the titular Orisha of the family, any individual may or may not have participated in the worship of that Orisha. Individuals may have served other Orisha as well as (or instead of) the titular Orisha or no Orisha at all. In addition, non-family members living in a compound (in-marrying wives, as well as unrelated outsiders) may or may not have participated in the service of the titular Orisha, and may or may not have continued in the service of other Orisha.

Individuals came to the worship of the Orisha in several ways. Children may be marked from conception or birth as the devotee of a particular Orisha; these people were said as having "come from heaven" worshipping that Orisha or as being "born by" that Orisha. Children born with deformities or with a caul are said to belong to Obatala. Children with a certain kind of hair belong to Dada, the sister of Shango. Children born after their mothers have made offering and petitions to an Orisha belong to that Orisha. The mothers of such children would serve the Orisha for them, taking them to festivals, making sacrifices on their behalf, and perhaps participating in rituals until the child is old enough to do this on their own. Parents or grandparents may choose to train one or more of their children or grandchildren to serve their own Orisha, whether the titular Orisha of the compound or another Orisha. This is the way the worship of the titular Orisha is passed from generation to generation within the family. Others within the compound—for example, a woman who brought the worship of her family Orisha with her when she married into the family—might assure the worship of her Orisha within the family by training one or more of her children in the rituals of that Orisha. If a person is having inexplicable problems in his or her life, divination might reveal that an Orisha is campaigning for his or her devotion. Even though no one within the family is currently a devotee of that Orisha, the indigenous understanding is that the Orisha had been worshipped by an ancestor and resents its recent neglect.

Although a Yoruba child would have been born into an Orisha-worshipping society, no one Orisha was universally worshipped. Although one might not participate in the worship of any Orisha, it was more common for individuals to worship several Orisha, coming to the worship of each in a different manner. An individual might be born worshipping an Orisha, be trained into the worship of another Orisha by a parent or grandparent, and may take up the worship of yet another Orisha based on a divination session. In the early twentieth century, William Bascom estimated that, at that time, the average person worship five different Orisha.[1]

When the hundreds of thousands of Yoruba-speaking people were brought to the Americas in the late eighteenth and early nineteenth centuries, the lineage system of worship and religious training could not be maintained. Families were ripped apart, and marriages among Africans and Afro-Cubans were difficult to establish and maintain. There were more African and Afro-Cuban women than men. At the same time, among the Spanish population, there were more men than women. This lead many of the women within the ranks of the *gente de color*, the free people of color, to become concubines of the Spanish men since legitimate marriages across these class lines were impossible. In spite of all these cultural difficulties, many of those who lived in the cities of Cuba were able to work together to recreate the worship of their Orisha. Unable to re-create the family structures they had known in Africa, they developed a new lineage system based on initiation rather than blood. Although the exact history has still not been fully identified, what was developed has become the current system of godparenthood. Under the guidance of one's godparents, one is reborn into a religious family and lineage tradition, and learns the rites and rituals of the Orisha.[2]

In Yorubaland, the senior priests and priestesses of an Orisha were responsible for initiating new members into the worship group, and for training and supervising them. Although there was coordination between many of the groups, each Orisha's worship community was independent and autonomous. However, as the religious system was re-created in Cuba, the worshippers of all the Orisha organized themselves into a single community under the leadership of senior priests and priestesses of different Orisha. These elders, many of whom had been born and trained in Africa, lead rituals and were responsible for initiating and training new devotees. These leaders worked together and, over time, developed a system of religious lineages based on initiation.

According to current understandings, everyone is born as the child of a specific Orisha who owns their head and is their primary protector. However, in order to become a worshipper of that Orisha or the Orisha in general, everyone needs a priest or priestess who can initiate her into the service of the Orisha and teach her the appropriate cultural and religious forms. With a few exceptions, both men and women can become priests of the Orisha and perform all of the ritual activities required of them. Since many of the first religious leaders in Cuba were woman and many of contemporary worshippers are women, I will prefer the female in this account of the person-to-person relationships, with the understanding that it applies equally to men and women. When I describe the relationships between individuals and their Orisha, I will prefer the male, again with the understanding that my description applies equally to men and women. Contemporary Santería initiations require four named actors (along with other members of the community): the *iyawo*, the *olorisha* who is the initiating priest or priestess who will be the iyawo's primary godparent, the *yubona* who is the second godparent, and the *oriate* who is the ritual specialist who conducts these ceremonies.

It is the primary godparent who provides the Orisha icons from which the initiate's icon are born, whose *ashé* vivifies these icons and empowers the ashé of the iyawo, and who has the primary responsibility for the training and religious supervision of the iyawo. All Santería initiations require that the new icons be empowered through contact with the old. It is only in the presence of the icons of the primary godparent that new icons can be consecrated, and only in the presence of the initiating priest that a new priest can be consecrated. Just as no child can be born without a mother, no one can be initiated and no icons can be animated without contact with an existing priest and her Orisha icons. Similarly, just as every child must have two parents, every ritual requires the participation of two priests who become the godparents of the initiate. The only requirement is that the godparents must be fully-crowned priests. Other characteristics, for example, their gender, chronological age, or race, are irrelevant. Importantly, these godparents need not be of opposite genders. The iyawo may have a padrino and a madrino (godfather and godmother), two padrinos or two madrinas.

The relationship between the initiate and her primary godparent is the most important human-to-human relationship in the religion. This is followed closely by the relationship between the initiate and secondary godparent (the yubona). The godparents are responsible for the initiate's spiritual and religious life. The initiate will be expected to salute them first when meeting them at later rituals or other events, and she will be expected to honor them on their own religious birthdays. When the initiate is a priest, the godparents will pay an important part in her own religious birthday celebrations, and if one or both survive the death of their godchild, they will be responsible for their godchild's funeral ritual.

Through this system of godparentage, new religious families are created. A priest who has initiated many godchildren becomes the head of her own extended religious family that includes not only her own godparents but also all of godchildren of her godparents. The godchildren of one's godparent become one's religious siblings, some older in the religion and, over time, some younger. Also included in one's religious family are the godparents of one's godparents (one's grandparents or *abuelos* in the religion) and one's godparent's religious siblings, who can be thought of as one's religious aunts and uncles, along with their godchildren, one's religious cousins. Just as one's personal family extends in all directions back into time, sideways to include cousins and others of one's generation, and into the future with the birth of new children into the family, so one's religious family also extends in every direction. For many people, one's religious family is more complex than one's personal family because of the greater number of relationally near individuals and because of the complexity of cross-initiations.

Because of the importance of one's religious lineage, new priests are encouraged to learn the names of their religious ancestors back to the founder of their religious line. Each ritual begins with the recitation of the names of the religious ancestors of the primary participants. Even when little is known about these ancestors beyond their names, each priest who has been initiated in a Cuban-based religious family knows that he or she is the member of a religious lineage that can be traced back to one of the original founders of the religion in Cuba. Members of other Orisha traditions may not trace their lineage back to Cuba, but all maintain this type of lineage system.

Participation in all of the Orisha traditions is shaped by the initiations one has undergone. Each initiation involves the devotee into a progressively more intense relationship with both the Orisha and the initiating godparents. For many people, the first initiations are those of Warriors and Necklaces. Although these rituals can be performed separately, many santeros prefer a single ceremony. If the same godparents present both the necklaces and the warriors, the new godchild comes away from the ceremony with two godparents whose hierarchy is easy to understand. However, since in most households women are not allowed to present warriors to devotees, when a woman wants to give warriors and necklaces to a new devotee, she must call in a priest to be the primary godparent for the warriors portion of the rituals. In this situation, the new godchild is left in the somewhat confusing situation of having two primary godparents, one for necklaces and one for warriors. If the two priests are from different religious families, which is common, the new godchild is left in the situation where she has responsibilities to two different religious families who may have minor (or even major) differences of practice and ritual.

The Necklaces ceremony brings the new devotee (often called an *aleyo*) into the Orisha community, and puts her under the protection of the Orisha and under the guidance of the primary godparent. While someone with necklaces can still only attend public rituals, she has taken the first step into the religious community. As a member of the household of her primary godparent, the devotee has some minor ritual responsibilities toward the primary godparent. She may also be expected to help out when the godparents have other ceremonies or celebrations. Although she is excluded from the majority of religious rituals, there is much secondary work, particularly in the kitchen and its environs, that she can do, from providing coffee and snacks during ritual breaks to processing the carcasses of sacrificial animals into dishes for the feasting that follows major rituals. Like a young child who learns about the world by working alongside her parents, the aleyo begins to learn about this religious tradition by working alongside her godparents and the other godchildren in the household.

The Warriors ceremony actually makes a devotee an Orisha worshipper. During this ritual, the aleyo actually receives the empowered icons of the Orisha Eleggua, Ogun, Ochosi, and Osun. With this ritual, she has taken the first step toward full participation in the religion. As an aleyo with warriors, the devotee has a similar level of social responsibility as one who has received necklaces. However, because she has actual Orisha living in her house, her ritual responsibility is higher. She must propitiate her warriors weekly, and may interact with them directly. In some households, the aleyo is taught to divine with coconut pieces so that these Orisha may communicate directly with her.

The relationship between the aleyo and her godparents is deepened with each of these rituals. The godchild has a responsibility to honor and respect the godparents, and they are expected not only to guide the aleyo's spiritual development, but also to begin teaching her about the rituals and values of the religion. In the ideal situation, these will be the godparents who will work with the aleyo throughout her lifetime, providing additional rituals and ceremonies as required. However, many godchildren choose to leave the religious household of these first godparents. There is little stigma attached to a godchild who chooses to leave his first religious family and associate herself with a different household. Each new ritual has the possibility of breaking the ties with a previous godparent and establishing ties with a new godparent. If a devotee chooses to leave the household of a godparent and associate herself with a new household, the new godparent may annul her relationships with the original godparents by "throwing away" or destroying the ritual paraphernalia received from them and re-initiating her with new warriors and necklaces. Although a devotee may associate herself with several godparents before making a final commitment to a religious family, there is a limit to the larger community's tolerance for fickleness. A devotee who is known to have moved from one house to another several times may be seen as unreliable and not welcomed in subsequent households.

The relationship between godchild and godparent becomes solidified and indestructible when the devotee decides that she has been called by the Orisha to become a priest. The godparents who place the Orisha in or on the devotee's head during the *kariocha* rituals establish a permanent relationship with the new initiate, now known as a *iyawo*. This ritual overrides all previous initiations and abrogates any previous godparent relationships so that after this ritual the initiate has no more obligations to any previous godparents. Although the iyawo as a new priest may participate in other rituals with other godparents, those relationships are additive, additions that cannot nullify the relationship between the priest and the kariocha godparents. Even if the priest severs her ties with her kariocha godparents and receive the pinaldo (Knife) ceremony from a different set of godparents, the kariocha ties are never completely dissolved. In such a case, the new godparents are viewed more as adoptive parents, those who take on the offspring of others.

Since the religious households of *babalawo* are only loosely connected to the households of *santeros*, babalawo and santeros cannot participate in each other's rituals. Warriors received from a babalawo cannot be used during the kariocha rituals, and a different set must be given to the devotee by a santero. Santeros cannot give the Hand of Orula or initiate a godchild into the mysteries of Ifa, since these are the exclusive privilege of the babalawo. Many babalawo marry fully-crowned Santería priestesses so that their godchildren can move between the realms of the babalawo and the santero while staying within the same general religious sphere. However, the relationship between the babalawo and his godchildren and that between them and his priestess wife are different and independent relationships. Each may have godchildren independent of the other, and each is entitled to different types of honor and respect.

Since many practitioners receive different rituals from different sets of godparents, both the godparents and the godchildren will introduce each other according to the highest initiation received. Thus, you may hear someone say, "she is my godmother for knife," "he is my godchild of warriors," or "he is my godchild in Ifa." The higher the ritual invoked, the more intense the assumed relationship between the godparent and godchild. By acknowledging their relationship to others, the godparent and godchild further solidify their bond, regardless of the bonds each may have with other sets of godchildren and godparents.

Having multiple sets of godparents, particularly having different godparents for kariocha and pinaldo, indicate disruptions in the religious family structure. Ideally, the godparent can call upon his or her godchild for both ritual and practical support. Similarly, the godchild should be able to call upon the godparent for both spiritual and practical assistance. Religious siblings and members of the wider religious community should be able to trust and respect each other and to rely upon each other in times of both religious and practical needs. However, many religious families fail to follow the ideal. In the United States, many godparents and godchildren are geographically separated, with godparents living in another state or even in Nigeria, Cuba, or another foreign country. As people's career and personal responsibilities take them away from their initiating communities, they may find it difficult to maintain their religious relationships. Ritual support may require that one or both of the parties travel, often long distances, to participate. Often godchildren establish alternative "adoptive" relationships in their new home areas, putting themselves under the protection and guidance of senior priests that have little or no relationship to their original godparents. Over time, the relationship between the godchild and these adoptive godparents may become stronger and more durable than that with the original but absent godparents.

Physical proximately doesn't ensure good relationships either. The ideal relationship is based on cultural forms that many American find difficult to maintain, and it is common to find godparents and godchildren who are alienated from each other. Santeros talk about losing respect for their elders, of disrespectful godchildren, and of a general loss of trust within the community. Disruptions within the community are usually described in terms of respect, or rather its loss. Godparents complain that their godchildren are disrespectful, while godchildren complain that their godparents either don't respect them as adults or that the godparents are no longer worthy of respect. Both godparents and godchildren feel as though they ought to be respected for their religious and initiatory status, regardless of their personal behavior. At the same time, both sides feel as though they need only respect others who act in a manner worthy of their respect. Often, the rhetoric of disrespect between the parties escalates until an unavoidable break occurs. Whereas, in traditional societies such as those found in pre-colonial Yorubaland and in colonial Cuba, respect is naturally afforded to persons because of age, social rank, or initiatory status, in the contemporary United States, respect must be constantly earned. Particularly in the religious sphere, respect is always contingent upon appropriate behavior, and those who act in an unacceptable manner risk the loss of the respect of others.

Another difficulty in the development of religious families in the United State is the tendency of American culture to support a vocabulary of family dysfunction that militates against using the natal family as a model of religious kinship. Without a model of a functioning personal family where elders are owed unconditional respect and children are given unconditional love, many Americans are at a loss when the relationships between godparents and godchildren are strained. Godchildren, many of whom are initiated as adults, chafe under the authority of their godparents, who may be chronologically younger than themselves. Godparents complain that their godchildren are disrespectful when they act according to the American ideals of autonomy, individualism, and self-reliance. Many practitioners seem unwilling or unable to fully commit to their new religious families in the manner expected by the ideal case. Godchildren leave their original godparents and form new "foster" relationships; godparents kick their godchildren out of their religious families, leaving them to fend for themselves. Even in the best of cases, our mobile society works against long-term and close relationships, as godchildren and godparents may live hundreds or even thousands of miles from each other.

Both godparents and godchildren bring into these relationships preexisting ideas of how others should act, with little regard for their own behavioral responsibilities. Godparents are expected to exhibit exemplary behavior and are often discounted when their feet of clay are revealed. Godchildren are expected to exhibit a level of deference unknown in other situations. Nowhere in American society is respect given or received merely on the strength on one's position: presidents can and have been impeached, and ministers and priests of the dominant religions can and have been defrocked and indicted for crimes against their parishioners. Santería ideology, however, says that practitioners owe each other respect as well as trust and reliability, not because of who they are or how they act, but because of their positions within the Santería hierarchy. By demanding respect from others while denying it to those whom they feel are not worthy of respect, santeros betray their lack of deep understanding of that ideology. These issues of mutual respect have become one of the most challenging areas of practice for Americans.

## THE ORISHA AS PARENTS AND GUARDIANS

The Orisha, as the deities of this religion, are multi-dimensional beings that represent the forces of nature, act as archetypes, and function as sacred patrons or "guardian angels" for devotees. As knowable aspects of Olodumare, the great God, they represent a level of power that is approachable through ritual, and thus are the focus of all religious action. When one kneels before Olodumare and chooses one's destiny for this lifetime, included in that destiny is the determination of one's Orisha guardians. These are the

Orisha who will be the special patrons of the individual throughout his life-time. If it is part of his destiny to become a priest in the tradition, he will be initiated as the priest of one of these Orisha, identified as the Orisha that "owns his head" (or destiny).

Before initiation and without any knowledge or understanding of the religion, everyone is born as a child of the Orisha, *omo Orisha*. Thus, one's first relationship with the Orisha is that of a child to a loving parent. Divination can determine which specific Orisha has chosen to accompany this child through his earthly journey, but even before that knowledge is obtained, the Orisha as a generalized force stand ready to guard and protect him. Lydia Cabrara, an early ethnographer of this religion in Cuba, was surprised when she was told by her Afro-Cuban informants that, in spite of being white and ignorant of the religion, she, like everyone else, had "un Santo y una Santa," a male and female Orisha who watched over and protected her "porque eran mis padres," because they were her parents.[3] Similarly, newcomers to the religion are often surprised to be told that they, too, are protected by Orisha who watch over and protect them in spite of their ignorance of the tradition.

Many elders discourage devotees from attempting to discover the identity of one's Orisha guardian, since this information isn't needed until one is preparing for initiation. However, it is common for both newcomers and established priests to want to know to whom one stands in this special relationship. In the same way that those who know astrology feel that they know something about an individual when they know his or her birth sign, practitioners believe that knowing one's Orisha guardian gives them insight into the person's personality. Independent of the divination session that establishes one's primary guardian, Orisha practitioners speculate on who "owns" a newcomer's head. As the child of an Orisha, the devotee is often said to exhibit the archetypal qualities of that Orisha, and one's personal characteristics are often used to guess the identity of one's Orisha guardian. Thus, a hot-blooded, macho man-about-town would be associated with Shango, while an earth mother-type would be associated with Yemaya.

However, it is important to realize that the identity of one's Orisha guardian, the Orisha that owns one's head, cannot be known without a special type of divination. One does not choose one's Orisha guardian based on personal preference or inclination, neither is one's personal Orisha determined by one's personality; rather, one's Orisha guardian, the Orisha of one's head, chooses who will be its worshipper and priest. The identity of the Orisha who has chosen one is identified through a formal divination session known as "marking the head," through the throw of cowry shells or kola nuts.

An Orisha may claim an individual for a variety of reasons. Although the personality one brings to the divination session may predispose one to an alliance with a particular Orisha, some individuals are chosen by an Orisha in opposition to their personal characteristics. Often the associations seem to be completely arbitrary, neither supporting nor challenging the devotee's personal self-concept. There doesn't appear to be any *necessary* relationship between the personality of the individual and his Orisha guardian.

It is also important to realize that, ideally, no consideration of one's gender or sexual orientation is made in the determination of one's Orisha guardian. That is, an individual presenting himself for divination is as likely to be given a male as a female Orisha, regardless of his own gender or sexual preference. Because the personality of the priest often correlates with that of the Orisha, one would expect that gay or effeminate men as well as most women would be associated with Oshun, the goddess of love and sexuality, or Yemaya, the maternal Orisha. Although in many communities this correlation does not hold, some diviners do attempt to assign these Orisha to obviously gay men. However, there is no requirement that one tell the diviner one's sexual orientation, and there are many gay men whose Orisha guardian is male, many straight men whose Orisha guardian is female, and many women whose Orisha guardian doesn't correlate with either their own gender or their sexual preference. In addition, the attributes associated with the Orisha are not universally projected onto a devotee relative to these gender correspondences or differences. That is, male Oshun priests are not *necessarily* perceived as effeminate, nor are female Shango priests necessarily seen as overly virile.

Many godparents are quick to take their new godchildren to the diviner to determine their guardian Orisha, believing that this knowledge will help them better guide the individual's spiritual development. Although the determination of one's Orisha guardian serves little ritual function until initiation is imminent, for many people, it serves an important part of their socialization into their Orisha community. Once that Orisha guardian has been determined, one is said to be a child not of the Orisha in general but of that Orisha in particular. Once one learns who "owns his head" there is a strong tendency to attribute behaviors to this correspondence. Thus, you will often hear even uninitiated devotees identifying themselves as the daughter of Oshun or the son of Obatala. And once the identification has been made it is very common for individuals to search their own lives and personalities for correspondences with this Orisha's stories and characteristics.

It is at the time of priestly initiation that the determination of one's Orisha guardian is most important, because each new priest is initiated as a priest of a particular Orisha. Initiation does more than solidify the relationship between Orisha and devotee. Although one always remains the child of his Orisha guardian, his new relationship as an initiated priest is expressed through the metaphor of marriage. During the initiation event and for a full year afterward, the new priest loses his given name and is simply called *iyawo*, that is, the new bride of the Orisha. He regains his given name at the end of this period called the *iyawoage*, but remains conceptually the "wife" of his Orisha guardian—regardless of his own gender or the gender of the Orisha guardian. In spite of the gender(s) assigned to them in the mythology, the Orisha are always considered male relative to their priests and priestesses. At the same time, in spite of often taking on the characteristics of their Orisha guardians, priests and priestesses are always considered female relative to those Orisha. As the wives of the Orisha, priests not only serve as caretakers of the Orisha and their devotee-children, they also serve as the vessels for their head Orisha, most radically during possession events.

During the initiation process, the Orisha is firmly seated in the devotee's head, so that not only is he the child and priest of the Orisha, but also its vessel, for it is after initiation that the new priest can manifest the Orisha directly through possession trance. The embodied Orisha can bless members of the community, offer healing, or counsel devotees in a particularly personal and physical way. For the duration of the possession event, it is the Orisha that actually speaks and acts using the body of the devotee.

Everyone is born *omo Orisha*, and through the ritual of initiation one can become *iyawo Orisha*, however, there remains other important familial relationships between priest and Orisha. At the completion of their iyawoage, fully-crowned priests (those who have completed all of the rituals associated with priestly initiation) may be known as *olorisha*, that is, "owners of Orisha." Here we see an interesting balance between the Orisha who "own" the priest (most obvious in the case of the Orisha guardian who is said to own the priest's head or destiny) and the priest who is said to "own" the Orisha to whom he has been initiated. The priest is responsible for serving and propitiating all of the Orisha that he has received either in his original initiation or in later rituals, all of the Orisha that he "owns." He may invoke them in divination, appeal to them for the good of himself, his family, or religious household, and give their ashé to others in the form of initiations or presentations.

If the priest chooses to become the godparent of a new priest, he vivifies the godchild's Orisha icons and empowers her as a new priest through the power of his own Orisha and the ashé they share with him. After someone has initiated another into the priesthood, he or she may take the title of *iyalosha* (mother of Orisha) or *babalosha* (father of Orisha). Now the priest stands not only as a child and wife of the Orisha, but as one of those who has given birth, as the spiritual parent of new devotees and their Orisha icons.

This suggests a movement toward an increasingly gendered view of devotees who begin as undifferentiated children (omo), become wives upon priestly initiation (iyawo), and fully-gendered parents when they reproduce, that is, create new members of the ritual family (as iyalosha or babalosha). At the same time, priests always remain *iyawo Orisha*, that is, wifely followers of the Orisha whom they serve.

Although every priest has two special Orisha who are considered to be his mother and father Orisha, each is initiated with five to seven Orisha, and most acquire additional Orisha throughout their lifetimes. Just as one has different relationship with the different members of one's birth family, many priests have different relationships with these different Orisha. Although the

Orisha of the head and the second Orisha parent may have primacy, often priests will identify another Orisha as their special Orisha, the one to whom they are most likely to appeal in times of need and the one to whom they are most likely to perform special rituals and ceremonies. Sometimes, this Orisha is identified in a divination session. At other times, the priest himself determines that he has a special relationship with an Orisha other than the Orisha of his head. Just as one's relationships with one's friends and relatives may wax and wane over time, so too these Orisha relationships may strengthen and weaken as one's life and circumstances change.

In an ideal world, a devotee's godparent wouldn't take him for the divination that determines the Orisha of his head until he is preparing for initiation. However, many people want to know who owns their heads, and many godparents take devotees to the diviner for this ritual long before they are interested in priestly initiation. Because of the nature of many communities, it is not uncommon for a devotee to have several godparents before the initiation, or for there to be many years between the time that his guardian Orisha is determined and the time he knocks on the door of initiation. Often it happens that the identity of the Orisha guardian changes as the devotee moves from godparent to godparent, or if there is a long time between the determination of the Orisha guardian and the actual initiation. Sometimes a devotee is told in a divination session that an Orisha "loves you very much." This formula is sometimes misinterpreted to mean that this Orisha owns one's head. So they are surprised if, at some future divination, a different Orisha is said to "love you very much" or, more importantly, to claim their head.

Devotees question why such changes take place. Were the earlier divinations wrong in their determination, or was the diviner incompetent? New godparents sometimes discredit the work of former godparents in order to solidify the new relationship, suggesting that the former godparent or the diviner they chose was mistaken or dishonest. When there has been a long time between the original determination and the final one, some priests say that the original Orisha got tired of waiting for the priest to decide to initiate, and gave up on him so that another Orisha had to step into the breach. And while one or more Orisha may love the devotee very much, they did not necessarily claim his head, as many have discovered.

Another way of looking at this discrepancy is to reconsider how such changes could happen within the limitations of one's destiny. The Yoruba idea of destiny is flexible. Rather than an immutable destiny that cannot be changed, according to this worldview, one can soften or strengthen one's destiny. Thus, it is possible to suggest that, as one moves through life, different Orisha may step forward to protect and help one manifest one's best destiny. At the same time, every decision one makes closes off some possibilities and improves others. Choosing to go to school rather than to work, to live in this place or that, to marry now or later, this person or another, all change the path of one's life. An Orisha who would walk with one under certain circumstances may defer to another under different circumstances. A superb coach might be the best mentor should one choose a career in sports, but not if one chooses to enter the business world. As one's life and one's associates, including one's godparents, changes the Orisha, claiming one's head may also change to reflect one's current situation, and best and most fulfilling destiny.

# Orisha Religion Today and Tomorrow

In this chapter, we're going to discuss some general issues that didn't fit nicely into any of the previous chapters, including discussions of syncretism, gender fluidity, and the place of women in these traditions. Finally, we're going to look at some of the ongoing controversies in these traditions. Alert readers will notice that several of the controversial issues also have syncretistic elements to them. How these issues are going to be resolved is still an open question that will require ongoing discussion among devotees and between communities of practitioners.

## SYNCRETISTIC ELEMENTS

When people are confronted with a new way of thinking that they find difficult to understand, they tend to use the ideas and concepts of a system they already know to form analogies with the new system. Sometimes, when there are many newcomers to a tradition, those analogies get passed from person to person until they become part of the standard explanation of the new system. Customs and rituals sometimes get integrated into systems of practice in a similar way. Early Christianity, for example, integrated Greek philosophical ideas that were foreign to most of the Jews of Jesus' time into their theology, while Christians incorporated some of the customs of their pagan neighbors into their own religious practices. Examples of incorporated customs include many of the northern European solstice rituals, including the Yule log and Christmas tree, mistletoe, and the gift-giving that have become an integral part of the celebration of Christmas. We call this integration or combination of alien beliefs and practices "syncretism."

Syncretism is formally defined as the attempt to combine two or more different systems of belief and practice together into a single system. Often the two belief systems are logically incompatible, although individual devotees seldom question the internal inconsistencies. Since traditions are often considered corrupted by their incorporation of elements from other traditions, to describe a religious tradition as syncretistic is considered derogatory, as it implies the betrayal of the tradition's original purity. Although all religious systems have syncretistic elements, many times, African-based traditions both on the continent and in the Americas are used as examples of syncretism, as though they are more likely to engage in this practice than other religious traditions. Santería has been described as a syncretistic religion that combines elements of West African Orisha cults and Spanish colonial Catholic religious practice. Practitioners are commonly accused of either corrupting Catholicism with their own cosmology, practices, and language, or inappropriately assimilating Catholicism into their practice of Orisha worship. The most commonly used example of this syncretism among Orisha devotees is the association of Catholic saints with the Orisha.[1]

All of the most common and many of the more obscure Orisha are associated with one or more Catholic saints. During times of persecution or in places where the Orisha icons are not appropriate, devotees have been known to substitute the appropriate saint's name or image for that of an Orisha. Outsiders see the saint and are pacified, while insiders know that the saint is merely serving as camouflage for the reality of the Orisha. All insiders know that the saints are not the Orisha, and when the time comes for a ritual or other event, they know which objects are sacred and contain the sacred presence of the Orisha (and must be propitiated during the ritual) and which are simply decorative (and can be ignored). For Cubans and others raised in a Catholic environment, the use of the saints is a simple and comfortable addition to their devotion to the Orisha; however, for Americans who were raised in Protestant or secular homes, the saints are as strange or stranger than the Orisha themselves. For African Americans and others for whom the African roots of these traditions are central to their practice, the saints and other elements from European or Catholic systems of thought are not only strange, but uncomfortable reminders of the colonial heritage of these traditions.

Accusations of syncretism usually center on ideas of purity. Syncretism, in this context, is often described as the attempt by practitioners of an incomplete or lesser tradition to assimilate the concepts and practices of a more advanced or more highly-developed tradition. Often, this assimilation is assumed to have taken place under duress. In the case of the Orisha traditions, this point of view is represented by the explanation that the Orisha devotees who were enslaved and brought to a foreign and repressive culture incorporated elements of that culture in order to survive. Early anthropologists saw this assimilation as a result of an incomplete understanding of the surrounding culture on the part of backward and ignorant peoples. The enslaved Africans didn't really understand the beliefs and practices of the Spanish colonial culture, so they took what they could understand, associating it with what they already knew. This point of view assumes that once these people (or their descendents) were fully assimilated into the Euro-American culture, appropriately educated, and fully converted to the dominate religion, they would let go of their previous syncretistic beliefs and practices. In this understanding, syncretism is an unfortunate but temporary state of affairs.

Insiders frame this story of syncretism somewhat differently. From the viewpoint of many devotees, there was, at some point in the past, a pure version of the tradition that has been degraded by the incorporation of foreign elements. Generally, this idealized past is thought to have existed in the precolonial Africa of the ancestors. When these African ancestors were enslaved and brought to the Americas, they were unable to continue to practice their own cultural traditions. Because of the tremendous repression of the surrounding culture, they appropriate elements from the surrounding Catholic Spanish culture in order to hide their real beliefs and practices. But these elements were merely camouflage necessary in the past, but no longer so, and easily dispensed with in the contemporary situation.

A third version of how and why this syncretism developed makes the incorporation of the Spanish and Catholic elements into the Orisha traditions more deliberate and less reactionary. As Henry Drewal says, the cultures of West Africa are open, flexible, and incorporative rather than closed, rigid, and conservative.[2] This means that people from these cultures are generally ready to take on new ideas and practices and incorporate them into their lives and cultures. It appears that the precolonial Yoruba-speaking peoples were quite willing to assimilate beliefs and practices of their neighbors into their own culture, taking them for their own. Some of this assimilation is remembered in the Ifa corpus; for example, there are suggestions that many of the Orisha had their origin not in Yorubaland, but in neighboring territories. Many Orisha are identified as having originally been from the Nupe area of what is now northern Nigeria,

When the Yoruba-speaking peoples were brought to Cuba, they did not see themselves as members of a single culture. In fact, many arrived in the Americas because of the wars going on between the different cities of what we now call Yorubaland. As they joined together in the social clubs and fraternities sponsored by the Cuban cabildos, they set aside their differences and began to work together to fashion new lives for themselves. In so doing, they brought together worship groups and secret societies that would never have worked together back in Africa. In addition to assimilating the beliefs and practices of their fellow Yoruba speakers, they also assimilated beliefs and practices from the surrounding European culture. Always willing to accept new ideas and concepts, they not only brought together their own disparate beliefs and practices, but also incorporated the images of the saints and other cultural elements from the dominant culture. In this version of the story, the incorporation of alien elements wasn't from ignorance or repression, but was freely undertaken by knowledgeable priests who deliberately chose what of the surrounding culture they wanted to incorporate into their own beliefs and practices.

According to this account, the associations between the saints and the Orisha were not random. Rather, the Catholic saints that were associated with the Orisha were deliberately chosen for the similarity of the saintly iconography to that of the Orisha. The matches made were not exact, and by analyzing what we know of each Orisha and the saints that have become associated with them, we can see what those early Afro-Cuban devotees thought was important and what was not. For example, it appears that color was one of the most important aspects of the Orisha, as many of the saints seem to have been chosen for the colors used in their iconography; for example, St. Barbara's red and white garments (Shango), the Virgin of Mercy's white clothes (Obatala), and the Virgin of Cobre's gold and white garments (Oshun). Other iconographic elements also appear important; all of the saints associated with Ogun, for example, are holding or using metal implements, including St. Peter with his large metal keys and St. George the Dragon-Slayer with his lance or sword. Gender, on the other hand, seems unimportant. Although there are no female Orisha represented by male saints, several of the male Orisha are represented by female saints, including Shango (St. Barbara) and Obatala (Virgin of Mercy). Sexuality also appears not to be important. St. Barbara, who was martyred by her father for refusing to marry, is associated with Shango, the lusty king with at least three wives (or, because monogamy was the standard in Cuba, a wife and several mistresses).

The saints are merely the most widely known examples of syncretism in the Orisha traditions. Some other things that have been described as syncretistic and have caused conflicts between Cuban and Cuban-identified practitioners in the United States and those with less of a tie to the island and its culture include the costumes used to dress iyawo, especially for the Middle Day presentation, and Orisha who have taken possession of devotees during drumming rituals; the use of Catholic holy water in rituals; the requirement in some communities that candidate for priestly initiation be baptized before the ritual and that they be taken to a church afterward.

Another adaptation made in the Americas that is also a syncretism of a sort is the tradition of initiating a priest with a set of five to seven Orisha during the kariocha ritual. Although the statement that in precolonial Yorubaland each village worshiped a single Orisha and that devotees only worshiped one or two Orisha is not completely accurate, the integration of the Orisha worship communities into a single community and the standardization of the initiation rituals is a Cuban innovation.[3] At least one American community, Oyotunji village and those associated with it, have returned to what they understand to be a more traditional form of initiation sometimes called "head and foot" initiation. In this form, rather than being initiated to one's head Orisha and a five or more other Orisha, one is initiated only to the Orisha of their head and Eleggua, the "foot" or foundational Orisha. More than any other disagreement between Cuban-based communities and Oyotunji-based communities, this diversity of initiation forms has caused a schism between them. According to Orisha traditions, one cannot participate in rituals one has not been initiated to. Thus, according to many santeros, priests initiated in the Oyotunji style cannot participate in any Cuban-style initiations because they have not received the appropriate rituals. This was a larger concern for Oyotunji initiates when there were fewer communities outside the village than there are today. However, it presents an ongoing problem for those who would like to see a unified Orisha community in the United States.

## GENDER FLUIDITY

Although typically the majority of devotees in a religious traditions are female, in most of the well-known so-called world religions, the leaders, whether they are called priests, imams, rabbis, ministers, or the like, are typically male. These traditions can be described as male-normative, in that the male forms the idealized devotee, and women must repudiate their female nature or accept a secondary position within the hierarchy. Religious women in the United States and some European countries have fought for the right to become religious leaders, but many of those who have become priests, bishops, or rabbis have discovered the so-called "stained-glass ceiling," an invisible barrier to the highest leadership positions in their religious communities.

Within Orisha traditions, on the other hand, qualities associated with being female form the ideal of religious practice for both men and women. These are female-based traditions in that they valorize female virtue and practices such that the female, rather than the male, is normative.[4] This remains true despite patriarchal overlays from Yoruba, Spanish Cuban, and American cultures. Orisha devotees use female roles and titles to suggest certain attributes and to perform activities associated with their religious practice. Although it is not necessary for male devotees to repudiate their masculine nature in order to participate fully within these communities, it *is* sometimes necessary for them to be able to move into female roles as part of their religious practice. Similarly, women priests are also required to move between gender roles, most obviously when they participate in possession activities, but also at other points in their religious lives. It is important to understand that, although male and females roles are essentialized such that certain characteristics are assigned to one gender and others to the other, these traditions are *not* normatively male. Unlike the idea more commonly presented in the Western philosophical tradition, women from this viewpoint are not considered defective men, nor are men considered defective women. Rather, men and women are complementary pieces of a cultural whole, and both have qualities that are necessary for the proper functioning of the world.

What this means is that both men and women are called upon to assume cross-gender roles; for example, when men become iyawo, the wife of an Orisha, and when women are possessed by a male Orisha. They must assume these roles without changing their own sex, gender, or sexual orientation. A man's masculinity is not automatically called into question when he joins these traditions, nor is a woman's female nature compromised when she assumes a leadership role within the religious household. At the same time, one is more likely to encounter openly gay, lesbian, transsexual, and transgendered persons as both devotees and as leaders within these communities than in many other religious traditions. Perhaps because of the cosmological understanding that everyone has chosen or been given a destiny for this lifetime, these sexual and gender variations are viewed as coming from and thus sanctioned by Olodumare. This doesn't mean that there aren't homophobic or insensitive individuals or communities—there are—but these positions are less common in Orisha-worshipping communities than elsewhere in American society. This is particularly true in *oriaté*-centered houses that have eschewed the authoritative leadership of a babalawo. Perhaps because the role of babalawo is forbidden to gay men (and in many communities, women), individual babalawo and the houses they head tend to be less open to men who don't fit within their idea of heterosexual norms. Although oriate-centered communities have been little studied by scholars, they encompass a large percentage of Orisha practitioners. In the absence of the strong male leadership provided by babalawo, openings are available in these communities for both women and gay men to assume positions of authority. Additionally, in the less homophobic environment that is more typical of oriaté-centered communities, all members can exhibit their own special gifts for the benefit of the community.[5]

## WOMEN AND GENDER

In spite of the female-normative nature of Orisha religion, there are roles that have conventionally been denied to women (and in some cases, to gay men) in these traditions. I've already mentioned that the practice of Ifa divination has, until recently, been limited to straight men. Women and gay men, even if they were marked by divination to go to Ifa, were denied that opportunity. Women and gay men are also excluded from the brotherhood of Aña, those who play the sacred bata at drumming rituals. Finally, women are generally discouraged from performing sacrifices that require the ritual known as *Pinaldo* (Knife) even if they have received the appropriate initiations. American women are challenging all of these limitations, but I want to focus on what is happening within the brotherhood of Ifa. (I will leave aside for the moment, limitation placed on gay men. Closeted gay men have never been excluded, and openly gay men are excluded on the grounds of their "effeminate" nature. So we can expect that as the position of women changes, theirs will as well.)

In spite of the fact that priests of Orula are generally excluded from the most important Orisha ritual, *kariocha*, they are often described in both the scholarly and popular literature as the high priests of the tradition. We should not be surprised, then, to find that, as American women gained greater gender equality in other parts of their lives, female Orisha devotees have begun to demand to be included in this high priesthood. Although Ifa has been a generally male bastion in both Yorubaland and in Cuba, there have always been positions for women within its ranks. The most important of these is that of *apetebi*, the handmaiden of the babalawo who is a necessary actor in all Ifa initiations. Generally, an apetebi was the wife or daughter of a babalawo. However, many women in the United States without a familial connection to a babalawo have been given this initiation and perform this service to the Ifa community. Additionally, as Ifa has grown and gained adherents in the United States, women have begun to be initiated *iyanifa* or *iyalawo*, that is, as priests of Ifa. These women are full priests of Ifa, and, with the appropriate training, can perform divination and many of the same rituals performed by their male counterparts. They are, however, excluded from the highest levels within the Ifa hierarchy.

At this point, it is important to distinguish between the communities of Ifa and all other Orisha communities. While Ifa communities in the Americas continue to exhibit the same claims of male superiority and supremacy found in some of the earliest records of the Ifa priesthood in Yorubaland, the other Orisha communities have always been female-oriented and female-led. In Yorubaland, the worship of most of the Orisha was lead by women; in Cuba, the earliest heads of Orisha communities were women, and today women continue to lead the majority of Orisha communities. Whereas women in Ifa communities are precluded from the highest levels of ritual participation, women in other Orisha communities can hold the highest office, *iyalosha*, mother of Orisha. Woman can be initiated to *pinaldo*, and, when they choose, can perform every type of sacrifice. Although men have dominated the role of oriate since Obadimille refused to train women, the earliest oriate were women, and contemporary woman are again being trained for this important role. The only role that has been slow to open to contemporary women is that of drummer. The brotherhood of Aña, the sacred drums, is closely allied with that of Ifa and has not yet welcomed women into their ranks. Although there are trained female drummers, no one has been willing to initiate them into the sacred drums. Gay men, too, have found it easy to make a place for themselves in the larger Orisha community, with many performing as babalosha of large religious communities. Since they are not precluded from pursuing a calling as an oriate, many fine diviners have followed that route instead of going into the brotherhood of Ifa.

## ONGOING CONTROVERSIES

Orisha religion in the United States faces several ongoing controversies in the twenty-first century, some internal and some in conjunction with the larger society. Externally, the use of animal sacrifice, possession trance, and the public's perception that Santería is a cult continue to plague devotees as they try to practice their religion. Many devotees have stories of rituals raided by opponents of sacrifice who want to save the animals. Devotees also freely discuss their fears of losing their jobs, homes, or children if outsiders discover their practice of the religion, and most can name someone in their community who has suffered just such a loss. Also of concern to devotees is the appropriation of the trappings of Santería by other groups, notably Spiritist groups and some Neo-Pagans.

Internally, several movements within the tradition also challenge devotees. For the most part, these are not challenges to the beliefs or practices of the tradition, but rather organizational challenges. As the religion has moved out of the Cuban and extended Latino communities and into the larger American society, non-Latinos have brought their own sensibilities to the tradition. This has led to two somewhat overlapping movements I call Protestantization and Africanization. The resolution of these controversies will determine the face of the tradition as it continues to grow and evolve.

### APPROPRIATION

As early as the 1960s, anthropologists began to describe a type of *Espiritismo* which George Brandon dubbed *Santerismo*. Santerismo is a term scholars used to describe a form of Spiritism that has incorporated elements of Santería into Puerto Rican Espiritismo beliefs and practices. This incorporation includes the use of beaded necklaces similar to those used in Santería, the addition of some Orisha into the pantheon of spirits, and the adaptation of the Santería religious kinship system—that is, identifying senior *espirististas* as *padrino* or *madrina*—and the identification of the core members of the congregation as *ahijados* (godchildren).[6] Within Santerismo, the Orisha/saints are not seen as deities, but as spirits that are more highly evolved than the spirits of ordinary people, but less highly evolved than the angels and other pure spirits that are closest to God. These spirits are useful for providing some types of healing, but are not as inherently good and powerful as the higher, purer spirits.

A common example of way the Orisha/saints have been incorporated into Santerismo is the so-called Seven African Powers or *Siete Potencias*

**Front of a Seven African Powers candle with Arma Christi and chromolithographs of Catholic Saints**

*Africanas.*[7] The image of these Powers are found on chromolithographs, tall, glass-encased candles commonly sold in *botanicas,* and grocery stories serving the Spanish-speaking community. In the center of the paper or silk-screen label on the front of the candle is an image of the crucifixion of Christ, complete with the *Arma Christi* (Instruments of the Passion, including hammer, nails, and scourge) and the word "Olofi" printed below. Surrounding the center image are seven medallions connected by a chain. Each medallion contains the picture of a Catholic saint, none of which is African or of African heritage. On the top of each medallion is the name of the Orisha generally associated with that saint. Although not all candles contain the same iconography a typical candle includes what appear to be St. Barbara (Chango), the Virgin of Charity of Cobre (the patron saint of Cuba who is associated with Oshun), Virgin of Regla (Yemeya), Our Lady of Mercy (Obatala), St. Francis

(Orula), John the Baptist (Ogun), and St. Anthony of Padua (Eleggua). Hanging from the chain connecting the lowest two medallions is a set of miniature tools including a sword, a battle-ax, and a lance, along with several types of hammers (the tools of Ogun). On the back of the candle is a prayer in Spanish, and often English as well, asking the "Seven African Powers" who surround Our Lord to intercede for the devotee. The juxtaposition of images suggests, incorrectly, that these candles are favored by either Catholics who, ignoring the African elements, may focus on the images of the Crucifixion and the saints, or Santería practitioners and devotees who may see past the Catholic images to find their own deities portrayed. However, this is not an example of syncretism between these two traditions, but rather between Santería and Espiritismo, and is a common image in Santerismo communities.

Both Orisha devotees and other espiritistas judge these practices harshly. Although many Orisha devotees are also practitioners of Espiritismo, from their viewpoint, the two systems of practice should be kept apart. Rituals should be held at different times, in different places. In addition, home altars and worship areas should be kept as separated as possible within the limitation of one's home or apartment. Santeros say that combining the two into a single system of beliefs and practices is improper. Santero also criticize espiritistas who include the Orisha in their pantheon as lesser spirits. For santeros, the Orisha are full gods who should not be invoked or manipulated by the uninitiated.

Criticisms from espiritistas fall into two major areas. Neither focuses on iconography, but rather other practices that have been taken from Santería. One is the practice of charging for spiritual services and the other is the dependence on so-called lesser spirits. Traditionally, spiritualists do not charge for their services, while all Santería rituals involve a monetary component known as the *derecho* (Sp. right, tax). Within Santería, the derecho pays for the goods and services needed to complete the ritual, as well as a payment to the priest performing it. Santerismo mediums have incorporated this right into their own religious practice in order to receive fees for their ritual work, much to the distress of mediums that view the derecho as a type of spiritual exploitation. The other major concern for many espiristas is the incorporation of Santería and its deities into Espiritismo. Because of its association with *brujería* (witchcraft), in the minds of many espiritistas, the rituals and practices of Santería are considered to involve an inappropriate use of "black magic" into what is generally seen as a purely spiritual practice.

Santerismo is generally found in Hispanic and usually Puerto Rican-identified communities. Another form of appropriation can be found in mainly non-Spanish-speaking, non-African-heritage communities, and that is the incorporation of the Orisha into the practices of Wicca and other contemporary Pagan groups. Contemporary Paganism is a general term for a diverse set of beliefs and practices influenced by ancient, usually pre-Christian religious cultures, including those of classical Greece, Rome, and

Egypt. Some Pagan groups also draw heavily on Celtic traditions or other less-known Indo-European cultures. Many Pagan groups and other like-minded individuals are wide-ranging in their search for the divine. Thus, it should not be surprising that, as the Orisha traditions gain public recognition, Pagans have begin to incorporate the Orisha into their pantheons. Many santeros find this disturbing. Since the requirements to work with the Orisha within the traditions are stringent and tied to the initiatory system, many devotees feel that outsiders who appropriate Orisha and their worship are being both foolish and risky.

From the point of view of Orisha devotees, it may be that the deities from other pantheons have been so weakened by the loss of their original communities that anyone is free to work with them. The Orisha, on the other hand, are still alive and powerful, and can be very dangerous for the inexperienced. The Orisha initiation system is designed to give practitioners both the spiritual protections and the knowledge to work with these powerful beings. In bypassing this system and working independently, *olorisha* believe that Pagans are putting themselves and their communities at risk. There is also an element of what scholars call "cultural appropriation" in the Pagan tendency to pick and choose without making a firm commitment to a community of practitioners. Although cultural appropriation can go both ways, in this context, the term refers to the situation where members of the dominant culture use ("steal") from a minority culture. Prominent examples include the performance of such Native American religious rituals as sweat lodges, pipe ceremonies, and vision quests by non-Native peoples, who live and practice outside of Native communities. From the point of view of Orisha devotees, ceremonies and rituals focused on their deities independent of the larger Orisha community are a similar form of cultural appropriation.

## PROTESTANTIZATION AND AFRICANIZATION

When Orisha devotees began to reestablish their traditional practices in colonial Cuba, they were not able to set up the kinds of communities they had known in Africa. Instead, they used the societal forms available to them. Without the foundation of multigenerational lineage groups living together in common compounds, they established ritually constructed families that were independent of the traditional relational lines of blood and marriage. Unable to develop their own towns governed by an *oba* and his ministers, they used the *cabildo* system to form their own cultural communities. Unable to restore the independent worship communities focused on discrete groups of Orisha, they developed a system whereby priests were initiated into the worship of a group of Orisha. The flexibility of the Yoruba-speaking peoples in Cuba enabled them to make the changes necessary to continue their worship of the Orisha in a new and often oppressive culture environment. The migration of the Orisha and their devotees to the United States in the mid-twentieth century has resulted in a new set of challenges to the organizational structure of Orisha-worshipping communities. The most prominent of these I have called Protestantization and Africanization.

*Protestantization* is the attempt to make Orisha worship communities conform more closely to the organizational structure of American Protestant churches. Although churches have a variety of governing forms, for many, the general structure includes one or more religious leaders (ministers, rabbis, imams, and the like) who are principally responsible for the spiritual life of the church, including regular religious services, marriages, funerals, and other activities of pastoral care, and a group of members who form the governing board that is primarily responsible for the secular life of the church, including finances, building maintenance, and the like. The religious leaders usually have close ties to the board, and may retain some secular responsibilities as well. In some cases, each church is independent, and there is no higher-level governing body that can exert authority over the local congregation. In other cases, there is a hierarchal relationship between the local congregations and regional, national and sometimes international organizations that assert political and ecclesiastical authority over the local congregation. Although many traditions have women ministers at the local level and in some cases at the higher governing levels, generally, leadership is a primarily male prerogative, and the majority of the leaders at all levels are men.

Orisha "churches" like the Church of the Lucumí Babalu Aiye Lucumí (CLBA) and the Lucumí Church of Orisha in New York City are examples of this movement of protestantization. They have chosen the term "church" to designate themselves, in spite of the Christian connotations the term has for many. Important to this movement is the establishment of "church" organizations that can be recognized both by the local authorities and the surrounding community, and a concurrent movement away from secrecy. The public face of CLBA, for example, is a storefront where it holds regular religious services for its members. Its leadership is divided into separate religious and administrative functions. CLBA is also attempting to function as a clearinghouse that certifies and registers priests. The development of a primarily male leadership within these organizations suggests a corresponding loss of status among female priests. Although Orisha churches tend to have a Cuban focus, often looking to the cabildos period for models of practice and structure, many reject the Catholic (Christian) trappings that found their way into the tradition in Cuba, and many have eliminated them, including the use of Catholic saints, holy water, and the like. Although protestant-style organizations may open their communities to scrutiny by the larger culture, as happened when CLBA established themselves in Hialeah, they also can provide increased legitimacy to the tradition as a whole, as CLBA did when they won their Supreme Court case.

Africanization is the desire to re-Africanize the tradition, removing cultural elements that are believed to have been added to the tradition during its sojourn in the Americas. Primarily found among African American devotees, Africanization efforts include the movement to replace Catholic and Spanish trappings with those from Africa, including the use of Yoruba rather than Spanish vocabulary, the production of Africanized images to replace Catholic ones, the incorporation of Africanized dress, and the return to Yoruba communities in Nigeria to receive initiations and teachings, and thus bypassing the Cuban community. Although the peoples of what has become Nigeria have been subjected to the efforts of Christian missionaries and European colonists since the time their first enslaved brethren left the continent, many modern American think that contemporary Yoruba peoples have retained a purer and more authentic version of Orisha worship. It comes as a surprise to many who travel to Nigeria to find that many contemporary Nigerians view these traditions as a part of their primitive and unenlightened past. Some people have even suggested that the traditions as they have been maintained in the Americas are in fact truer to the original traditions than the vestiges left in Nigeria.

Be that as it may, the aim of Africanization is to construct religions and social communities that are modeled on an idealization of Yoruba culture. The work of anthropologists and others who documented Yoruba culture in the late nineteenth and early twentieth centuries provides the basis for this movement. Although Oyotunji Village and it many daughter communities are the most prominent example of this movement, many others also espouse some of its central ideas. This movement, too, has shifted away from secrecy and to put a more public face on the religion.

## FINAL WORDS

The Orisha traditions are among the fastest growing religious traditions in the United States today. Every week, more and more people from all social, racial, and economic groups are discovering these traditions, and seeking and receiving initiations. Where once these traditions were limited to the Cuban-exile communities in Miami, New York, and Los Angeles, today there are communities in most major and many smaller communities from coast to coast. The diversity of membership has lead to diversity of practice as different communities of devotees attempt to integrate this tradition into their busy contemporary lives. Devotees have found that the Internet and other electronic media provide them with a way to communicate among themselves, not only across the country, but also around the world. Different communities of practice have developed as different groups have begun to interpret the teaching in new and innovative ways. I have spotlighted Oyotunji village as one of the oldest of these innovative groups, but there are many others around the country. One of the questions of the future of these traditions will be to what extent these different communities will continue to see themselves as members of the same religious family and to what extent different groups will diverge from each other. There are both centripetal (pulling together) and centrifugal (pulling apart) forces acting on these groups. Whether the forces holding the groups together are stronger than those pulling them apart is still unknown. What is certain is that the religion of the Orisha will continue to grow and develop in the United States and around the world.

# Glossary

The terminology used by Orisha practitioners is a mix of Yoruba (designated as Yr.), Spanish (Sp.), a creolized version of Yoruba known as Lukumi (Lk.), and English words. In addition, this glossary contains some Kongolese (Kg.) words.

**abo faca (Lk.)**   Hand of Orula for men. Also called *awofaka*.

**aborisa (Yr.)**   Used by some contemporary practitioners to designate someone who participates in the religion but has not undergone the *asiento/kariocha* ceremony.

**adimu Orisha (Lk.)**   "Orisha one embraces," Orisha received outside of kariocha ritual. See also *santo lavado*.

**aiye (Yr.)**   Visible world, this world, the earth. Opposite of *orun*, the invisible world. Also *aye*.

**Ajalamo (Yr.)**   Maker of heads/destinies.

**aje (Yr.)**   Witch, witches; more correctly, those who possess witchcraft substance.

**ajogun (Yr.)**   "Warlords," forces of nature that challenge the balance of the cosmos.

**akpwon (Lk.)**   Singer who is the master of ceremonies for drumming rituals.

**alaafin (Yr.)**   Ruler of the city of Oyo.

**aleyo or alejo (Lk.)**   "Stranger-resident-in-the-House." Person who has received the first initiation of *ilekis/collares/*necklaces.

**Aña (Lk.)**   Spirit inhabiting sacred drums.

**ángel guardián (Sp.)**   "Guardian angel," one's primary Orisha.

**apetebi (Yr.)**   Female ordained to her patron divinity who serves the Ifa order.

**arun (Yr.)**   Disease. One of the ajogun, forces of destruction.

**ashé (Yr.)**   Power, energy, blessings; energy of the universe; ritual power; also name of empowered material.

**asiento (Sp.)**   From *asentar*, to put, set, place; initiation ceremony to make or crown a priest; puts or seats the Orisha in the head of the devotee.

**awofaka (Lk.)**   See *abo faca*.

**aworo (Yr.)**   Orisha priest, sometimes translated "fetish priest" in eighteenth century documents.

**aye (Yr.)**   Visible world. See *aiye*.

**awon iya wa (Yr.)**   "Our mothers," that is, the witches, also *iyami* or *eleye*.

**babalawo (Yr.)**   "Father of secrets," priest of Orula/Orunmila, the owner of Ifa, the highest form of divination.

**babalosha (Yr.)**   "Father of Orisha," male priest.

**Babluaiye (Lk.)**   "Father ruler of the world," Orisha of smallpox. Also known as Sopona (Yr.), Obaluaiye.

**bata (Yr.)**   Consecrated ritual drums.

**bembe (Lk.)**   Drum ritual, used interchangeably with *tambor*.

**bontanica (Sp.)**   Store catering to Orisha devotees and practitioners of other Latino magical traditions

**boveda (Sp.)**   "Vault," Spiritist home altar.

**brujería (Sp.)**   Witchcraft (also *brujo/a*, witch).

**brujo/a (Sp.)**   Witch, one who practices witchcraft

**buba (Yr.)**   Woman's blouse or man's shirt.

**cabildo (Sp.)**   Church chapter house, town council; in Cuba, the social clubs for *gente de color*.

**camino (Sp.)**   Road or path; advocation of an Orisha. Some Orisha have many caminos, others have only one.

**casa de Orisha (Sp.)**   House of the Orisha, home shrines that replace the cabildos in late nineteenth century Cuba

**cascarilla (Sp.)**   White chalk-like material made from eggshells. See *efun*.

**cofa (Lk.)**   See *ikofa*.

**collares (Sp.)**   Necklaces, strand of colored beads representing an Orisha, also called *eleke* or *ileki*.

**cuchillo (Sp.)**   Knife ((Yr.): *pinaldo*). Ritual that bestows the right to sacrifice animals with a knife. Considered the culmination of one's priestly initiation.

**curandero/a (Sp.)**   Native healer.

**derecho (Sp.)**   "right, tax." Payment made for ritual services.

**día de media (Sp.)**   "Middle Day" of initiation ritual when iyawo is presented to the community.

**diloggun (Lk.)**   16, from (Yr.): *medilogun*; divination system using 16 cowry shells.

**ebo (Yr.)**   Sacrifice; offering or work given to Orisha or *egun*.

**ebo eje (Yr.)**   Blood sacrifice.

**efun (Yr.)**   White chalk used in rituals.

**egba (Yr.)**   Paralysis. One of the ajogun, forces of destruction.

**egun (Lk.)**   Ancestor, sometimes used interchangeably with *muerto* (dead person).

**Egungun (Yr.)**   Spirit of the ancestors honored in ritual masquerade.

**eleda (Yr.)**   "Creator," one's ancestral guardian soul. See also emi, ojiji.

**eleke (Yr.)**     Bead; single strand of colored beads representing an Orisha. Also called *collar* or necklace.

**Eleggua (Lk.)**     Trickster Orisha, guardian of the crossroads, one of the Warrior Orisha. Also known as Elegba, Elegbara, or Eshu.

**eleye (Yr.)**     "Owner of birds," the witches, also *iyami* or *awon iya wa.*

**emi (Yr.)**     Breath, vital force; one of a person's souls. See also ojiji, eleda.

**epe (Yr.)**     Curse. One of the ajogun, forces of destruction.

**ese (Yr.)**     Generalized term for human affliction. One of the ajogun, forces of destruction.

**espiritista (Sp..)**     Spiritist practitioner.

**Espiritismo (Sp.)**     Kardecian spiritism.

**Espiritismo de Caridad (Sp.)**     Spiritism of charity.

**Espiritismo de Cordon (Sp.)**     Spiritism of the Chain.

**Espiritismo del Mesa (Sp.)**     Spiritism of the table, or scientific Spiritism

**Espiritismo Cruzado (Sp.)**     Crossed or mixed Spiritism.

**Eshu (Yr.)**     Trickster Orisha often conflated with Eleggua.

**ewe (Yr.)**     Prohibitions, taboos.

**ewon (Yr.)**     Imprisonment. One of the ajogun, forces of destruction.

**fila (Yr.)**     Man's hat.

**fundamento (Sp.)**     Basis, foundation; the stones and tools enclosed in the altar containers that serve as residence for the Orisha.

**funfun (Yr.)**     White, cool, or peaceful.

**gele (Yr.)**     Head wrap.

**gente de color (Sp.)**     "People of color"; name given to former slaves and their descendants in Cuba.

**guerreros, los (Sp.)**     The Warriors. The Orisha Eleggua, Ogun, Ochosi, and Osun. Usually received as part of a single ritual of the same name.

**hacer el santo (Sp.)**     To make the saint, see *asiento.*

**herramienta (Sp.)**     Tool, the metal or wooden implements of the Orisha.

**ibeji (Yr.)**     Twins. Deity of twins.

**ibori (Yr.)**     Cowry encrusted container that serves to represent one's *ori* in Yorubaland.

**Ifá (Yr.)**     Divination system invoking the wisdom of Orula/Orunmila; performed only by a *babalawo.* Also another name for the Orisha Orula/Orunmila.

**igbodu (Yr.)**     Sacred grove, site of religious activity.

**ikofa (Lk.)**     Hand of Orula for woman. Also called *cofa.*

**iku (Yr.)**     Death. One of the ajogun, forces of destruction.

**ilé (Yr.)**     Earth/town/household, within Santería a religious family.

**ile Orisha (Lk.)**     "Household of the Orisha," religious family.

**ileke (Yr.)**     Bead; single strand of colored beads representing an Orisha. Also called *collar* or necklace.

**ipele (Yr.)**     Woman's shawl.

**ire (Lk.)**     Good luck.

**iro (Yr.)**     Woman's wrapper.

**itá (Lk.)**     From Yr. *itan*, story, history; *diloggun* divination performed as part of *asiento* initiation, tells the initiate's past, present and future.

**italero (Lk.)/(Sp.)**     "One who performs ita," a diviner trained in cowry shell divination. Although *ita* refers only to divination done in conjunction with initiations and other rituals involved the sacrifice of four-legged animals, the term *italero* is often used to denote anyone who reads the shells. Often conflated with *oriaté*.

**itotele (Lk.)**   "He who follows in rank," middle-sized bata drum.

**iwe pele (Yr.)**   Gentle character.

**iwe rara (Yr.)**   Good character.

**iya (Yr.)**   Mother; also the title of all adult women who are assumed to have borne children. Also name of largest of the bata drums.

**iyalawo (Yr.)**   "Mother of the secrets," title of female Ifa priest, see also *iyanifa*.

**iyalode (Yr.)**   "Titled market woman," head of marketplace, sometimes used to designate leaders of the witches.

**iyalosha (Yr.)**   "Mother of Orisha," female priest.

**iyami (Yr.)**   "Our mothers," that is, the witches, also *awon iya wa* or *eleye*.

**iyanifa (Yr.)**   "Mother of Ifa," title of female Ifa priest, see also *iyalawo*.

**iyawo (Yr.)**   "Bride younger than speaker, wife"; in Santería, a new initiate of either sex.

**iyawoage (Yr.)/(Sp.)**   Yearlong liminal period after the *asiento*, during which one is subject to a long list of restrictions.

**Iyawo Orisha (Yr.)**   Wife of an Orisha, initiated priest.

**kariocha (Yr.)**   To place the Orisha (on/in the head), priestly initiation.

**Jakuta (Yr.)**   Thunder deity whose worship was assimilated into that of *Shango*.

**jubona (Yr.)**   The second godparent at Santería initiations, see *ojugbona*.

**letra del ano (Sp.)**   "Letter of the year." Divination performed at New Year.

**limpieza (Sp.)**   "Cleansing," ritual bath.

**Limpieza de sangre (Sp.)**   "Purity of blood," marker of religious ethnic purity in early Modern Spain.

**Lukumí (Lk.)**   Creolized Yoruba language developed in Cuba; alternative name for Santería. Also *Lucumí*.

**madrina (Sp.)**   Godmother.

**Marielitos (Sp.)**   Cuban refugees who left Cuba through the Port of Mariel in the 1980s

**matanza (Sp.)**   Sacrifice.

**medilogun (Yr.)**   See *diloggun*.

**misa blanca (Sp.)**   "White mass," Spiritist séance.

**misa espiritual (Sp.)**   Spiritual mass or séance.

**muerto (Sp.)**   Dead person, usually used to designate the spirit of a dead person.

**nfumbi (Kg.)**   Spirit of a dead person in Regla de Congo.

**nganga (Kg.)**   Cauldron that serves as a sacred site in Regla de Congo. Also call prenda.

**oba (Yr.)**   "Ruler," chiefly title; within Santería, a title given to an *oriaté*.

**Obatala (Yr.)**   "Ruler of the white cloth," wisest and oldest of the Orisha.

**obi (Yr.)**   Kola nut; in Cuba and the U.S., coconut pieces used for divination; also name of Orisha associated with coconut divination.

**ocha (Lk.)**   Contraction of *Orisha*, used to designate both the religion (see *Regla de Ocha*) and its deities.

**Ochosi (Lk.)**   Hunter Orisha, one of the Warrior Orisha. Also known as Oshosi, Ossoosi.

**odu (Yr.)**   Letter or number determined by either diloggun or Ifa divination.

**ofo (Yr.)**   Loss. One of the ajogun, forces of destruction.

**Ogun (Yr.)**   Orisha of iron, a blacksmith, one of the Warrior Orisha.

**ojiji (Yr.)**   Shadow, one of a person's souls. See also *emi, eleda*.

**ojugbona (Yr.)**   "One who clears the road," "Eyes of the road," or "witness," the second godparent at Santería initiations. Also *jubona, yubona*.

**okonkolou (Lk.)**   "He who is small/young," name of smallest bata drum.

**Olodumare (Yr.)**   Great God, deity behind the Orisha. Olodumare is only propitiated through the Orisha. Also known as Olorun, Olofi, although these are often considered separate members of a divine trinity reminiscent of the Christian trinity.

**Olofi (Lk.)**   Supreme ruler, title of *Olodumare*.

**Olokun (Yr.)**   Orisha of the depths of the ocean.

**olori (Yr.)**   "Owner of ori or destiny," Another name for the ancestral soul, eleda. See also eleda, emi, ojiji.

**olorisha (Yr.)**   "Owner of Orisha," priest of Orisha religion.

**Olorun (Lk.)**   Owner of heaven, title of *Olodumare*.

**oluku mi (Yr.)**   "My friend," believed to be the source of Lucumí as the name of the Yoruba people.

**omiero (Lk.)**   Spiritually charged herbal infusion.

**omo (Yr.)**   Child.

**omo-ile (Yr.)**   Child of the house.

**omo-orisha (Yr.)**   Child of an Orisha.

**onisegun (Yr.)**   Herbalist, native doctor, master of medicine.

**opa egun (Lk.)**   Staff of the ancestors.

**opele (Yr.)**   Divination chain used by a *babalawo*.

**opon Ifa (Yr.)**   *Ifá* divination board.

**oran (Yr.)**   Big trouble. One of the ajogun, forces of destruction.

**Ori (Yr.)**   Head, personal destiny, one's personal Orisha.

**ori-inu (Yr.)**   Inner head, destiny.

**oriaté (Lk.)**   Head or ruler of the [divination] mat, highly-trained diviner, and ritual specialist who presides over the initiation of Santería priests and other rituals. Also *oba oriate*.

**oriki (Yr.)**   Praise song sung to honor Orisha and other important persons

**Orisha (Yr.)**   Deities of the Yoruba traditional religion and Santería. Also *orisa* (Yr.), *oricha* (Sp.).

**Orula (Lk.)**   Deity of divination, owner of Table of *Ifá*. Also known as Orunmila.

**orun (Yr.)**   Invisible world, heaven, sky. Opposite of *aiye*, the visible world.

**orun bururu (Yr.)**   "Bad orun," celestial rubbish heap.

**orun rere (Yr.)**   "Good orun," heaven.

**Orunmila (Yr.)**   Deity of divination, owner of Table of *Ifá*. Known in Santería as Orula.

**oshe (Yr.)**   Double-headed axe that is the trademark of Shango.

**Oshun (Yr.)**   Orisha of rivers and sweet water, love, children. and the pleasures of life.

**osogbo (Lk.)**   Bad luck.

**Osun (Yr.)**   Protector Orisha, one of the Warrior Orisha.

**Oya (Yr.)**   Orisha of the whirlwind, owner of the cemetery.

**padrino (Sp.)**   Godfather.

**Palo (Sp.)**   *Reglas de Congo*, central African-based religions in Cuba including Palo Monto and Palo Mayombe.

**palero/a (Sp.)**   Priest of Palo Monte and its related religions.

**pataki (Lk.)**   Story or legend, usually associated with the diloggun.

**pescado y jutia (Sp.)**   Dried fish and rat powder.

**pinaldo (Yr.)**   Knife. See *cuchillo*.

**plaza (Sp.)**   "Market place," fruit, and other offering spread on the floor in front of a *trono*.

**prenda (Sp.)**   "Pledge." See nganga.

**Regla de Congo or Regla de Kongo (Sp.)**   "Way or rule of the Congo people," also known as *Palo Monte* and *Palo Mayombe*.

**Regla de Ocha (Sp.) & (Yr.)**   "Way or rule of the Orisha," also known as *Santería*.

**rogación (Sp.)**   "Rogation or petition," head blessing ritual.

**rompimiento (Sp.)**   "Breaking," cleansing ritual.

**Santería (Sp.)**   Conventionally translated as "way of the saints," common name for followers of Orisha religion in Cuba and the U.S. See also *Regla de Ocha*, *Lucumí*.

**Santerismo (Lk.)**   Version of Espiritismo that incorporates elements of Santería.

**santero/a (Sp.)**   "Maker or seller of saints"; within Santería, refers to a devotee, more properly only to an initiated priest.

**santo/a (Sp.)**   "Saint or holy being"; used in Santería to refer to the Catholic saints associated with the Orisha; often used as generic term referring to the Orisha themselves.

**santo lavado (Sp.)**   "Washed Orisha," Orisha received without full blood sacrifice.

**se Orisa (Yr.)**   To make, do, or work the Orisha. Pronounced "shai Orisha".

**Shango (Yr.)**   Fourth king of Oyo, Orisha of thunder and lightning. Also *Sango* (Yr.), *Chango* (Sp.).

**shekere (Yr.)**   Type of musical instrument that has beads or shells woven around the outside of the gourd as noisemakers.

**sokoto (Yr.)**   Men's pants.

**tambor (Sp.)**   Drum ceremony to invoke the Orisha. Also called *bembe*.

**traje del desayuno (Sp.)**   Morning or breakfast dress. Gingham outfit worn by a new initiate before noon on the so-called "middle day."

**traje del medio (Sp.)**   Middle Day dress. Fancy outfit worn by a new initiate during the public presentation on the "middle day."

**trono (Sp.)**   Throne, altar built to honor one or more Orisha or as part of an initiation.

**Yemaya (Yr.)**   "Mother whose children are like the fishes," Orisha of the ocean and maternal protection.

**Yansan (Yr.)**   "Mother of nine," praise name of Oya.

**yubona (Yr.)**   The second godparent at Santería initiations. See *ojugbona*.

# Notes

## CHAPTER 1: INTRODUCTION

1. Sandra T. Barnes, ed., *Africa's Ogun: Old World and New* (Bloomington, IN: Indiana University Press, 1997).

2. Mary Pat Fisher, *Living Religions* (Upper Saddle River, NJ: Prentice-Hall, 2006).

3. David D. Brown, *Santeria Enthroned: Art, Ritual, and Innovation in an Afro-Cuban Religion* (Chicago: University of Chicago Press, 2003).

4. Central Intelligence Agency, *World Fact Book: Nigeria* (June 29, 2006 2006 [cited July 4 2006]); available from http://cia.gov/cia/publications/factbook/geos/ni.html.

5. [D]ice Oddedei: "hacer Santo es hacer rey, y kariocha es una ceremonia de reyes, como las del palacio del oba lucumi," Lydia Cabrera, *El Monte (Igbo, Finda, Ewe Orisha, Vititi Finda): Notas Sobre Las Religiones, La Magia, Las Supersticiones Y El Folklore De Los Negros Criollos Y Del Pueblo De Cuba* (Miami, FL: Ediciones Universal, 1975).

6. For more information about Haitian vodun, see Karen McCarthy Brown, *Mama Lola: A Vodou Priestess in Brooklyn* (Berkeley: University of California Press, 1991); Maya Deren, *Divine Horsemen: The Living Gods of Haiti* (New Platz, NY: McPherson, 1983); Zora Neale Hurston, *Tell My Horse: Voodoo and Life in Haiti and Jamaica*, ed. Henry Louise Gates, Jr. (New York, Grand Rapids, Philadelphia, St. Louis, San Francisco, London, Singapore, Sydney, Tokyo, Toronto: Harper & Row, 1990); Joseph M. Murphy, *Working the Spirit: Ceremonies of the Africa Diaspora* (Boston: Beacon Press, 1994); Anthony B. Pinn, *Varieties of African American Religious Experience* (Minneapolis, MN: Ausburg Fortress Publishers, 1998). For information about Voodoo in New Orleans, see Ina Johanna Fandrich, *The Mysterious Voodoo Queen, Marie Laveaux: A Study of Powerful Female Leadership in Nineteenth-Century New Orleans* (New York: Routledge, 2005); Carolyn Morrow Long, *A*

*New Orleans Voudou Priestess: The Legend and Reality of Marie Laveau* (Gainesville: University Press of Florida, 2006); Martha Ward, *Voodoo Queen: The Spirited Lives of Marie Laveau* (Jackson, MI: University Press of Mississippi, 2004).

7. Fernando Ortiz, *Los Negros Brujos* (Reprint, Miami: Ediciones Universal, 1973).

8. A search of Lexis Nexis, a popular searchable archive of content from newspapers and magazines, yields many articles associating "voodoo or Santería" with the unexplainable, for example, the Tampa police spokesman who said, "We are just leaning toward it being cult related or involving Santeria or some voodoo because we don't have any other reasonable explanation." Candace J. Samolinski, "Scholar Calls Santeria, Voodoo Theory Unfair," *The Tampa Tribune*, July 3, 2006.

9. Henry John Drewal. "Interpretation, Invention, and Re-Presentation in the Worship of Mami Wata." *Journal of Folklore Research* 25, no. 1–2 (1988): 101–39, 132.

10. Church of the Lukumi Babalu Aye CLBA (http://www.church-of-the-lukumi.org/) maintains a list of priests who have been certified by their organization. The Organization of Lukumi Unity, a networking site for practitioners of all the forms of Orisha religion (http://www.lukumiunity.org/), also has a directory of resources, including information posted by diviners and others. However, these organizations list only a small, self-selected group of priests. Many good, hardworking, knowledgeable priests have not chosen to seek certification from these sources.

## CHAPTER 2: HISTORY OF THE TRADITION

1. William Bascom, *The Yoruba of Southwestern Nigeria* (New York: Holt, Rinehart and Winston, 1969); The Rev. Samuel Johnson, *The History of the Yorubas: From the Earliest Times to the Beginning to the British Protectorate*, trans. Dr. O. (ed.) Johnson (Lagos: C.M.S. (Nigeria) Bookshops, 1960).

2. George Brandon, *Santeria from Africa to the New World: The Dead Sell Memories* (Bloomington, IN: Indiana University Press, 1993).

3. Roger Bastide, *African Civilizations in the New World*, trans. Peter Green (New York: Harper & Row, 1971).

4. William R. Bascom, *The Sociological Role of the Yoruba Cult-Group*, ed. Ralph Linton, vol. 46, *American Anthropologist* (Menasha, WI: American Anthropological Association, 1944).

5. Bascom, *The Yoruba of Southwestern Nigeria; Bascom, The Sociological Role of the Yoruba Cult-Group;* Stephen S. Farrow, *Faith, Fancies and Fetich or Yoruba Paganism* (Brooklyn, NY: Athelia Henrietta Press, Inc., 1996), 85.

6. For a detailed description of the development of Afro-Cuban cabildos, see Brown, *Santeria Enthroned: Art, Ritual, and Innovation in an Afro-Cuban Religion*, especially chapters 1 and 2.

7. For an excellent analysis of this period, see Stephan Palmié, *Wizards and Scientists: Explorations in Afro-Cuban Modernity and Tradition* (Durham and London: Duke University Press, 2002), especially chapter 2.

8. Frernando Ortiz, "Los Cabildos Afro-Cubanos," *Revista Bismestre Cubana* XVI (1921).

9. Brown, *Santeria Enthroned: Art, Ritual, and Innovation in an Afro-Cuban Religion*, 99.

10. Brown, *Santeria Enthroned: Art, Ritual, and Innovation in an Afro-Cuban Religion*, 108–9.

11. For a more detailed description and analysis of the development of the religion during this period, see Brown, *Santeria Enthroned: Art, Ritual, and Innovation in an Afro-Cuban Religion*, especially chapters 1 and 2.

12. J.D.Y. Peel, "The Pastor and the Babalawo: The Interaction of Religions in Nineteenth-Century Yorubaland," *Africa* 60, no. 3 (1990).

13. Brown, *Santeria Enthroned: Art, Ritual, and Innovation in an Afro-Cuban Religion*.

14. Miguel Ramos, "The Empire Beats On: Oyo, Batá Drums and Hegemony in Nineteenth-Century Cuba" (Master of Arts in History, Florida International University, 2000).

15. Brown, *Santeria Enthroned: Art, Ritual, and Innovation in an Afro-Cuban Religion*.

16. Brandon, *Santeria from Africa to the New World: The Dead Sell Memories*.

17. Information from Kamari Maxim Clarke's *Mapping Yorùbá Networks* and Carl Hunt's *Oyotunji Village* as well as the Oyotunji African Village website (http://www.oyotunjivillage.net/) and the Roots & Rooted Indigenous spirituality site's article about Oba Adedunmi and Oyotunji Village (http://www.rootsandrooted.org/oyotunji.htm), Karmari Maxine Clarke, *Mapping Yorùbá Networks: Power and Agency In the Makings of Transnational Communities* (Durham: Duke University Press, 2004); Carl M. Hunt, *Oyotunji Village: The Yoruba Movement in America* (Washington, D.C.: University Press of America, Inc., 1979).

18. Information about Church Lukumi Babalu Aye from the church website (http://www.church-of-the-lukumi.org/).

19. Linda Greenhouse, "Court, Citing Religious Freedom, Voids a Ban on Animal Sacrifice," *New York Times*, June 12, 1993.

## CHAPTER 3: COSMOLOGY

1. The name "Star Wars" and all logos, characters, artwork, stories, information, names, and other elements associated with it are the sole and exclusive property of Lucas Online, a division of Lucasfilm Ltd.

2. Joseph M. Murphy, *Santería: African Spirits in America* (Boston: Beacon Press, 1993), 130, 147 quoting Pierre Verger.

3. Joseph M. Murphy, *Santería: African Spirits in America* (Boston: Beacon Press, 1993), 131.

4. For an in-depth analysis of Olodumare, see Ìdòwú, E. Bolájí. *Olódùmarè: God in Yorùbá Belief.* New York: Wazobia, 1994.

5. E.T. Lawson, *Religions of Africa: Traditions in Transformation* (San Francisco: Harper & Row, 1984).

6. P.R. McKenzie, "Yoruba Òrìsà Cults: Some Marginal Notes Concerning Their Cosmology and Concepts of Deity," *Journal of Religion in Africa* VIII, no. Facs. 3 (1976).

7. Pierre Verger, *Notes Sur Le Culte Des Orisa Et Vodun À Bahia, La Baie De Tous Les Saints, Au Brésil Et À L'ancienne Côthe Des Esclaves En Afrique* (Dakar: I. F. A. N., 1957).

8. See McKenzie, P.R. "Yoruba Òrìsà Cults: Some Marginal Notes Concerning Their Cosmology and Concepts of Deity." *Journal of Religion in Africa* VIII, no. Facs. 3 (1976): 189–207.

9. Brandon, *Santeria from Africa to the New World: The Dead Sell Memories.*

10. William Bascom, "Yoruba Concepts of the Soul," in *Men and Cultures. Selected Papers of the Fifth International Congress of Anthropology and Ethnological Sciences*, ed. Anthony F.C. Wallace (Philadelphia: University of Pennsylvania Press, 1960).

11. Segun Gbadegesin, *African Philosophy: Traditional Yoruba Philosophy and Contemporary African Realities*, vol. 134 (New York: Peter Lang, 1991).

12. Wándé Abímbólá, "Ifa: A West African Cosmological System," in *Religion in Africa: Experience and Expression*, ed. Thomas D. Blakely, Walter E.A. van Beek, and Dennis L. Thompson (Portsmouth, NH: Heinemann, 1994).

13. Hallen, B., and J.O. Sodipo, *Knowledge, Belief & Witchcraft* (London: Ethnographica, 1986), 102.

14. Anne Llewellyn Barstow, *Witchcraze: A New History of European Witch Hunts* (San Francisco: Pandora, 1994); Richard E. Greenleaf, *The Mexican Inquisition of the Sixteenth Century* (Albuquerque: University of New Mexico Press, 1969); Henry Kamen, *The Spanish Inquisition: An Historical Revision* (London: Weidenfeld & Nicolson, 1997).

15. Martha O. Loustaunau and Elisa J. Sobo, *The Cultural Context of Health, Illness, and Medicine* (Westport, Connecticut, London: Bergin & Garvey, 1997).

## CHAPTER 4: THE ORISHA AND THEIR MYTHOLOGY

1. For more information about individual Orisha, see Barnes, ed., *Africa's Ogun: Old World and New*; William Bascom, *Shango in the New World* (Austin: University of Austin, 1972); Diedre L. Bádéjo, *Òsun Sèègèsí: The Elegant Deity of Wealth, Power and Femininity* (Trenton, NJ: Africa World Press, Inc., 1996); Judith Gleason, *Oya: In Praise of the Goddess* (Boston: Shambhala Publications, Inc., 1987); John Mason, *Olóòkun: Owner of Rivers and Seas* (Brooklyn, NY: Yorùbá Theological Archministry, 1996); Joseph M. Murphy and Mei-Mei Sanford, eds., *Òsun across the Waters: A Yoruba Goddess in Africa and the Americas* (Bloomington: Indiana University Press, 2001); Robert D. Pelton, *The Trickster in West Africa* (Berkeley: University of California Press, 1980); Lloyd Weaver and Olurunmi Egbelade, *Yemonja Maternal Divinity: Tranquil Sea Turbulent Tides* (Brooklyn, NY: Athelia Henrietta Press, 1998).

2. E. Bolájí Ìdòwú, *Olódùmarè: God in Yorùbá Belief* (New York: Wazobia, 1994).

3. Joseph M. Murphy, "Oshun the Dancer," in *The Book of the Goddess, Past and Present: An Introduction to Her Religion*, ed. Carl Olson (New York: Crossroad, 1983).

4. Joseph M. Murphy and Mei-Mei Sanford, "Introduction," in *Òsun across the Waters: A Yoruba Goddess in Africa and the Americas* (Bloomington: Indiana University Press, 2001).

5. Joseph M. Murphy, "Oshun the Dancer," in *The Book of the Goddess, Past and Present: An Introduction to Her Religion*, edited by Carl Olson, 190–201 (New York: Crossroad, 1983), 195.

6. Henry John Drewal and John Mason, eds., *Beads, Body and Soul: Art and Light in the Yorùbá Universe* (Los Angeles: UCLA Fowler Museum of Cultural History, 1997).

7. "Mandingo" is used to refer to the Mande peoples of West Africa. Mande can be found in almost every country in West Africa.

8. For more information about Sopona and smallpox, see Johnson, *The History of the Yorubas: From the Earliest Times to the Beginning to the British Protectorate*; Ìdòwú, *Olódùmarè: God in Yorùbá Belief.* Although the knowledge was discounted, Cotton Mather learned about inoculations from his African servant in the 1700s and promoted the practice in his sermons.

## CHAPTER 5: DESTINY, DIVINATION, AND SACRIFICE

1. Greenhouse, "Court, Citing Religious Freedom, Voids a Ban on Animal Sacrifice."

2. Robert Ferris Thompson, *Flash of the Spirit: African and Afro-American Art and Philosophy* (New York: Random House, 1984).

3. Special thanks to Olamidé, Mary Curry (ibaye) for explaining these distinctions to me.

4. 'Wande Abimbola, "The Bag of Wisdom: Òsun and the Origins of the Ifá Divination," in *Òsun across the Waters*, ed. Joseph M. Murphy and Mai-Mai Sanford (Bloomington, IN: Indinana University Press, 2001).

5. All of these rituals are described in "Initiation Rituals."

6. Greenhouse, "Court, Citing Religious Freedom, Voids a Ban on Animal Sacrifice"; Linda Greenhouse, "High Court Is Cool to Sacrifice Ban," *The New York Times*, Nov 5, 1992.

7. Emile Durkheim, *The Elementary Forms of Religious Life* (New York: The Free Press, 1915); Sigmund Freud, *Totem and Taboo* (New York: W.W. Norton & Company, Inc., 1950); Rene Girard, *Violence and the Sacred* (Baltimore and London: The Johns Hopkins University Press, 1977); Robert G. Hamerton-Kelly, ed., *Violent Origins* (Stanford, Calif.: Stanford University Press, 1987).

8. John Dunnill, "Communicative Bodies and Economies of Grace: The Role of Sacrifice in the Christian Understanding of the Body," *The Journal of Religion* 83, no. 1 (2003); Hamerton-Kelly, ed., *Violent Origins.*

## CHAPTER 6: LIFE, DEATH, AND THE AFTERLIFE

1. Biographical information from the Translators Preface to *The Spirits Book* Allan Kardec, *The Spirit's Book* (São Paulo, Brazil: Lake-Livraria Allan Kardec Editîra Ltda., 1972).

2. Allan Kardec, *The Spirit's Book* (São Paulo, Brazil: Lake-Livraria Allan Kardec Editîra Ltda., 1972), 12.

3. Armando Andres Bermundez, "Notas Para La Historia Del Espiritismo En Cuba," *Etnologia y folklore* 4 (1967).

4. There has also been some appropriation of Santería elements into the form of Espiritismo that was brought to the United States by Puerto Ricans. George Brandon calls this *Santerismo*, a combination of Santería and Espiritismo, Brandon, *Santeria*

*from Africa to the New World: The Dead Sell Memories,* see also Andrés Isidoro Pérez y Mena, *Speaking with the Dead: Development of Afro-Latin Religion among Puerto Ricans in the Unites States* (New York: AMS Press, Inc., 1991).

5. For more information about Kongolese cosmograms, see Thompson, *Flash of the Spirit: African and Afro-American Art and Philosophy.*

6. Joseph Hilgers, *Novena in Catholic Encyclopedia* (Online Edition) [Webpage] (Robert Appleton Company, 10/06/05 2003 [cited 1/2 2006]); available from http://www.newadvent.org/cathen/11141b.htm.

7. Allan Kardec, *Coleccion de Oraciones Escogidas* (Bronx, NY: De Pablo International Inc., 1990); Allan Kardec, *Collection of Selected Prayers* (Bronx, NY: De Pablo International Inc., 1989). A new English translation has also recently been published: Candita C. Gual, *Collection of Selected Prayers: Devotion Manual: A Spiritualist Prayer Guide* (New York: iUniverse, Inc., 2006).

8. For excellent histories of this region, see Anne Hilton, *The Kingdom of Kongo,* ed. John D. Hargreaves and George Shepperson, *Oxford Studies in African Affairs* (New York: Oxford University Press, 1958); Kairn A. Klieman, *"The Pygmies Were Our Compass": Bantu and Batwa in the History of West Central Africa, Early Times to c.1900 C.E.,* ed. Allen Isaacman and Jean Allman, *Social History of Africa* (Portsmouth, NH: Heinmann, 2003).

9. Palmié, *Wizards and Scientists: Explorations in Afro-Cuban Modernity and Tradition.*

## Chapter 7: Religious Rituals

1. Clarke, *Mapping Yorùbá Networks: Power and Agency in the Makings of Transnational Communities.*

2. Ericka Bourguignon, *Possession* (San Francisco: Changler & Sharp Publishers, Inc., 1976).

## Chapter 8: Initiation Rituals

1. For a personal account of the warrior ceremony, see chapter 2, Michael Atwood Mason, *Living Santería: Rituals and Experiences in an Afro-Cuban Religion* (Washington and London: Smithsonian Institution Press, 2002).

## Chapter 9: The Religious Family

1. Bascom, *The Sociological Role of the Yoruba Cult-Group.*

2. For a more detailed description of this institution, see Mary Ann Clark, "Godparenthood in the Afro-Cuban Religious Tradition of Santería," *Journal of Religious Studies and Theology* 22, no. 1 (2003).

3. Lydia Cabrera, *Yemayá Y Ochún* (New York: Eliseo Torres, 1980).

## CHAPTER 10: ORISHA RELIGION TODAY AND TOMORROW

1. One of the first to document these associations and the text to which many subsequent texts refer is Melville J. Herskovits, "African Gods and Catholic Saints in New World Negro Belief," *American Anthropologist* 39, no. 4 (Part 1) (1937). Others who have suggested that these associations are integral to the religion include Bastide, *African Civilizations in the New World.*

2. Drewal, Henry John. "Interpretation, Invention, and Re-Presentation in the Worship of Mami Wata." *Journal of Folklore Research* 25, no. 1–2 (1988): 101–39, 132.

3. For examples of the suggestion that only one or two Orisha were worshiped by individuals in Yorubaland, see Bastide, *African Civilizations in the New World*; Bádéjo, *Òsun Sèègèsí: The Elegant Deity of Wealth, Power and Femininity*; Gary Edwards and John Mason, *Black Gods—Orisa Studies in the New World* (Brooklyn, NY: Yoruba Theological Archministry, 1985); Conrad E. (Awo Fayomi) Maugé, *The Yoruba Religion: Introduction to Its Practice* (Mount Vernon, New York: House of Providence, 1993); Murphy, *Santería: African Spirits in America.* See also Bascom, *The Yoruba of Southwestern Nigeria; Bascom, The Sociological Role of the Yoruba Cult-Group.* Bascom discovered in his research that generally Yorubaland devotees worshiped one to five Orisha.

4. For a more complete and nuanced statement of this argument, see Mary Ann Clark, *Where Men Are Wives and Mothers Rule: Santería Ritual Practices and Their Gender Implications,* ed. Stephen Angell and Anthony Pinn, *The History of African-American Religions* (Gainesville: University Press of Florida, 2005), especially chapter 8.

5. As Randy Conner argues, not all communities are as open to gay, lesbian, bisexual, and transgendered participation as this account suggests. See Randy P. Conner and David Hatfield Sparks, *Queering Creole Spiritual Traditions: Lesbian, Gay, Bisexual, and Transgender Participation in African-Inspired Traditions in the Americas* (New York: Harrington Park Press, 2004).

6. Brandon, *Santeria from Africa to the New World: The Dead Sell Memories.* See also Pérez y Mena, *Speaking with the Dead: Development of Afro-Latin Religion among Puerto Ricans in the Unites States.*

7. See Mary Ann Clark, "Material History of American Religion Project: Seven African Powers: Hybridity and Appropriation" (1999).

# Bibliography

Abimbola, 'Wande. "The Bag of Wisdom: Òsun and the Origins of the Ifá Divination." In Òsun across the Waters, edited by Joseph M. Murphy and Mai-Mai Sanford, 141–54. Bloomington, IN: Indinana University Press, 2001.

———. "Ifa: A West African Cosmological System." In Religion in Africa: Experience and Expression, edited by Thomas D. Blakely, Walter E. A. van Beek and Dennis L. Thompson, 101–16. Portsmouth, NH: Heinemann, 1994.

Bádéjo, Diedre L. Òsun Sèègèsí: The Elegant Deity of Wealth, Power and Femininity. Trenton, NJ: Africa World Press, Inc., 1996.

Barnes, Sandra T., ed. Africa's Ogun: Old World and New. Bloomington: Indiana University Press, 1997.

Barstow, Anne Llewellyn. Witchcraze: A New History of European Witch Hunts. San Francisco: Pandora, 1994.

Bascom, William. Shango in the New World. Austin, TX: University of Austin, 1972.

———. "Yoruba Concepts of the Soul." In Men and Cultures. Selected Papers of the Fifth International Congress of Anthropology and Ethnological Sciences, edited by Anthony F. C. Wallace, 401–10. Philadelphia: University of Pennsylvania Press, 1960.

———. The Yoruba of Southwestern Nigeria. New York: Holt, Rinehart and Winston, 1969.

Bascom, William R. The Sociological Role of the Yoruba Cult-Group. Edited by Ralph Linton. Vol. 46, American Anthropologist. Menasha, WI: American Anthropological Association, 1944.

Bastide, Roger. African Civilizations in the New World. Translated by Peter Green. New York: Harper & Row, 1971.

Bermundez, Armando Andres. "Notas Para La Historia Del Espiritismo En Cuba." Etnologia y folklore 4 (1967): 5–22.

Bourguignon, Ericka. *Possession*. San Francisco: Changler & Sharp Publishers, Inc., 1976.

Brandon, George. *Santeria from Africa to the New World: The Dead Sell Memories*. Bloomington, IN: Indiana University Press, 1993.

Brown, David D. *Santeria Enthroned: Art, Ritual, and Innovation in an Afro-Cuban Religion*. Chicago: University of Chicago Press, 2003.

Brown, Karen McCarthy. *Mama Lola: A Vodou Priestess in Brooklyn*. Berkeley: University of California Press, 1991.

Cabrera, Lydia. *El Monte (Igbo, Finda, Ewe Orisha, Vititi Finda): Notas Sobre Las Religiones, La Magia, Las Supersticiones Y El Folklore De Los Negros Criollos Y Del Pueblo De Cuba*. Miami, FL: Ediciones Universal, 1975.

———. *Yemayá Y Ochún*. New York: Eliseo Torres, 1980.

Central Intelligence Agency. 2006. World Fact Book: Nigeria. In, http://cia.gov/cia/publications/factbook/geos/ni.html. (accessed July 4, 2006).

Clark, Mary Ann. "Godparenthood in the Afro-Cuban Religious Tradition of Santería." *Journal of Religious Studies and Theology* 22, no. 1 (2003): 45–62.

———. "Material History of American Religion Project: Seven African Powers: Hybridity and Appropriation." 1999.

———. *Where Men Are Wives and Mothers Rule: Santería Ritual Practices and Their Gender Implications*. Edited by Stephen Angell and Anthony Pinn, *The History of African-American Religions*. Gainesville, FL: University Press of Florida, 2005.

Clarke, Karmari Maxine. *Mapping Yorùbá Networks: Power and Agency In the Makings of Transnational Communities*. Durham: Duke University Press, 2004.

Conner, Randy P., and David Hatfield Sparks. *Queering Creole Spiritual Traditions: Lesbian, Gay, Bisexual, and Transgender Participation in African-Inspired Traditions in the Americas*. New York: Harrington Park Press, 2004.

Deren, Maya. *Divine Horsemen: The Living Gods of Haiti*. New Platz, NY: McPherson, 1983 (1953).

Drewal, Henry John. "Interpretation, Invention, and Re-Presentation in the Worship of Mami Wata." *Journal of Folklore Research* 25, no. 1–2 (1988): 101–39.

Drewal, Henry John, and John Mason, eds. *Beads, Body and Soul: Art and Light in the Yorùbá Universe*. Los Angeles: UCLA Fowler Museum of Cultural History, 1997.

Dunnill, John. "Communicative Bodies and Economies of Grace: The Role of Sacrifice in the Christian Understanding of the Body." *The Journal of Religion* 83, no. 1 (2003): 79–93.

Durkheim, Emile. *The Elementary Forms of Religious Life*. New York: The Free Press, 1915.

Edwards, Gary, and John Mason. *Black Gods—Orisa Studies in the New World*. Brooklyn, NY: Yoruba Theological Archministry, 1985.

Fandrich, Ina Johanna. *The Mysterious Voodoo Queen, Marie Laveaux: A Study of Powerful Female Leadership in Nineteenth-Century New Orleans*. New York: Routledge, 2005.

Farrow, Stephen S. *Faith, Fancies and Fetich or Yoruba Paganism*. Brooklyn, NY: Athelia Henrietta Press, Inc., 1996 (1926).

Fisher, Mary Pat. *Living Religions*. Upper Saddle River, NJ: Prentice-Hall, 2006.

Freud, Sigmund. *Totem and Taboo.* New York: W.W. Norton & Company, Inc., 1950.

Gbadegesin, Segun. *African Philosophy: Traditional Yoruba Philosophy and Contemporary African Realities.* Vol. 134. New York: Peter Lang, 1991.

Girard, Rene. *Violence and the Sacred.* Baltimore and London: The Johns Hopkins University Press, 1977.

Gleason, Judith. *Oya: In Praise of the Goddess.* Boston: Shambhala Publications, Inc., 1987.

Greenhouse, Linda. "Court, Citing Religious Freedom, Voids a Ban on Animal Sacrifice." *The New York Times,* June 12 1993.

———. "High Court Is Cool to Sacrifice Ban." *The New York Times,* Nov 5, 1992 1992, 25, col 1.

Greenleaf, Richard E. *The Mexican Inquisition of the Sixteenth Century.* Albuquerque: University of New Mexico Press, 1969.

Gual, Candita C. *Collection of Selected Prayers: Devotion Manual A Spiritualist Prayer Guide.* New York: iUniverse, Inc., 2006.

Hallen, B., and J.O. Sodipo. *Knowledge, Belief & Witchcraft.* London: Ethnographica, 1986.

Hamerton-Kelly, Robert G., ed. *Violent Origins.* Stanford, Calif.: Stanford University Press, 1987.

Herskovits, Melville J. "African Gods and Catholic Saints in New World Negro Belief." *American Anthropologist* 39, no. 4 (Part 1) (1937): 635–43.

Hilgers, Joseph. 2003. Novena. In *Catholic Encylopedia,*ed. K. Knight. Online Edition, Robert Appleton Company, http://www.newadvent.org/cathen/11141 b.htm. (accessed 1/2, 2006).

Hilton, Anne. *The Kingdom of Kongo.* Edited by John D. Hargreaves and George Shepperson, *Oxford Studies in African Affairs.* New York: Oxford University Press, 1958.

Hunt, Carl M. *Oyotunji Village: The Yoruba Movement in America.* Washington, D.C.: University Press of America, Inc., 1979.

Hurston, Zora Neale. *Tell My Horse: Voodoo and Life in Haiti and Jamaica.* Edited by Henry Louise Gates, Jr. New York, Grand Rapids, Philadelphia, St. Louis, San Francisco, London, Singapore, Sydney, Tokyo, Toronto: Harper & Row, 1990 (1938).

Johnson, The Rev. Samuel. *The History of the Yorubas: From the Earliest Times to the Beginning to the British Protectorate.* Translated by Dr. O. (ed.) Johnson. Lagos: C.M.S. (Nigeria) Bookshops, 1960 (1921).

Kamen, Henry. *The Spanish Inquisition: An Historical Revision.* London: Weidenfeld & Nicolson, 1997.

Kardec, Allan. *Coleccion De Oraciones Escogidas.* Bronx, NY: De Pablo International Inc., 1990.

———. *Collection of Selected Prayers.* Bronx, NY: De Pablo International Inc., 1989.

———. *The Spirit's Book.* São Paulo, Brisil: Lake-Livraria Allan Kardec Editîra Ltda., 1972.

Klieman, Kairn A. *"The Pygmies Were Our Compass": Bantu and Batwa in the History of West Central Africa, Early Times to c.1900 C.E.* Edited by Allen Isaacman and Jean Allman, *Social History of Africa.* Portsmouth, NH: Heinmann, 2003.

Lawson, E.T. *Religions of Africa: Traditions in Transformation*. San Francisco: Harper & Row, 1984.

Long, Carolyn Morrow. *A New Orleans Voudou Priestess: The Legend and Reality of Marie Laveau*. Gainesville: University Press of Florida, 2006.

Loustaunau, Martha O., and Elisa J. Sobo. *The Cultural Context of Health, Illness, and Medicine*. Westport, Connecticut, and London: Bergin & Garvey, 1997.

Mason, John. *Olóòkun: Owner of Rivers and Seas*. Brooklyn, NY: Yorùbá Theological Archministry, 1996.

Mason, Michael Atwood. *Living Santería: Rituals and Experiences in an Afro-Cuban Religion*. Washington and London: Smithsonian Institution Press, 2002.

Maugé, Conrad E. (Awo Fayomi). *The Yoruba Religion: Introduction to Its Practice*. Mount Vernon, New York: House of Providence, 1993.

McKenzie, P.R. "Yoruba Òrìsà Cults: Some Marginal Notes Concerning Their Cosmology and Concepts of Deity." *Journal of Religion in Africa* VIII, no. Facs. 3 (1976): 189–207.

Murphy, Joseph M. "Oshun the Dancer." In *The Book of the Goddess, Past and Present: An Introduction to Her Religion*, edited by Carl Olson, 190–201. New York: Crossroad, 1983.

———. *Santería: African Spirits in America*. Boston: Beacon Press, 1993.

———. *Working the Spirit: Ceremonies of the Africa Diaspora*. Boston: Beacon Press, 1994.

Murphy, Joseph M., and Mei-Mei Sanford. "Introduction." In *Òsun across the Waters: A Yoruba Goddess in Africa and the Americas*, 1–9. Bloomington, IN: Indiana University Press, 2001.

———, eds. *Òsun across the Waters: A Yoruba Goddess in Africa and the Americas*. Bloomington: Indiana University Press, 2001.

Ortiz, Fernando. *Los Negros Brujos*. Reprint, Miami: Ediciones Universal, 1973 (1906).

Ortiz, Frernando. "Los Cabildos Afro-Cubanos." *Revista Bismestre Cubana* XVI (1921): 5–39.

Palmié, Stephan. *Wizards and Scientists: Explorations in Afro-Cuban Modernity and Tradition*. Durham and London: Duke University Press, 2002.

Peel, J.D.Y. "The Pastor and the Babalawo: The Interaction of Religions in Nineteenth-Century Yorubaland." *Africa* 60, no. 3 (1990): 338–69.

Pelton, Robert D. *The Trickster in West Africa*. Berkeley: University of California Press, 1980.

Pinn, Anthony B. *Varieties of African American Religious Experience*. Minneapolis, MN: Ausburg Fortress Publishers, 1998.

Pérez y Mena, Andrés Isidoro. *Speaking with the Dead: Development of Afro-Latin Religion among Puerto Ricans in the Unites States*. New York: AMS Press, Inc., 1991.

Ramos, Miguel. "The Empire Beats On: Oyo, Batá Drums and Hegemony in Nineteenth-Century Cuba." Master of Arts in History, Florida International University, 2000.

Samolinski, Candace J. "Scholar Calls Santeria, Voodoo Theory Unfair." The Tampa Tribune, July 3, 2006, 5.

Thompson, Robert Ferris. *Flash of the Spirit: African and Afro-American Art and Philosophy*. New York: Random House, 1984.

Verger, Pierre. *Notes Sur Le Culte Des Orisa Et Vodun À Bahia, La Baie De Tous Les Saints, Au Brésil Et À L'ancienne Côthe Des Esclaves En Afrique.* Dakar: I.F. A.N., 1957.

Ward, Martha. *Voodoo Queen: The Spirited Lives of Marie Laveau.* Jackson, MI: University Press of Mississippi, 2004.

Weaver, Lloyd, and Olurunmi Egbelade. *Yemonja Maternal Divinity: Tranquil Sea Turbulent Tides.* Brooklyn, NY: Athelia Henrietta Press, 1998.

Ìdòwú, E. Boláji. *Olódùmarè: God in Yorùbá Belief.* New York: Wazobia, 1994.

## Online Resources

Among the many face-to-face communities that also have a presence on the web are Oyotunji Village (http://www.oyotunjivillage.net/) and the Church of the Lucumí Babalu Aye (CLBA, http://www.church-of-the-lukumi.org/). CLBA also maintains a list of priests who have been certified by their organization.

The Organization of Lucumí Unity, a networking site for practitioners of all the forms of Orisha religion (http://www.lukumiunity.org/), also has a directory of resources including information posted by diviners and others. However, there is no indication on the site that anyone has verified the information posted.

Individual practitioners also have sites. Among the best are Eledá.org (http://ilarioba.tripod.com/) by Willie Rasmos, a long-time oba oriate out of the Miami area, and OrishaNet (http://www.orishanet.org/) by Baba Eyiogbe, a babalawo in Seattle.

OrishaList, currently housed in Yahoo Groups, is one of the oldest of the Internet forums devoted to the discussion of Orisha religion (http://groups.yahoo.com/group/Orisalist/). It has an active community of over 500 members who discuss a variety of African traditions from both African and American perspectives.

Other discussion groups can also be found on the Yahoo Groups site (http://groups.yahoo.com/).

# Index

# About the Author

MARY ANN CLARK is both a scholar and practitioner of Santería. In addition to teaching in the Religious Studies Program at the University of Houston and the School of Human Sciences and Humanities at the University of Houston Clear Lake, she is the coordinator of the Council of Societies for the Study of Religion. She is the author of *Where Men are Wives and Mothers Rule: Santería Ritual Practices and Their Gender Implications*, as well as several articles, book chapters, and book reviews.